KNITTING
BASICS

KNITTING BASICS

ALL YOU NEED TO KNOW ABOUT
KNITTING STITCHES AND TECHNIQUES

MELODY LORD

MURDOCH BOOKS

Contents

Introduction

The dwarfs said, 'If you will take care of our house, cook, make the beds, wash, sew and knit, and if you will keep everything neat and clean, you can stay with us and you shall want for nothing.' *Jacob and Wilhelm Grimm, HOUSEHOLD TALES, 'Little Snow-White'*

My first knitting lesson was not a great success. Tired of me whining to be taken to the swimming pool or the shops on one of those hot summer holidays, my grandmother made an attempt to keep me still and quiet for a short time by teaching me the rudiments of knitting. I suppose it worked, although I don't recall knitting more than a few rows of that scarf or whatever it was that I began but never finished.

I can still picture my grandmother, sitting in her favourite silk brocade armchair under the lamp, contriving jumpers, hats and other garments for her multitude of grandchildren—I was one of twenty-one cousins on the maternal side. Gran would sit and knit and recite poetry she'd learned in her own childhood, about the giant Pindunderagig, with eyes so big, or Little Orphan Annie.

Despite my initial lack of success, which was mainly due to a lack of patience and persistence, I remained interested in the art of winding wool around a pair of needles and creating something that could be worn by a baby, a child, or even a teapot.

When my youngest sister was born, my mother knitted her a very stylish outfit consisting of a pair of purple leggings (with feet in) and a purple jumper with a large golden sunflower on the front. Seeing this marvel of stitchery, I begged, again, to be taught how to knit. My mother helped me to begin an orange cardigan for my favourite doll, a miniature

baby doll called Sweet April, and this time I actually managed to finish the task, although I dare say that Mum did most of the decreasing and probably half of the knitting, by the time she picked up all my dropped stitches and corrected my other mistakes. Still, I remember how proud I felt showing off April's new outfit to my friend—whose own Sweet April doll delighted in the nickname 'Fatigue', pronounced 'Fatty-goo'.

Once the skill was acquired, there was no stopping me. I soon found that I could knit while I read, which allowed me to enjoy two of my favourite activities at once. I knitted at school—sitting on the weatherboard verandah at lunchtime—on the school bus, in the car, in front of the television. I haunted the yarn section of our small town's only department store, tore patterns out of magazines and invented my own designs according to the colours and yarns that I could get my hands on.

When I was at university, I knitted while I studied. I took on my first commissions—not for profit: I loved knitting so much that I told friends that I'd knit whatever they wanted if they bought the wool. My housemate wanted a gorgeous black mohair cable knit, my boyfriend a Fair Isle vest to wear to work.

I knitted my mother a tea cosy that looked like a miniature jumper for the teapot, except that one sleeve was long and thin for the spout, and the other sleeve was wide and short for the handle. My sister liked it so much she asked me to knit her a tea cosy that she could wear as a jumper!

Knitting is so much like second nature to me now, it would be rare to find me without a project on the go. Having furnished my family and everyone I know with more knitwear than they know what to do with, I spend quite a lot of my knitting time these days creating blankets, hats and scarves for charity. Two of my favourite knitting causes are Wrap with Love (http://www.artsandcraftsnsw.com.au/Wrap.htm) and the Victoria-based group Knit One Give One (http://www.knitonegiveone.org/). It's a challenge to come up with classic and comfortable designs for those who need a bit of extra warmth, but I love to think that the warmth of my thoughts as I knit is tied up in the scarf that keeps off the chill for an unknown person far away.

No limits

There was a time in the recent past when knitting was out of fashion. Knitting was seen as a skill relegated to the pre-feminist days when women didn't work outside the home, and hand-knitted jumpers and scarves took on an overtone of poverty as mass-produced knitwear hit the shelves of stores. Ironically, as machine knits became more inexpensive, the cost of knitting by hand—in terms of both time and dollars—became prohibitive. You could buy a good quality jumper in a department store for less than the price of the wool to knit it yourself, and wear it to the office the same day.

The last few years have, thankfully, seen the resurrection of knitting as a craft. People have learned to value the skill and creativity that goes into a hand-knitted garment, and yarns and patterns have caught up with the fickle moods of modern fashion too. Now you can seek out Internet-based communities of like-minded knitters, or gather in your local café or pub for a Stitch 'n' Bitch session. You can even participate in the slightly underground movement known as 'yarnbombing', in which you knit a cover for a local landmark and sneak out at a quiet moment to sew your creation over the parking meter, statue or other feature.

Once almost exclusively considered women's work, knitting is also being taken up by men and boys— such as my own son, who has accompanied me to many a knit-in, although he's yet to complete a project on his own. Designer Kaffe Fassett is one of my favourite knitting dudes, although there are a growing number who are happy to show off their work on the Internet, if you're interested.

This may be the future of knitting but, in the meantime, you're keen to get started. So let's do it! In this book I'm drawing on my own experience of learning to knit, trying to cover the basic knowledge that I learned from my mother and grandmother, or picked up along the journey. The best advice I can give to a knitting novice is to find a friend who can knit (it's not difficult—just hang around a yarn store and ask questions, or strike up a conversation with a public knitter on the train or at a café). Begin with a small, easy project so that you get the thrill of achievement: there a quite a few in this book for you to try. Don't expect your work to be perfect first go, and don't give up!

1

Getting organised

* Don't drop a stitch

* Storing your stash and other stuff

* Becoming a knitter

The portable craft

Maman would bring her knitting to the garden and watch them. *Willa Cather,* ONE OF OURS

One of the great advantages of knitting is that you can take it with you, almost wherever you go. The trip from my rural home to the high school I attended involved a one-hour school bus trip, which was the perfect opportunity to pull out my latest knitting project and work away while I chatted with the friends who joined me during the trip. Later, commuting to work by train afforded me the opportunity to increase my wardrobe and occupy my time creatively. My father actually banned me from knitting in the car, pointing out that knitting needles were potentially dangerous missiles—in the event of an accident—and they were to be carried in the boot.

These days, you're much more likely to find me knitting while I'm watching television. I've never quite got the hang of simply sitting in front of a television screen and doing nothing. If I'm not knitting, I'm crocheting, embroidering or sewing: I can't bear to sit still without using the time to create something pretty or useful.

This also goes for football matches. I do enjoy the quality time I get to spend with my partner and son, cheering on our favourite team (Go, Newtown!), especially on a sunny winter's day when the wind-chill factor is low. If it's warm enough to get the gloves off, it's the perfect time to knit a beanie or a scarf—especially if it's in the team colours (see the Quick-knit footy scarf pattern on pages 12–13). On really cold and wet days, it's too hard to knit. That's when you wrap up in the woollies you've made at past matches and concentrate on keeping warm and dry.

Quick-knit footy scarf

This scarf is knitted flat on a circular needle, so it's easy to carry your project with you. Knit it in your team's colours, and then wear it at the game.

YOU WILL NEED:

* Two 50 g balls of 8-ply wool yarn in the first colour (celery)
* Two 50 g balls of 8-ply wool yarn in the second colour (aqua)
* One 50 g ball of 8-ply wool yarn in the third colour (white)
* One 5.5 mm (UK 5, US 9) extra-long circular knitting needle
* One 6 mm (UK 4, US 10) knitting needle for casting on and off
* Wool needle for darning ends
* Large crochet hook
* Scissors

CONSTRUCTION:

There is no need to knit a tension square as a small amount of variation in size won't matter.

Use the 6 mm knitting needle to cast the stitches onto the 5.5 mm circular needle so that the cast-on row is nice and loose. (The circular needle is needed to hold the large number of stitches but the scarf is knitted flat, not in the round.) Cast on 175 stitches in the first colour (see page 67), keeping the tension loose.

Working in garter stitch (knit every row; see page 73), knit 12 rows in the first colour. Break off the yarn, leaving a tail about 10 cm (4 in) long.

Join the second colour (see page 87) and knit 10 rows of garter stitch. Break off the yarn.

Join the third colour and knit 8 rows of garter stitch. Break off the yarn.

Join the second colour. It's a good idea to use the second ball of yarn (even though you have some yarn left in the first ball) because this will minimise the number of tails you need to darn in after you've finished and ensure that you don't accidentally run out of yarn halfway through a row. Knit 10 rows of garter stitch. Break off the yarn.

Join the first colour (use the second ball). Knit 12 rows of garter stitch.

Use the 6 mm knitting needle to cast off the stitches loosely (see page 94), and then break off the yarn. Darn the tails of the yarn into the back of the work (the back is the side where you can see the colour change interlinked) using a wool needle. See pages 102–103 for instructions.

To add the fringe, cut twelve 30 cm (12 in) lengths of each colour of yarn. Gather a bundle of two pieces of each colour (six strands) and fold the bundle in half. Use a large crochet hook to pull the folded end through the knitted fabric at one corner of the scarf. Slip the cut ends of the strands through the folded loop and pull the loop tight. Repeat this process at the other corner of the scarf and at the end of each row where the colour changes. Repeat at the other end of the scarf.

Lay the scarf flat on a table and comb out the fringe with your fingers. Trim the ends of the strands of yarn so that they are all the same length.

Now wrap the scarf around your neck and cheer on your team! You should have enough yarn left over to knit yourself a beanie or a pair of mittens.

Simple drawstring bags are great for toting small projects around.

Rubber point protectors prevent stitches from slipping off.

Don't drop a stitch

The most important thing to think about when carting your knitting around with you is to keep it neat, clean and in one place. You don't need to take the whole project with you: just pack enough yarn to keep you busy (you'll gradually learn how long it takes you to get through a ball), your needles, your pattern and a pair of snips if you think you'll need them. (Leave the rest of your yarn supply and any completed sections of the project at home.) You can pack all of this into a special knitting tote or slip it into a cotton drawstring bag.

The item in a knitting project with the most potential for mess is the ball of yarn. As you knit and the thread unwraps, the ball turns and spins. If you drop the ball or it falls, it will unroll and can tangle or run away, gathering dirt as it goes. The easiest way to avoid this is to start knitting using the end of the thread inside the ball.

① Leave the ball of yarn in its paper wrapper, if you can. Some labels go through the middle of the ball, and you may have to remove them. Insert your fingers into the centre of the ball from one end.

② Carefully draw out a small amount of yarn from the middle of the ball.

③ Tease out the yarn you've removed until you find the end. Use this end to begin knitting.

④ The ball will sit still as the yarn comes straight out of the middle, and so you can tuck it inside your knitting bag or sit it in a clean container to protect it from gathering dirt (see page 32).

Another trick to prevent travelling disasters is to use needle-point protectors. These are small rubber caps that fit onto the point of the needle to prevent the stitches sliding off if your knitting gets jostled around in transit. You can buy them from craft stores or make your own by poking the end of the needle into a small plastic eraser.

When you bring your knitting home, make sure you keep all the parts of the project together. There's nothing worse than having to hunt through a basket of yarn for the last ball of the stuff you're using and then having to untangle it. Or having to turn the house, car and your handbag upside down because you can't find a sleeve that you finished two weeks ago. A large project bag with lots of compartments for everything you need for your project solves this problem, but you don't have to buy an expensive, custom-made knitting bag. A canvas shopping bag, a cardboard box (preferably with a lid) or a wicker basket will do just as well.

Before you begin a project, make sure you've got everything you need to complete it: pattern, yarn and needles of the correct size and shape, plus scissors, stitch holders, stitch markers, cable needles and more. Keep it all together, in one place (except when you take it with you to work or while you're on the bus or at the football).

Storing your stash and other stuff

It might seem strange to a beginner that people can collect yarn obsessively. 'Surely,' you think, 'you just buy what you need for a project and then make the project.' I am here to tell you that it is not so. Here's how it begins.

You go to the yarn store to purchase materials for your next project. While there, you spot a beautiful yarn in your favourite colour, with an absolutely entrancing texture. It's impossible to resist fondling the balls of yarn and, while doing so, imagining the perfect garment or accessory you could make with

it—after you've finished the one you're about to start, of course. So you guess how much yarn you think you'll need for whatever it is you think you'll make with the new yarn, add a ball or two just in case, and walk out of the store with enough yarn for two projects, not one.

TIP
Circular needles (see page 23) can be used for ordinary knitting too. They are easier to carry around than long, straight needles because they wrap around the yarn ball and take up less room in your project bag.

Don't assume it ends there. Finally, you finish the first project. If you're lucky, you won't have spotted any more 'must have' yarn in the meantime. Now, you start looking for a pattern for the exquisite yarn you bought. Found one? Drat, you're a ball short, and the yarn store has sold out of the particular colour and dye lot you bought. So you buy a slightly different colour that is just as gorgeous to make the new project, and put the other yarn away until you find the perfect pattern for it.

While you're at the yarn store, naturally, you spot a new yarn with a really amazing texture that would look fabulous knitted up, and so you snap up some of that and take it home to your growing stash. In the meantime, you've got one and a half balls left over from your original project; it's not enough to make anything with, but it's too nice to throw away. So you buy some more yarn with a contrasting colour or texture and plan to make a project with the first colour as a stripe or motif—sometime.

You can see how it happens.

Getting organised

15

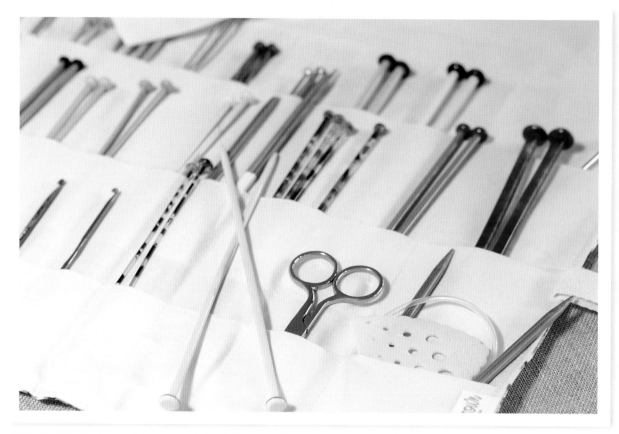

A needle roll with layers of long pockets for knitting needles and other accessories helps keep your stuff organised.

The most important thing about storing your stash is keeping the yarn free from dust and dirt, tangles and getting mixed up. You also want to keep track of the colour (especially of the dye lot—see page 41), composition and ply of the yarn. The little paper labels that tell you all the pertinent information do tend to slip off and you can't rely on your memory for all the details.

Clear plastic ziplock bags are fantastic for yarn storage. You can get them in sizes large enough to fit all the yarn you'll need for a project, or small enough to keep just the remains of one ball of yarn with its label. You can stack the bags of yarn on a shelf or stand them upright in a large storage box so that it's easy to see at a glance what you've got.

A cosy basket of odds and ends looks inviting and fun. I have one near my favourite knitting spot, and it's where I toss odd balls of yarn that are left over from other projects or that friends and relatives have given me. I don't worry too much about keeping the labels, because I use the contents of the basket for small projects—knitted egg cosies, crocheted flowers and curly decorations for hair clips and headbands—or for charity knits, such as beanies for Knit One Give One or blanket squares for Wrap With Love.

Storing your knitting accessories is easier. If you're like me, and you love to have all your knitting needles and crochet hooks right in front of your eyes, you can stand them in a large jar or vase on a shelf. For neatniks, a cardboard or plastic box is a good way to keep them all in one place so that they're easy to store. If you're keen on order, a needle roll with long, narrow pockets for pairs of needles makes it easy to find the size you want instantly. You can make your own to accommodate your growing collection of needles, or buy one ready-made.

Other knitting necessities tend to be small and easy to lose, but they're also easy to store. An old biscuit tin, a shoe box, or a clear plastic storage container (aren't those ones with different-shaped compartments delicious?) will keep all your bits and bobs together.

A magazine storage box is the perfect receptacle for patterns and knitting magazines.

Becoming a knitter

Once you've been knitting for a while, you'll find that your fingers do most of the work without you needing to think about it. It's like when you drive home from the supermarket and arrive at your house without remembering much of the trip. You've done it so many times you could do it with your eyes closed. Knitting is the same: even if I'm watching television or chatting to a friend, I can tell immediately if a stitch doesn't feel right or slips off the needle, and I stop to correct whatever is wrong. With time, you will be able to do this, too.

In the meantime, you need three things to get you from wool to wearable: patience, practice and pride.

PATIENCE

At first, knitting seems difficult and, at the same time, tedious. You wonder if you'll ever get the hang of transferring a stitch from one needle to the next, or remembering a five-line repeat without looking at the pattern every other stitch. After hundreds of stitches, the fabric hanging from your needle is only

a few centimetres long. It's finger-numbingly boring, and you haven't even finished the ribbing.

PRACTICE

You will get faster and more confident, and this will make your task easier and the time will start to fly. You'll get better at the tricky bits and your memory for stitch patterns will improve as various designs become more familiar. You'll learn which yarns are easy to knit and which require a little more care and attention to avoid splitting the thread or dropping stitches. As Lady Catherine de Bourgh told Elizabeth Bennet in Jane Austen's *Pride and Prejudice*: 'I often tell young ladies that no excellence … is to be acquired without constant practice.'

PRIDE

Mostly, you'll learn to be proud of what you make. You'll love the textures and colours that wool and other yarns bring to your creations, and celebrate the quirky little touches that make your garments unique. When you present a loved one with a handmade scarf, or receive a compliment for your stylish new jumper, you'll feel that bubbling sensation in your chest that makes you want to shout, 'I made it myself!' What more can you ask for?

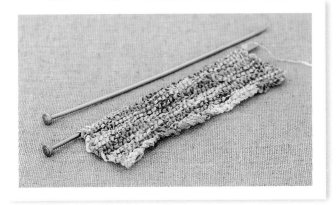

2

Knitting necessities

✳ Knitting needles ✳ Specialty needles ✳ Accessories
✳ Measuring devices ✳ Scissors and implements
for sewing up ✳ Knick-knacks

Pins and needles

Frau Dörr was knitting with big wooden needles on a blue woolen jacket for her husband, and the work, as yet quite shapeless, lay on her lap like a great fleece. There was but little talk, and so nothing was to be heard but the clicking of the needles ...

Theodor Fontane, TRIALS AND TRIBULATION

Buy only what you need. Even though knitting needles can be relatively inexpensive, there's no need to rush out and buy one of every possible size and shape before you begin your first project.

Knitting needles

If you're lucky, you might receive an assortment of needles from an elderly relative who no longer needs them. A good proportion of mine were inherited from my Great-Aunt Hazel. Other sources of knitting paraphernalia are second-hand shops and charity shops—you can often buy collections of needles, and sometimes yarn and patterns too, quite cheaply.

Knitting needles range in size from thin needles as fine as wire to thick ones that resemble broom handles. The rule of thumb is that the finer needles are for finer yarns and the larger needles are for thicker yarns, although finer yarn knitted on thicker needles can give an interesting net-like effect.

If you're using second-hand needles you will definitely need a needle gauge (see next page) to work out what size they are, as markings can become difficult to read after much use. Simply slide a needle through the holes in the gauge until you find the one that fits best. This will give you the diameter of the needle in millimetres or the size in US or UK numerals. (Most needle gauges have all three measurements marked.)

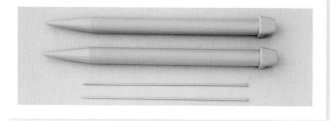

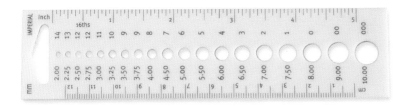

A needle gauge—this one has both metric and imperial sizes and useful rulers on the edges.

A standard knitting needle (sometimes called a knitting pin) has a knob or head at one end and a point at the other end. The head holds the stitches on the needle so that they don't slide off as you work, while the tapered point is used to assist the needle to pass between the yarn and the other needle as you knit. The point should be sharp, so as to slide easily between the needle and the yarn, but rounded so as not to split the yarn as you poke it through. Knitting needles are sold and used in pairs of the same size (unless you want to mix up the tension for a weird and random fabric effect).

The shaft of the needle can be any length, although it is usually between about 25 cm (10 in) and 40 cm (16 in) in length. The stitches scrunch up on the shaft of the needle, and so the width of your knitting is not necessarily limited by the length of the needle, although for really large numbers of stitches (such as for shawls and blankets) you can choose to use circular needles (see next section).

The diameter of the shaft is measured in millimetres, and it is the size of this diameter that determines the size of the stitches you make. Standard needle diameters range from 2 mm to 25 mm; however, very fine needles and larger novelty needles are also sometimes found. The size is usually marked somewhere on the needle, either on the head or on the shaft. Most new knitting needles are sold and marked in metric sizes, even in the United States, but some, especially second-hand needles, will be marked only in the old-fashioned sizes. If your needles are marked with a numeral that is not followed by 'mm', chances are it is either a UK or US gauge size. This is where a needle gauge is invaluable for ensuring that you get the correct size for your project.

The numerals for the UK sizes correspond to the standard gauges for the wires that were used to make steel needles: the smaller the needle, the larger the number. The US system works in the opposite way, with larger needles having larger numbers. The table on page 22 gives conversions for the three standard sizing systems.

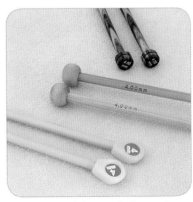

The gauge of the needle is usually marked near the head.

NEEDLE SIZE (MM)	UK GAUGE	US SYSTEM
2.0	14	0
2.25	13	1
2.5	--	--
2.75	12	2
3.0	11	--
3.25	10	3
3.5	--	4
3.75	9	5
4.0	8	6
4.5	7	7
5.0	6	8
5.5	5	9
6.0	4	10
6.5	3	10½
7.0	2	--
7.5	1	--
8.0	0	11
9.0	00	13
10.0	000	15
12.0	--	17
16.0	--	19
19.0	--	35
25.0	--	50

Needles made, top to bottom, of plastic-coated wire, glass, steel, plastic, cellulose acetate, aluminium, bamboo, faux tortoiseshell, casein.

COMPOSITION OF NEEDLES

It's widely believed that knitting began in the Middle East and spread throughout the world via the Mediterranean trade routes in the Middle Ages. The earliest needles were probably lengths of bronze wire, although the technique of knitting with a frame, nails and a hook (see French knitting, page 114) was also used.

Needles made of bone and wood would have been used for coarser stitches and, later, needles made from ivory and tortoiseshell were much sought after. Modern needles are still made of metals such as steel and aluminium, but also of wood and bamboo, glass, and plastics such as cellulose acetate and casein.

Different knitters will prefer their needles in different materials. I tend to choose aluminium or steel if I have the correct size, because I like the rigidity and strength of the needles and the way the yarn slips on and off. Some knitters like the warmth of natural materials, such as wood, bamboo or casein (plastic made from milk protein), and they are highly recommended if you have arthritis or repetitive strain injury. Plastic needles are perfectly fine to use, especially in larger sizes where the weight of metal or wooden needles would be more of a strain; however, they do tend to break more easily. I also find that I knit with slightly looser tension on plastic needles than on metal, and this can be either good or bad, depending on the project.

The best idea is to try a few different sorts of needles and see which material suits you best. Needles are generally quite inexpensive, and your collection can never be too big, anyway!

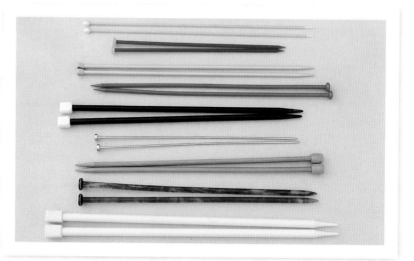

Speciality needles

There are some other types of knitting needles that will come in handy for creating certain projects. Once again, you don't need to rush out and buy pairs of every type and size. Just wait until you have a project that requires them before adding to your stock of knitting needles.

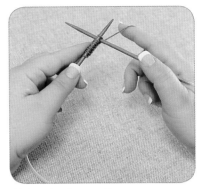

CIRCULAR NEEDLES

Circular needles are useful for knitting in the round (see page 90), as well as knitting large numbers of stitches that won't fit on a standard pair of needles. They are also great for taking your knitting with you, as the flexible central part can easily be curled up to take up less space in a bag.

Using circular needles.

Circular needles consist of a pair of pointed shafts, like a pair of standard needles, joined together by a flexible cable (usually made of nylon or plastic). The needle shafts are the same sizes as standard needles, although the flexible cable is thinner. Don't be concerned that this will affect your tension, as the stitches must pass over the needle shafts as you knit them, ensuring that your tension remains even.

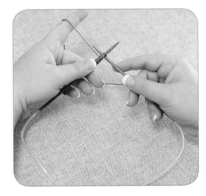

The length of the flexible cable determines the number of stitches the needles can hold. The pattern you are using will usually indicate the length of the cable that is required, ranging from about 22 cm to more than a metre. There are also circular needle systems available that have interchangeable points and lengths of cable: you can purchase a set of needle shafts with a screw mechanism in the non-pointed ends, along with a set of different lengths of cable that slip into the screw mechanism. This is very economical in the long term if you think you're going to be doing a lot of circular needle knitting, although it's quite expensive to get the initial set-up.

You can use a circular needle in place of a pair of standard knitting needles, simply knitting across your right-side row, turning the work, and knitting back across the wrong-side row. If you are knitting in the round, you cast on the required number of stitches and then—instead of turning around and knitting back across the cast-on stitches—you knit into the first stitch you cast on, making a circle of knitting. All rows are then knitted as though they are right-side rows, and you simply continue knitting until the work is the required length (see page 91 for more details about knitting in the round). The thing about knitting this way is that it's easy to forget which row you're up to or where the

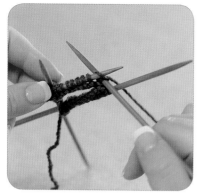
Using a set of four DPNs.

pattern repeat starts. If it's important to keep track, slip a stitch marker (see page 26) onto the right-hand needle at the end of the cast-on row, and transfer the stitch marker to the right-hand needle each time you come to it to keep track of the number of rows.

DOUBLE-POINTED NEEDLES

Double-pointed knitting needles (you'll see these abbreviated as DPNs) are mainly used for knitting in the round. They are like standard knitting needles in shape and size, but with a point at both ends of the shaft.

These needles are useful for knitting small items in the round that are too small for a circular needle: items such as socks, collars and cuffs, for example, are often knitted on DPNs. They can also be used for other purposes, such as knitting alternate rows of different yarns (see page 41), or (for more advanced knitters) two-colour brioche stitch (see page 194).

Knitting with double-pointed needles may seem tricky at first, and naturally you will be worried about dropping stitches off the ends of the non-active needles. This is less likely to happen than you think, as the tension of the yarn is generally enough to make sure the stitches stay put. The trick is to make sure that you don't have too many stitches on any one needle.

DPN work is usually done with four or five needles: three or four to hold the work and one to knit onto. The stitches are divided as evenly as possible between the needles, preferably at the start of a pattern repeat if there is one (that just makes it easier to keep count). Try not to have more than about 30 stitches on each needle: if you have more than that, it will probably be more efficient to use a circular needle anyway.

Practice will teach you the best way to hold double-pointed needles: I prefer to work with the two active needles tucked under the ends of the non-active ones, and allow the non-active ones to fall behind my work. Some people like to hold the non-active needles parallel to the active ones but just a little below the knitting row. You'll soon discover which method suits you. See page 91 for more instructions about knitting with DPNs.

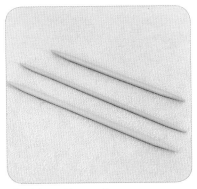

Straight cable needles.

Cable needles with a bend.

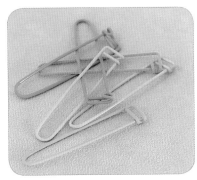

Safety-pin style stitch holders.

CABLE NEEDLES

Cable needles are short, double-pointed needles that are used for holding slipped stitches out of the way temporarily while you are knitting twists and cables (see Chapter 9: Twisted stitches, page 160). Some cable needles are simple, straight shafts with a point at each end, while others have a bend in the middle to help keep the stitches in place. I prefer the straight ones—I just find them easier to use—but the bendy ones are great if you are cabling for the first time to give you more confidence that you won't drop your stitches.

The needles do come in different sizes, although it is not essential to use a cable needle with the exact diameter of the knitting needles you are using. You can also use a stitch holder or even a large safety pin to hold your slipped stitches if you don't have a cable needle.

Accessories

STITCH HOLDERS

Stitch holders usually look like giant safety pins. You slip stitches that you are not using onto the pointed end and hook the catch closed to make sure the stitches don't go anywhere. They are used to hold stitches that you will knit up later in the project; for example, to hold stitches

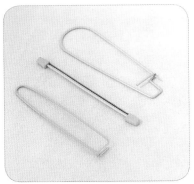

Stitch holders, safety-pin style and bar-and-spring type.

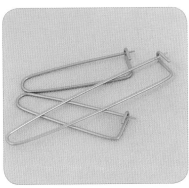

Stitch holders of different sizes.

Stitch markers in various sizes.

A stitch marker on the needle.

Decorative stitch markers.

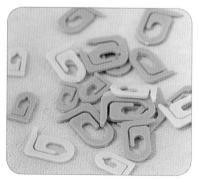

Row markers.

across the neck of a jumper while you continue knitting to shape the shoulders. (They can also be used if you want to put a project aside for a while, and use the needles to knit something else.)

Another type of stitch holder is like a short bar with a cap on each end held in place by a spring. Remove one cap, slip the stitches onto the bar and replace the cap. The advantage of this type of stitch holder is that you can slip the stitches back onto a needle from either end, depending on which way you want to knit them.

STITCH MARKERS

Keeping count of your stitches is the hardest part of knitting, especially if you're working with a large number of stitches. Stitch markers are a wonderful invention and will save you a lot of time and effort in your knitting. Most stitch markers are small plastic or metal rings that simply slip over the knitting needle between stitches. When you reach the marker in your knitting, transfer it from one needle to the other to keep the place, and continue knitting.

Basic circular markers, novelty shapes and even pretty beaded rings are available from most knitting supply shops, but it's easy to make your own: a small safety pin slipped over the needle does just as well, as does a loop of contrast-coloured yarn.

ROW MARKERS

Counting rows is just as tedious as counting stitches, and so using a row marker can also make knitting easier. Simple markers with an opening on one side are hooked around the last stitch in the row you want to mark (either the first row or last row of a repeat, for example). Some markers look like plastic paperclips; others have a lobster-claw clasp like jewellery.

Improvising your own row marker is easy, too: the ubiquitous safety pin can be used, as can a real paperclip. The simplest way to mark a row is to tie a short length of contrast-coloured yarn through the end stitch. You can easily cut this off later.

ROW COUNTERS

Once you have your rows and stitches marked, you still need to keep track of how many rows you've worked since you placed the marker. The simplest type of row counter is a piece of paper and a pencil: you just make a mark on the paper when you reach the end of each row.

However, this isn't always practical, particularly if you're knitting on the bus or in a cosy hammock.

A mechanical row counter that slips over your knitting needle or attaches to your knitting is the answer. The usual counter is a small plastic barrel that slips onto your knitting needle and has little windows showing the numbers from 0 to 9 and a toothed wheel on each end. At the end of the row, you simply turn the wheel so that the next number appears in the window.

There are also row counters with a trigger mechanism, so that you press the lever with your thumb at the end of each row to click the numbers over. These can be quite cute, in the shape of a frog, beetle or piece of fruit, and they usually hook over the end of your needle or can be pinned to your work or your clothing like a brooch.

POINT PROTECTORS

Point protectors are small rubber caps that can be placed over the points of knitting needles when they are not in use, so that the needles don't poke through things they shouldn't or become blunt. You might also find them useful for slipping onto the ends of double-pointed needles while you knit to prevent dropped stitches, especially if you're just starting to learn how to use DPNs.

A piece of soft pencil eraser or even a lump of reusable adhesive can also be used as a point protector.

SAFETY PINS

With a multitude of emergency uses, safety pins are a must for a knitter's supply kit: use them as stitch holders for small numbers of stitches; slip a closed pin over a knitting needle to use as a stitch marker; pin one to the end of a row to use as a row marker; pin pieces of a project together so they don't get lost while you're knitting the next piece; or even pin projects together while you sew or knit them up.

Measuring devices

NEEDLE GAUGES

A needle gauge, as described at the beginning of this chapter, is a small metal or plastic strip with a series of holes through which knitting needles can be passed to check their diameter. Many straight-edged needle gauges are rulers as well, making them doubly useful. Most are

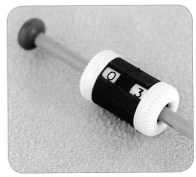
A row counter helps you keep track.

Different-sized row counters.

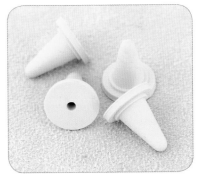
Rubber point protectors.

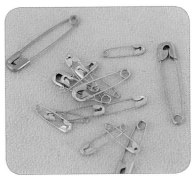
Safety pins of various sizes.

Flexible tape measure.

Retractable flexible tape measure.

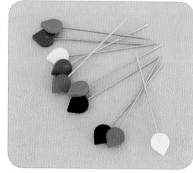
Knitter's pins.

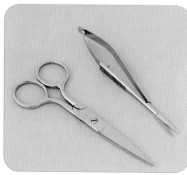
Scissors and snips for cutting yarn.

marked with both millimetre diameters and either UK gauge or US system numbers. Some have all three.

RULERS

A short, non-flexible ruler is useful for measuring tension squares, where you need to accurately count how many stitches and rows you will knit for every 10 cm (4 in) of fabric (see page 62). This is one of the most important steps in knitting, so make sure you have a good metal, plastic or wooden ruler. A short one, about 15 cm (6 in) long, will fit easily into your knitting project bag or accessories box.

TAPE MEASURES

A flexible tape measure is useful for measuring both bodies and knitted fabric. You need to be able to take basic size measurements from the person for whom a garment is intended, as well as to measure the length and width of your knitting as you work.

Choose a dressmaker's measuring tape that is at least a metre (a yard) long: a metre and a half is better. If you have a retractable tape, it will be easier to store, although the kind that you simply roll up around your fingers and secure with a rubber band is fine.

PINS

Pins are used for marking out tension squares as well as for holding knitted fabric together while you assemble your finished project. It is possible to use ordinary dressmaker's pins—the longer the better, and preferably the ones with plastic heads—but these are very fine and likely to get lost in the knitted fabric. Knitter's pins are longer and thicker and have larger heads so that they are less likely to disappear. The points are usually quite blunt, to avoid splitting the yarn.

Scissors and implements for sewing up

SCISSORS AND YARN CUTTERS

Naturally you will need a small pair of scissors for cutting yarn. Choose a good quality pair that fits naturally in your hand, and don't use them for anything else but cutting your knitting yarns. (Cutting paper and other substances blunts them more quickly.) A pair of dressmaker's thread snippers is a good alternative.

You can also use thread cutters with sharp blades concealed inside plastic or metal casings. These are especially good if you are taking your knitting with you, as they can be worn around your neck like a pendant, or pinned to your clothing or inside your project bag so that they won't get lost or dropped down behind the bus seat.

WOOL NEEDLES

To sew the pieces of your knitted project together, you will generally use the same yarn you have been knitting with (except perhaps in the case of novelty yarns, where you might use a plain yarn in a matching colour) and a wool or darning needle. Wool needles are large sewing needles with a blunt point and a large eye. They come in various sizes for different weights and thicknesses of yarn, so choose a suitable size and thread the yarn through the eye. See pages 102–103 for tips on sewing up projects.

CROCHET HOOKS

Many knitters also crochet; however, even if you don't intend to learn that skill, a crochet hook will come in handy for picking up dropped stitches (see page 88), or it can be used in place of a cable needle or stitch holder at a pinch. Crochet hooks are available in different diameters, much the same as knitting needles; a medium-sized hook (about 3.5 or 4 mm diameter) is handy to have around.

BUTTONS

Most knitted garments and items fit without separate closures, such as zippers and buttons, because they are designed to stretch and spring back into shape. Cardigans and jackets often have buttons (or, occasionally, zippers) and buttonholes worked into the knitted fabric or stitched on afterwards. Sometimes, buttons are purely for decoration.

When choosing buttons for knitted items, keep in mind that the texture of knitted fabric is usually chunkier and rougher than woven fabrics. Search out larger buttons, made of more interesting materials, like wood, shell, clay and bone. Or choose funky novelty buttons to adorn your knitted hat or handbag—they don't have to be functional. You can really let your imagination go wild and woolly!

Safety cutter with concealed blade.

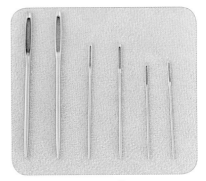

Wool or darning needles.

Crochet hooks, various sizes.

Buttons for decoration or fastenings.

Knitting necessities

29

Knitting basics

Felted pin and needle holder

A knitted and felted needle holder is a great way to store your pins and needles. It would be a good idea to read Chapter 13 about felting before you start this project.

YOU WILL NEED:

* One ball of 8-ply feltable wool yarn in the cover colour (blue)
* One ball of 8-ply feltable wool yarn in the inside colour (off-white)
* 4 mm (UK 8, US 6) knitting needles
* Washing machine, hot water and detergent
* Embroidery cotton or wool in a contrasting colour
* Knitter's pins and wool needle
* Scissors

CONSTRUCTION:

Cast on 35 stitches in one colour of yarn and knit in stocking stitch (1 row knit, 1 row purl) for about 15 cm (6 in). Cast off. Repeat the process with the contrasting colour for the reverse side.

Put the rectangles of knitted fabric in the washing machine with some detergent and run a hot water wash cycle. Remove the felted fabrics from the machine and dry them flat or in a tumble dryer.

Trim the fabric pieces so that they are the same size and pin them together with the wrong sides facing each other. Work blanket stitch around the outer edges using embroidery cotton or wool. Stitch down the centre of the 'book' as well, using back stitch or running stitch. You could add some embroidery to the cover if you like.

Stick pins and darning needles into the felt to keep them secure.

Takeaway coffee cups used as yarn holders.

Yarn bobbins.

Knick-knacks

Browsing through a knitting supply shop, you may be surprised by the different types of knick-knacks that are available for knitters. None of these is really necessary (usually you can come up with an inexpensive alternative from items you already have at home) but they can be fun and frivolous.

Yarn bobbins are useful for holding small amounts of yarn while you work with multiple colours or textures, as well as for storing small amounts of leftover yarn in case repairs are needed later.

You can buy cute plastic shapes, but you could also cut small rectangles of corrugated cardboard from an old box to serve the same purpose.

A **wool winder** that clamps onto the edge of a table (see page 249) is great for rewinding balls of yarn, but you can simply wrap the yarn around your fingers to get it started and then wind the rest of the ball by hand.

Graph paper is useful for drawing up patterns and motifs, when you're ready to start creating your own patterns. You can also use graph paper to help you keep count of stitches or rows.

Yarn containers with a hole in the top for dispensing yarn smoothly can be bought in most craft shops, or you can use clean takeaway coffee cups to hold average-sized balls. Wash the cups thoroughly if they've already been used for coffee, and use the end of a spoon handle to slightly enlarge the sipping hole in the lid so that the edges don't catch the yarn. Carefully pull the end of the yarn from the centre of the ball (see the instructions on page 14) and then place the ball in the coffee cup.

Pompom discs, various sizes.

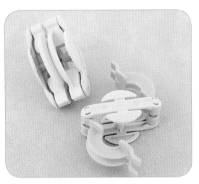
Pompom makers.

①

②

③

④

Thread the end of the yarn through the sipping hole, attach it to your work and start knitting!

Plastic pompom discs or donuts in various sizes, or a fantastic contraption like the ones pictured here that makes wrapping the yarn even easier, can be bought these days. Pompoms are a fun thing to make with knitting yarn, and a great way to use leftovers of your favourite yarns. You'll probably remember making them as a child, using two donuts of stiff card.

If you're using the donut method, cut the yarn into approximately 2-metre lengths to make it easier to work with. You'll need three or four of these lengths per pompom. If you're using a pompom maker, you can work with the yarn as it comes off the ball.

① Wrap the yarn firmly but not too tightly around the donut or the arms of the pompom maker until you've got a nice thick coverage all the way around the circle.

② Place the point of a pair of scissors into the yarn, between the two halves of the pompom maker or donut, and carefully cut the yarn all the way around the circle.

③ Slip a doubled length of yarn between the two halves of the donut or pompom maker and around the pompom, tying it firmly in a knot. Wrap it around and knot it again just to make sure.

④ Carefully slip the two halves of the pompom maker or donut off the ends of the pompom, fluff it into shape and trim off any protruding threads with scissors.

Knitting necessities

Retro cafetière cosy

Have fun making a bunch of pompoms and then use them to decorate this retro-style coffee cosy.

YOU WILL NEED:
* One 50 g ball each of five different retro colours in 8-ply wool yarn
* Pair of 4 mm (UK 8, US 6) knitting needles
* 3 cm (1¼ in) pompom maker or two cardboard disks with a diameter of about 4 cm (1½ in) and a 2 cm (¾ in) hole in the centre
* 4 mm crochet hook (optional)
* Wool needle
* Scissors

CONSTRUCTION:
First, make the pompoms. Make two of each colour and then another two from your favourite colours (you'll need twelve altogether).

Measure the height of your cafetière to work out the number of stitches you need to cast on. I used 30 stitches for a twelve-cup pot (which measures about 15 cm (6 in) between base and lip). Knit in garter stitch (every row knit: see page 73), changing colours after two rows.

When you change colour, loosely knot the ends of the yarn and leave a tail of about 10 cm (4 in) dangling at the edge of the fabric. Work the colours in any order; you can repeat them in the same order every 10 rows or change them at random.

Measure the circumference of your cafetière to work out how many rows you need to knit. Because the fabric will stretch, take off a few centimetres from the total measurement to allow for that.

My pot measures 35 cm (14 in), but I knitted only 32 cm (12½ in) of fabric. Cast off.

Press the fabric lightly with a steam iron on a wool setting to block it, if you wish. Knot each pair of thread ends firmly and lay the tails flat, at right angles to the edge of the fabric. Comb them out with your fingers and then trim them all to an even length (about 4 cm or 1½ in).

Choose one yarn colour to make the ties. I crocheted chains about 15 cm (6 in) long (45 chain), but you could also plait or twist the yarn. Make six ties, with a 10 cm (4 in) tail of yarn at each end. Using a wool needle and the tail of the yarn, stitch one end of each tie to the knitted fabric, one at each corner and one in the centre of each end. Darn in the end of the tails.

Thread the wool needle with the other tail of yarn at the loose end of the tie and then pass the needle through the centre of a pompom, then back through the last chain stitch of the tie. Repeat with another pompom, fasten the yarn and hide the tail in the tie or one of the pompoms. Repeat for all of the ties and pompoms.

Place the cosy around the cafetière (note that I've used the 'wrong side' of the knitting as the outside, to break up the stripes even more) and tie it on around the handle.

Make a pot of coffee and enjoy it while it's hot.

3
Fabulous fibres

* A good yarn * Ply your trade

* Dye lots * Hanks, balls and skeins

* Wool and other animal fibres

* Cotton, bamboo and plant fibres * Synthetic fibres

* Paper, plastic and other materials

Tactile textiles

The web of life is of a mingled yarn, good and ill together.

William Shakespeare, ALL'S WELL THAT ENDS WELL

A good yarn

A knitter's greatest pleasure is the look and feel of the multitude of different yarns that can be turned into fabulous garments and accessories. Traditionally, knitters have used spun woollen fibres to create their projects. Wool works well for knitted fabric because it is elastic (so it can be easily manipulated and yet hold its shape), warm and—to a large extent—weatherproof. It is also a renewable resource: you shear the sheep and then the wool grows back. However, there are many other fibres from animals and plants, and other materials that are suitable for knitting, and they all have their uses in the myriad projects you can produce with a pair of needles and a good yarn.

Ply your trade

When you're reading a pattern or shopping for yarn you will notice that the fibres usually come in twisted ropes of various thicknesses. The term 'ply' is traditionally used to describe the number of individual strands of filament that are twisted into the yarn. So, 3-ply is three strands of filament, 5-ply is five strands, and so on. In general, the larger the number of the ply, the thicker the yarn.

There are also some other common names for different weights and thicknesses of natural and synthetic yarns that you might come across instead of the ply measurement. The different names may depend on where the yarn was produced (or, if you're reading a pattern, where the pattern was printed). The table on the next page outlines some of the terms you might see and their equivalents, along with the main uses of these thicknesses of yarn.

Not all yarns are labelled with their ply, as they may have been created by a slightly different process: the twist may be looser to allow more bulk, or the filament may be thicker to begin with. With synthetic and novelty yarns, there may not even be a spinning and twisting process. You can generally work out the roughly equivalent ply of the yarn by noting the size of knitting needle that is recommended by the manufacturer, or by knitting a tension square (see page 62 for more information).

NATURAL AND SYNTHETIC SPUN FIBRES

PLY	ALSO KNOWN AS	NEEDLE SIZE	MAINLY USED FOR
2-ply	Lace weight	2.25 mm	Machine knitting, lacy work
3-ply	Baby	3 mm	Baby's clothing, socks and lacy work
4-ply	Sport, fingering	3.25 mm	Baby's and children's clothing, socks
5-ply	--	3.75 mm	Children's clothing, some women's wear; 5-ply yarn is used frequently in Australia but is rare elsewhere
8-ply	DK (double-knitting)	4 mm	Most knitting projects: clothing and accessories
10-ply	Aran, worsted	5 mm	Fisherman's ganseys, adults' clothing, soft furnishings
12-ply	Chunky, bulky	5.5 mm	Adults' clothing, novelty knitwear, accessories, soft furnishings
14-ply or larger	Super chunky, super bulky	7 mm or larger	Adults' clothing, novelty knitwear, accessories, soft furnishings

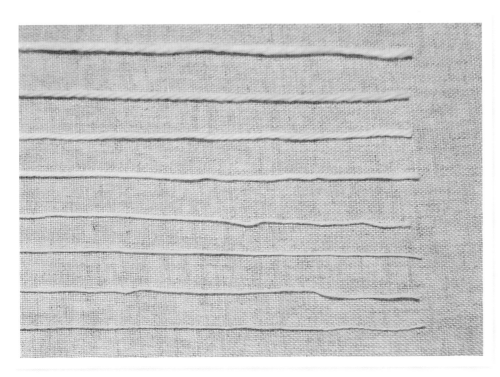

Wool yarn, from top to bottom: 14-ply, 12-ply, 10-ply, 8-ply, 5-ply, 4-ply, 3-ply, 2-ply.

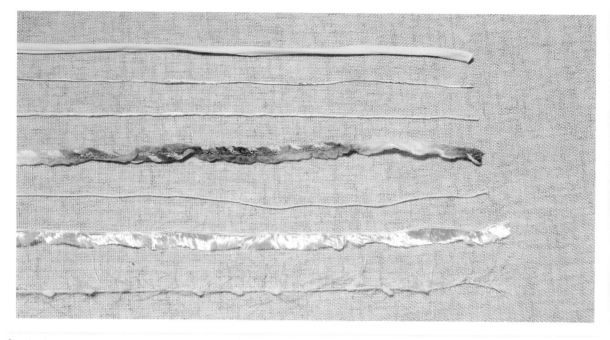

Synthetic and novelty yarns, top to bottom: fabric, paper, bamboo, stitched roving, cotton, eyelash, slubby yarn.

Reading a label

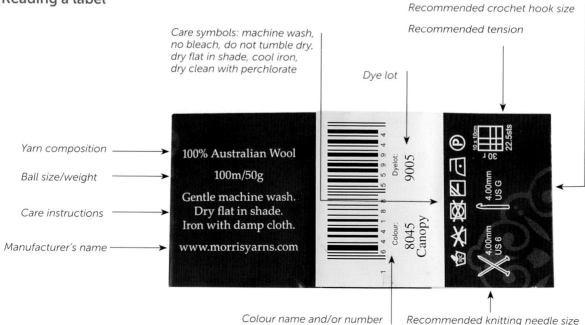

Recommended crochet hook size

Recommended tension

*Care symbols: machine wash,
no bleach, do not tumble dry,
dry flat in shade, cool iron,
dry clean with perchlorate*

Dye lot

Yarn composition

Ball size/weight

Care instructions

Manufacturer's name

100% Australian Wool

100m/50g

Gentle machine wash.
Dry flat in shade.
Iron with damp cloth.

www.morrisyarns.com

Dyelot: 9005

Colour: 8045 Canopy

10 x 10cm   22.5sts

30 r

4.00mm US G

4.00mm US 6

Colour name and/or number

Recommended knitting needle size

Different dye lots of the same shade may have subtle colour differences.

Dye lots

When you look at the label on the yarn you've selected, you'll see lots of information about using and caring for the fibres. One of the most important things to note is the dye lot. When yarns are dyed—particularly natural fibres such as wool, silk, linen, cotton and bamboo—natural variations in the composition of the fibres and the way they absorb the dye can result in slight differences in colour. This is why manufacturers indicate a dye lot as well as a colour number on the label. Yarn from the same dye lot is more likely to match than the same yarn dyed with the same dye recipe on a different day.

When you purchase yarn for a project, it's important to get enough yarn from the same dye lot to complete the whole thing; however, if you do run out of yarn or need to use some yarn from a different dye lot, there are some ways of minimising obvious colour changes.

COLLARS AND CUFFS

If you don't have quite enough yarn to finish a garment, you can sometimes save the project by knitting all the main parts in the original colour and then switching to a new dye lot to knit the finishing touches, such as the neckband. If you know before you start that you're going to have to switch dye lots, you could even knit sections such as ribbing around the bottom edge and on the cuffs in the different dye lot.

BLENDING

If you have roughly equal amounts of different dye lots, try knitting with two balls of yarn at once (one from each dye lot). To do this, use double-pointed needles or a circular needle so that you can knit from either end of the work.

① Work 1 row with one yarn and then join the next yarn and work the next row (see page 87 for joining yarn). Note that we have used two different colours (not just different dye lots) to make it easier to see what is happening.

② Don't turn the work but go back to the first yarn and work the next row with the first yarn.

③ Now turn the work and work the next row with the second yarn. Without turning the work, go back to the first yarn and work another row with the first yarn, and so on. (You will end up working 2 rows in the same direction, one with each dye lot and then turning and working 2 rows in the opposite direction, one with each dye lot.)

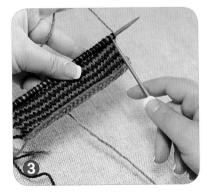

Hanks, balls and skeins

When yarn is spun and dyed, it is usually wound into large hanks, which are several hundred metres of yarn wound in large loops and twisted into a loose braid. If you are buying yarn in bulk directly from a spinner or dyer, you might see yarn in hanks. Before they get to the yarn shop, however, hanks of yarn are usually rewound in smaller, more manageable amounts. Sometimes yarn is wound onto a wooden, cardboard or plastic bobbin or cone for more support.

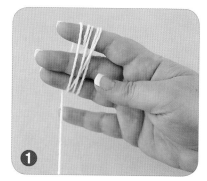

Mostly, yarn is wound into easy-to-use balls or skeins. By definition, a skein is a coil of yarn that is wound without any central support, and so most balls of yarn you see in stores are technically skeins. We're going to use the terms interchangeably in this book, but 'ball' is the most common term and so that's what will mostly be used.

Balls or skeins of wool are generally sold by weight, and the most common size is 50 grams; however, larger 100-gram, 200-gram and even 1-kilogram balls can be purchased, as well as smaller 20- or 25-gram balls. (In the United States, yarn is often sold in ounces or by the number of yards in the skein or ball, as well as by weight in grams. Fifty grams is just under 2 ounces; 100 grams is about 3½ ounces.) The weight of the skein is marked on the label, and the label will also usually indicate the number of metres or yards of yarn in the ball.

If you buy yarn in hanks, you'll need to wind it into smaller balls or skeins before you begin knitting, just to make it more manageable. You can do this by hand, or use an inexpensive mechanical yarn winder (available from your knitting supply shop).

① If you're winding from a hank of yarn by hand, begin by untwisting the hank and asking a helper to hold the loop open for you, or place it over the back of a chair, for example. Wind the yarn loosely around three fingers, making about a dozen loops. It's important not to stretch the yarn as you wind it.

② Holding the loops between your fingers and thumb, begin wrapping the yarn across the loops and around two fingers. Keep the yarn loose—you don't want to stretch it or cut off the circulation in your fingers!

③ When the yarn starts to form a ball shape, remove it from your fingers and turn it in your hand as you continue to loop the yarn over the ball, to get an even coverage. Note that you can't use the yarn from the centre of a hand-wound ball like this.

14-ply wool.

4-ply wool.

2-ply wool.

Wool and other animal fibres

Yarns made from animal hair such as wool have many of the properties that made them so useful to the animal from which they have been shorn. The hollow fibres are good insulators, keeping in body warmth and keeping out cold air; they absorb water readily, are not easily flammable and are generally soft and luxurious to touch.

WOOL

Wool is the fibre from sheep and, while some breeds of sheep are particularly known for their longer wool fibres (making them easier to comb and spin), all wool has the same basic characteristics: warmth, strength and elasticity. In addition, wool can absorb up to a third of its own weight in moisture before it feels wet, and while it is wet, it retains its insulating abilities. That's why wool is preferred for winter wear such as jumpers, scarves, gloves and hats.

Wool fibres have scales on the outside and a natural crimp, both of which help in the making of knitted fabric by encouraging the fibres to cling together and retain their shape; however, these are also what makes wool prone to felt up when it is washed and dried incorrectly. Some manufacturers apply a special process to the wool fibres to either remove the scales in an acid bath or coat the fibre

with a polymer, so that the wool can be washed in a washing machine and, in some cases, even tumble-dried. (See Chapter 11 for washing advice and Chapter 13 for more information about felting woollen fibres.)

Wool is shorn from live sheep and sorted for quality. When it arrives at the mill, it is processed by scouring with soapy water to remove impurities such as seeds and burrs; this also removes the greasy natural lanolin that coats the fibres. (Lanolin is a rich moisturiser that is often used in cosmetics such as hand-creams.)

Combing and carding are the next processes, designed to remove broken fibres and to line all the fibres up in the same direction, ready for the next stage of the process, roving. Roved wool is a loose bundle of clean, tangle-free fibres that are ready to be dyed. You can purchase wool roving in hanks (people who make felt use roved wool to make fabric, see page 233), either pre-dyed or ready to dye and spin if you are so inclined. Wool is often dyed before it is spun to get the most even colour effect, although the dye can be added at any stage of the process—after spinning but before plying, for example, or even after it has been wound into a ball or knitted into a fabric.

Roved wool is spun, either by hand using a spindle, on a spinning wheel or by machine, to create thin filaments of yarn that can be used on their own or twisted together (plied) to make thicker yarn.

Wool can be recycled, even after it has been made up into garments and worn. Rags are shredded and reduced back to fibre, which can then be carded, roved and spun into new yarn. Sometimes old wool is mixed with new wool in the spinning process. This is why you will see some wool labelled 'Pure New Wool': that means that no recycled wool is included in the yarn.

Knitting with wool is easy because the elasticity of the yarn assists you in making the stitches, allowing you to easily slide the point of one needle into a stitch on the other needle, for example. It is generally soft and somewhat smooth to the touch, despite all the childhood complaints I made to my mother about woollen jumpers being scratchy and uncomfortable.

Occasionally, wool fibres are blended with other fibres during the spinning or plying process, in order to improve the quality in some way. Other animal fibres, such as mohair, alpaca and cashmere (see below), add softness and smoothness to wool. Synthetic fibres mixed with wool can increase its durability and make it easier to care for: most synthetic fibres can be machine washed, for example (see page 214). They can also increase the softness of the yarn to the touch and hold dye well, giving a greater range of colours.

OTHER ANIMAL FIBRES

Mohair, alpaca, cashmere and angora are all popular spinning and knitting fibres that come from animals other than sheep. Mohair and cashmere are from goats, while vicuñas and alpacas give their name to their own fur. Angora fibres come from soft, fluffy rabbits. These fibres are often blended with wool to combine the best qualities of both fibres.

It is possible to comb and spin fibres from other animals, too. I have heard of people spinning fur shed from the winter coat of their pet dog, and I once had a friend who cut off many years' growth of hair and had her mother spin it into a yarn for her.

12-ply wool and alpaca blend.

Mohair and silk.

100 per cent cotton.

Silk

Silk comes from the cocoon of the silk moth (*Bombyx mori*) and is known as one of the most luxurious fibres in the world. Its beautiful, smooth feel comes from the long, fine fibres that are carefully wound off the cocoon before its occupant breaks free and spoils the fibres. (Unfortunately, this means death for the larva inside the cocoon.) Silk is strong, about twice as strong as a steel filament of the same diameter, and has all the desirable insulating properties of an animal-based yarn, although it is not as elastic or hard wearing as wool. Silk fibres plied together can make a lovely yarn, or they can be plied with wool and other yarns to make the finished product easier to care for than pure silk. The hot-water bottle cover on page 76 is knitted with hand-dyed silk yarn.

Cotton, bamboo and plant fibres

Fibres from plants—such as cotton, linen, hemp and bamboo—have long been used to help clothe human beings, usually through the process of weaving them into strong, smooth fabrics. Plant fibres, while they have some elasticity, owe their strength to solid cellular walls so they tend not to stretch much. Plant fibres are breathable: they allow body heat and moisture to be taken away from the body rather than kept in, and so these fibres are perfect for summer knitwear.

COTTON

Cotton is a popular fibre for knitting, although these days it is being pushed aside by bamboo, which has very similar characteristics and seems to offer a more sustainable method of production (see page 47). Cotton is the fibrous padding inside the seed pod or boll of the cotton plant (*Gossypium* species). When the bolls of the crop are ready to open and release their ripened seeds, the harvester comes along and collects them all for use in fabric making and other purposes. The seeds are removed and turned into cottonseed oil and animal feed.

Cotton is lustrous (smooth and shiny) and absorbent but is highly flammable. The fibres are prepared for spinning and knitting in much the same way as wool: they are combed, carded and roved before dyeing and spinning into yarn. Cotton accepts dye readily, and so a wide range of colours is attainable. It is soft to the touch, making it a pleasure to knit with. The main drawback of using cotton for knitted fabric is the weight of the yarn, combined with lower elasticity: garments can be

Fabulous fibres

Knitting elastic.

quite heavy and will tend to hang on the body and lose their shape, so steer clear of very tailored designs and stick to more casual looks when you are knitting with cotton.

Cotton can be blended with a synthetic fibre such as Lycra, or elastane, to give more elasticity; another alternative is to purchase knitting elastic—a very fine elastic thread that looks like a sewing thread on a spool—and knit this along with the cotton yarn for areas such as ribbing bands and necklines where you need the fabric to hold its shape.

RAYON

Although rayon is a manufactured fibre, it is made from cellulose, which is the important ingredient in cotton fibre (more than ninety per cent), as well as other plant fibres. This means that rayon has all the properties of a natural plant fibre and cannot be considered truly synthetic.

The process of converting cellulose into rayon was first invented in the mid-nineteenth century but was not efficient enough for widespread use until the twentieth century. The manufacturing process involves chemically dissolving cellulose in a solvent and spinning out filaments of the viscous solution that results (hence, rayon is sometimes known as viscose).

Rayon has the same comfort properties as cotton: it is soft, smooth, absorbent and comfortable. Rayon on its own lacks elasticity, but it is often blended with other fibres in knitting yarn.

LINEN AND HEMP

Like bamboo, linen and hemp are fibres that come from the stems of their respective plants. Linen comes from the flax plant (*Linum usitatissimum*), while hemp comes from the same plant as marijuana (*Cannabis sativa*)—although the plants grown for fabric are a different subspecies that has been bred so that the active ingredient of the drug is not produced.

The plants are harvested and then go through some deliciously named processes to prepare the fibre: retting, a sort of fermentation of the plant stems to break down the fibre bonds; scutching, crushing between rollers to remove the woody parts; and heckling, combing the fibres to line them all up ready for dyeing, spinning and weaving or knitting.

Both linen and hemp fibres are strong (two to three times stronger than cotton) and comfortable to wear; being quite absorbent they are useful in hot weather for wicking moisture away from the skin while allowing air to pass through the fabric and cool the body. They are not highly elastic, and so once again you might need to consider the way the finished garment will hang, although yarns made from linen and hemp are not usually as heavy as cotton yarn.

For knitting, these fibres are usually blended with other natural or synthetic fibres to improve elasticity and ease of care.

Bamboo viscose and wool blend.

BAMBOO

In an economic climate where we are constantly looking for sustainable crops and ecologically sound farming techniques, bamboo fibre is emerging as a new champion, overtaking cotton as the most popular summer yarn for knitters. It can also be woven into fabric in the same way as cotton and used for other fibrous needs, such as quilt batting, insulation and much more. Bamboo is a grass and the fibres come from new growth above ground. This means that it can be harvested without killing the plant, which will immediately begin to regrow from its underground stem.

The plant stems are treated in much the same way as flax and hemp to create a fibre for carding, dyeing and spinning; however, bamboo can also be used as the base fibre for rayon production, and there have recently been complaints that bamboo-based rayon is being marketed as bamboo yarn in order to tap into the eco-friendly market, although the manufacturing process is very different. You might see some yarns labelled as 'rayon (from bamboo)'.

Bamboo yarn has all the same characteristics as cotton and can be treated in much the same way once it is spun into yarn and knitted into fabric.

Synthetic fibres

The invention of synthetic fibres in the early twentieth century brought about a revolution in the manufacture of clothing and fabrics. One of the first fibres to be mass-produced, nylon, was immediately taken up by manufacturers of knitted stockings as it had all the desirable properties—smoothness, elasticity, washability—that silk and wool (fibres that had formerly been used in stockings) lacked. During World War II nylon came into its own: at the beginning of the war, eighty per cent of fabric was cotton, nearly twenty per cent was wool and the very small

100 per cent acrylic bulky yarn.

100 per cent acrylic 8-ply.

8-ply nylon and wool blend.

Wool, acrylic and nylon novelty yarn.

remainder accounted for all other fabric fibres. By 1945 synthetic fibres, including nylon, represented a quarter of fabric production.

Although manufactured fibres such as rayon were already in use, nylon was the first truly synthetic fibre made from a petrochemical base. The development of polyester fibres in the 1950s allowed synthetic fibres to take over from cotton and wool as the main source of fibre. Synthetic fibres are soft to the touch, colourfast and resistant to damage by hot water and sunlight, and therefore they are easy to care for when they are knitted into a fabric. They are usually coloured early in the manufacturing process, which makes for very even and non-fading colour. They do not readily accept dye once they are spun.

Acrylic fibres are another form of synthetic fibre, first produced by the nylon producer Du Pont in 1941 and patented under the name Orlon. These fibres are light, soft and warm, with a wool-like feel. They are generally inexpensive and are machine washable, with good wrinkle resistance; some knitters prefer them, particularly for babies' and children's garments that require regular washing. On the other hand, acrylic yarns have a tendency to fuzz or develop little 'pills' (balls of matted fibre) and can retain static electricity—have you ever removed an acrylic jumper in a dark room? It's quite a sight!

NOVELTY YARNS

Synthetic fibres are the basis of many of the fantastic and gorgeous novelty yarns that you will find in your yarn store or knitting supplies shop. Fringes of eyelashes, slubs of chenille, meshes of silky ribbons and combinations of lumps and strings and glitter make shopping and knitting so much fun. Most novelty yarns have the bonus characteristic of being quick to knit up on large needles, so that you can walk out of the shop with your exquisite yarn one day, knit it the next and wear it as soon as you like.

Paper, plastic and other materials

Knitters are becoming more adventurous and turning their needles to materials other than the traditional natural and synthetic fibres. While these materials can look great, they can be difficult to work with and require quite a lot of patience. Some will not be washable at all, so choose carefully what you are going to make with them.

FABRIC YARNS

The ultimate in recycling, turning a knitted or woven fabric into knitting yarn, is simple. You can purchase fabric yarn already cut and prepared, or take an old T-shirt and carefully cut it into strips about 2.5 cm (1 inch) wide. If you cut it around in a single spiral, you'll save yourself having to join the yarn so often. Cut across the fabric, and the strip will naturally roll in to hide the raw edges. Knit on large needles (10 mm or larger) to make handbags, cushions, rugs, hats and scarves. You could make clothing, but it will be quite heavy and awkward to wear.

100 per cent polyester eyelash yarn.

Nylon textured yarn.

Woven cotton fabric strips.

Cotton jersey fabric strips.

Fabulous fibres

Paper yarns.

Paper string.

Plastic bag yarn.

PAPER YARNS

Paper is fragile and liable to tear, but if it is twisted together in a paper string you will have some success with knitting it. You can purchase yarns made from recycled newspaper and other paper, or use paper string. There are also yarns that are made to look like paper; however, these are basically a rayon fibre made as a flattened filament rather than a rounded, plied yarn. If you want the paper look, these are perhaps a better choice as they can be laundered (carefully) and they are finer and easier to knit than real paper. Knit paper on large needles if you are using twisted paper yarn, or finer needles for the rayon paper yarns. Paper can be used for novelty items, such as grocery bags, sunhats, scarves and knitted furnishings.

Knitting basics

PLASTIC YARN

You could say that most synthetic yarns are plastic, but in this case we are talking about yarn made from household plastics such as plastic shopping bags. This is a kind of short-term recycling, in which used plastic bags are cleaned, dried and cut into narrow strips for knitting.

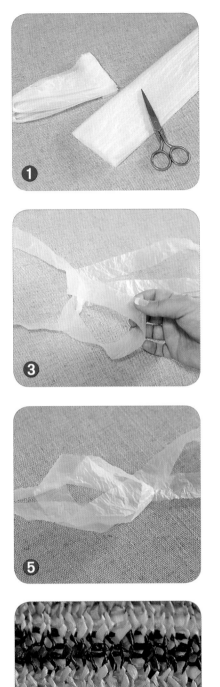

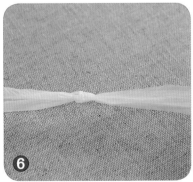

① The easiest way to make plastic yarn is to fold the clean, dry bag in quarters lengthwise, and then cut off the base and the handles.

② Cut 2.5 cm (1 in) strips across the bag and then open out the loops of plastic.

③ Join the loops into lengths of yarn by passing a second loop through the first one.

④ Pass one end of the second loop through itself.

⑤ Gently pull the two loops in opposite directions until they form a small knot.

⑥ Pull the knot until it is quite small, but don't pull too hard, or the plastic will break.

⑦ Knit plastic yarn with large needles to create shopping bags, raingear (hats and coats), bags, belts and other fun accessories.

Fabulous fibres

Knitted Tie

BLUEBELL CREPE

ALL ... PROOFED

MATERIALS

Bluebell

Patons Beehive or Queen Bee Knitting Needles.

1 ball

1 pair on 1: ... age 19.

Continue in plain smooth fabric, inc.
once at each end of needle in every row
until there are 41 [B—45] [C—...] sts.
Cast on 22 [B—23] [C—24] sts., beg.
... row, ... 4 sts. at beg. fol-
... row. (67 [B—72] [C—77] sts.).
... K.2. ... Knit last 4 sts.
Next row.—P... cast on 2 sts., pur...
... of row.
Work 8 rows without ... ping.
Inc. o... ... edge ... next and eve...
follow... [B—82] ... sts. on ... here are 7...
same time ... sts. in every ... whilst ...
... in every ... ... le as be-
previous butt... ... 20 ... ... from ...
tonholes.) ... but-
Shape neck by ... ng 4 ... at b...
of next row, ... K.2 ... ... ck edg...
in next 8 row ... ... 5] sts.).
Shape armho ... —70 ...
Next row.—Cast off 10 [B—11] ... [C—12]
sts. knit to last 2 sts., K.2 tog.
Dec. once at each end of needle in ...
... row until 40 [B—44] [C—48] ...
... ain.
Continue dec. once at neck edge only
... every following 4th row until 32 [B—3...]
[C—3...] sts. remain, then in every fo...
... lowing ... row until 27 [C—33] ...
sts. rema...
Work 6 [B—8] [C—10] rows without ...
shaping.
Shape shoulder ... as follows:—
... st row.—Work ... last 9 [B—10] [C—11]
... turn.

(Continued on page 18)

(Continued on page 18)

Pat...
Needles...
Loose Knitters—1 pair No. 10 ... Bee Knitting
Average Knitters—1 pair No. ...
Tight Knitters—1 pair No. ...
Needle size in instructions is ...
Average Knitters.
Needle size depends upon your ...
which should be 13½ sti... ... nsion,
inches in width, measured ... to 2
smooth fabric. Check ... plain
page 19.

Five Small Buttons.

ABBREVIATIONS: See ...

Instructions are for ... size A.
Larger sizes B and C ... ... own thus
[B . .] [C . .] ... ... one set of
figures is given, this ... to all sizes.

THE LEFT FRON... ... size No. 9
Needles, cast on 3 ...

1st row.—Knit.
2nd row.—Inc. on... ... st.,
once in last st.
3rd row.—Inc. onc... ... st.,
once in last st.
4th row.—Inc. ... ... st.,
... st., K.3, inc. ... ... first st., P.5, inc.
once in last st.

1st row ... ... to end of ro...
Rep. 1st row ... ... Following ...
... m commencem ... ... k m ...
... ceed as follows:
... (K.1, P.1) t ... ... ime ...
... p.s.s.o., (P.1, ... hre ...
... d of row.
2nd row.—K.1. * P... K...
... to end of row.
... 2nd row six times.
... (K.1, P.1) twice, K...
... lip 1, P.2 tog. p.s.s.o., (K...
... twice ...
... P.1.
... Rep. 1 ... (K...
7th row.— ... d row seven times.
... (K.1, P.1) twice, ... lip 1,
... 2 tog ... ... p.s.s.o., (P.1, K.1) tw...
... p. 2n ... row tw...
... ins. fr... row until work mea...
... in last dec. Cast off in M...
Swit...

4

Choosing and reading a pattern

✳ Choosing a pattern

✳ Measurements ✳ Common abbreviations

✳ Knitting a tension square ✳ Substituting yarn

A pattern to follow

Out of a drawer she had taken a white stocking with a red bird pattern on it, which she was now knitting; the long-legged creatures might have represented herons or storks ... 'Where have you learned that, Elke?' 'This? From Trin Jans out there on the dike; she can do all sorts of things.'

Theodor Storm, THE RIDER ON THE WHITE HORSE

Choosing a pattern

Sometimes, the pattern comes first. You see a picture in a knitting magazine or a pattern book in a knitting supplies store and think, 'I want to make that'. That's the easy way; then you only have to seek out the required brand and quantity of yarn, pick up your needles in the correct size and start knitting.

At other times, the yarn comes first. You find a colour or texture that appeals to you with its luxurious look and feel and then start to think about how you could use it to knit a garment or an accessory, or a bit of soft furnishing for your home. Yarn manufacturers often publish books of patterns for particular yarns in their range, and sometimes they will give away a free pattern with the purchase of a certain amount of yarn. These days, most manufacturers have websites on which they offer patterns and advice for knitting with their yarns, too.

A third way of deciding what to knit is the most difficult: deciding first on the type of garment you want to knit, searching out a pattern that most closely resembles what you have in mind, and then finding the yarn to suit. This is when you'll spend hours trawling through knitting websites and yarn stores, looking for the perfect pattern. Perhaps when you have more knitting experience, you'll feel confident enough to combine features from different patterns or even to create your own patterns. In the meantime, you'll need to learn the arcane language of the knitting pattern and what the various abbreviations and symbols mean.

READING A PATTERN

The sample pattern below shows the type of information you will find in a standard knitting pattern. This is an example only, not a complete pattern.

To fit chest	81	86	91 cm
	32	34	36 in
Actual size	84	89	94 cm
	33	35	37 in
Length	60	61	62 cm
	23½	24	24½ in
Sleeve length	44	44	44 cm
	17½	17½	17½ in

Sizing information

Manufacturer's yarn name 50 g balls

Colour or shade name   13   14   15 balls

Yarn requirements

1 pair each of 4 mm (No 8) and 3.75 mm (No 9) knitting needles

Needle size

TENSION

The recommended tension for this design is 20 stitches to 10 cm (4 in).

Tension details

BACK

With 3.75 mm needles, cast on 82 [86, 94] sts.

Row 1: (Right-side row) K2, * P2, K2 *, rep * to * to end.

Row 2: P2, * K2, P2 *, rep * to * to end.

Rep these 2 rows for 5 cm (2 in) ending 2nd rib row. Inc 1 st each end of the last row for 1st and 2nd sizes only (84 [88, 94] sts).

Change to 4 mm needles. Beg K row, work in st st until work measures 39 cm (15½ in) ending P row.

Knitting instructions for first garment piece

Shape armholes

Cast off 4 [5, 6] sts at beg next 2 rows, then 2 sts at beg of next 2 foll rows (72 [74, 78] sts). Dec 1 st each end of every alt row 6 [6, 7] times (60 [62, 64] sts). Cont straight until armholes measure 18 [19, 20] cm (7 [7½, 8] in) ending P row.

Shape back neck and shoulders

Next row: K22 [22, 22], turn work and complete this side first.

* Cast off 2 sts (neck) at beg of the next row, then 4 sts (shoulder) at beg of foll row. Rep these 2 rows twice more. P 1 row to shoulder edge. Cast off rem 4 [4, 4] shoulder sts.

Slip centre 16 [18, 20] sts on holder for neckband. With right side facing, rejoin yarn to neck edge of rem sts. Rep as given from * to end, reversing shapings.

Instructions for shaping the garment piece

FRONT

Work the same as back until armholes measure 13 [14, 15] cm (5 [5½, 6] in).

Knitting instructions for second garment piece

Measurements

To ensure that the finished garment fits you or the intended wearer correctly, it's important to know certain body measurements when deciding on a size. Most knitted garments are jumpers or tops, and so the most important measurement is the chest or bust measurement. Use a flexible tape measure held lightly around the chest just below the arms, with the arms hanging down over the tape measure. The tape should pass across the widest part of the chest, usually in line with the nipples. Don't pull it tight: the tape should just sit against the body.

The next most important measurement is the length, which is measured from the nape of the neck to either the waist or the hip, depending on the requirements of the pattern. If the garment has sleeves, you will also need to know the sleeve length, which can be measured either from the point of the shoulder to the wrist or from the underarm to the wrist (take both measurements, just to be sure).

Other measurements you might need or want to take, for checking your knitting as you go, include the waist or hip measurement, the circumference of the arm and the depth of the neckline, particularly if the garment you are knitting is quite fitted.

If you are making a knitted garment other than a jumper or top, you might need other measurements: waist and hip circumference, and waist to knee measurement, for a skirt; foot measurements and ankle to knee measurements, for socks; head circumference, for a hat; and even inside leg measurements for a pair of knitted leggings or pants.

BASIC MEASUREMENTS FOR WOMEN

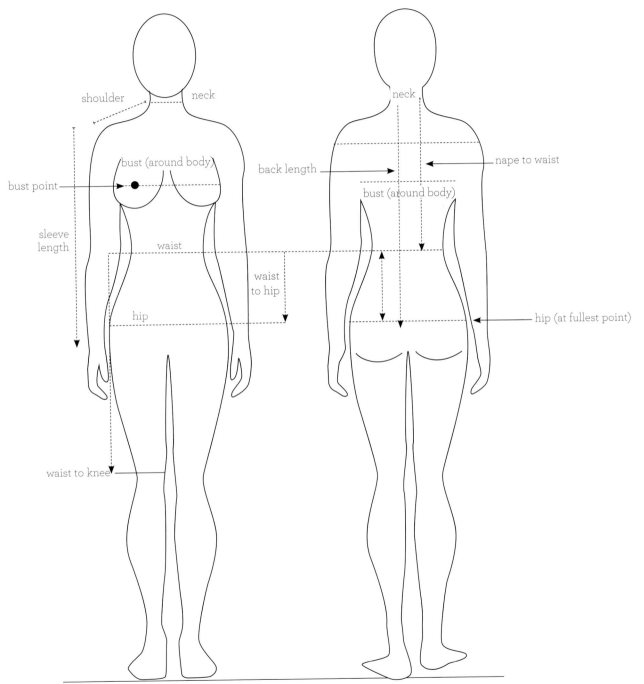

shoulder neck

neck

bust (around body)

bust point

sleeve length

waist

waist to hip

hip

waist to knee

back length

nape to waist

bust (around body)

hip (at fullest point)

BASIC MEASUREMENTS FOR MEN

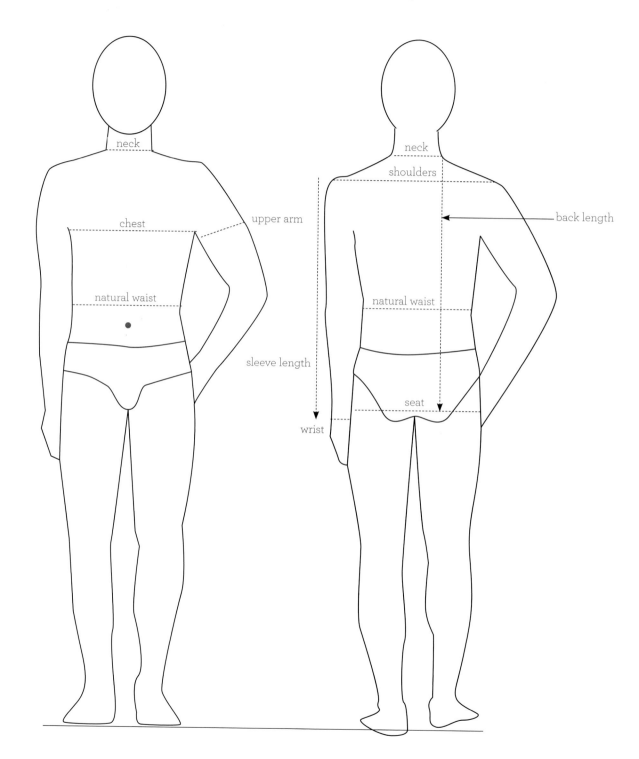

Knitting basics

Common abbreviations

Most knitting patterns or pattern books will give a list of abbreviations used and what they mean at the beginning of the pattern or book, or sometimes at the end. The most common abbreviations are shown in the following table.

ABBREVIATION	WHAT IT MEANS	SOMETIMES CALLED
alt	alternate	
beg	beginning	
CN	cable needle	
cont	continue	
dec	decrease	
DK	double knitting (yarn type)	
DPN	double-pointed needle	
foll	following	
fwd	forward	
inc	increase	
incl	including	
K	knit	right-side stitch
K1	knit 1 stitch	knit 1 right-side stitch
K2tog	knit 2 stitches together	
LH	left-hand	
M1	make 1 extra stitch	
MB	make bobble	
no	number	
P	purl	wrong-side stitch
P1	purl 1 stitch	knit 1 wrong-side stitch
p2sso	pass 2 slipped stitches over	
P2tog	purl 2 stitches together	
patt	pattern	
pb	place bead	
pfb	purl into the front, then the back of the stitch	
psso	pass slipped stitch over	
rem	remaining	

ABBREVIATION	WHAT IT MEANS	SOMETIMES CALLED
rep	repeat	
rev st st	reverse stocking stitch	reverse stockinette stitch/wrong-side stitch
RH	right-hand	
RS	right side	
sk	skip	
skpo	slip 1, knit 1, pass slipped stitch over	
sl	slip	
sl1	slip 1 stitch	
SSK	slip 1 stitch knitwise, slip another stitch knitwise, place the left-hand needle through the front of the slipped stitches and knit the 2 together	knit 2 stitches together through back of loops
SSP	slip 1 stitch knitwise, slip another stitch knitwise, return the stitches to the left-hand needle and purl the 2 together	purl 2 stitches together through back of loops
st	stitch	
sts	stitches	
st st	stocking stitch	stockinette stitch/right-side stitch
tbl	through back of loop	
tog	together	
WS	wrong side	
wyib	with yarn at the back of the work	wyb
wyif	with yarn at the front of the work	wyf
yb	yarn back	
yfwd	yarn forward	
yon	yarn over needle	
yrn	yarn round needle	

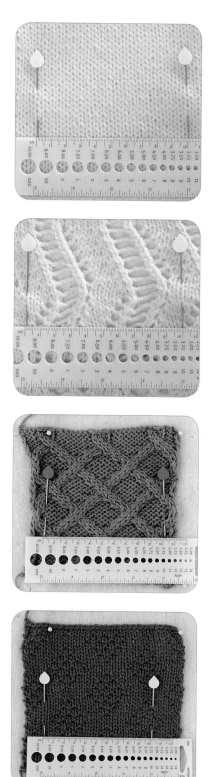

Knitting a tension square

When you choose a pattern and yarn, the first thing you must do is to knit a tension square to check that your stitches are the same as the ones in the sample. This is because, even with the same yarn and the same size needles, some knitters keep their yarn tension tighter and therefore their stitches are smaller, while others hold the yarn more loosely and make larger stitches. Don't be complacent either, thinking that you always knit with the same tension: you might find that with different yarns or patterns your tension varies. It can even vary on different days or depending on the time of day you're knitting!

A tension square is a small sample of knitting using the yarn, the needles and the stitch pattern you intend to use to create the project. Most patterns will give a recommended number of stitches and rows to knit for the square: it needs to be larger than 10 cm (4 in) because that is the standard length over which you will count the stitches and rows. For example, for 8-ply wool yarn knitting on 4 mm needles, the usual tension is 22 stitches and 30 rows to a 10 cm square. To measure this, you knit a square of, say, 30 stitches and 40 rows.

After you have cast off, lay the square on a flat surface and spread it out evenly using your fingers. If you lay it on a towel or other soft surface, you can pin the corners out to help keep it flat. Using a small metal, plastic or wooden ruler and knitting pins, mark 10 cm across the middle of the sample square. Now count the number of stitches between the pins. Do the same for the number of rows.

TROUBLESHOOTING

Too many stitches

If your sample square has more stitches and rows over 10 cm, your tension is tighter than recommended. The best way to solve this problem is to use needles a size larger than those recommended in the pattern. For example, use 4.5 mm needles instead of 4 mm needles. (If the pattern includes ribbing knitted on smaller needles, increase the size of those as well.) Make sure you knit a second sample square with the larger needles to check that your tension is now correct.

Not enough stitches

If your sample square has fewer stitches and rows over 10 cm than the pattern recommends, your tension is looser. Once again, the simple solution is to use needles a size smaller than those recommended in the pattern, and knit a second sample square to check your tension.

Alternatively, you could choose to make the garment a size smaller than you originally intended (or, if your tension is tight, a size larger); however, this may change the quantity of yarn required for the project.

GETTING ON WITH IT

Once you're happy with the tension of your knitting, set the tension square aside and begin the garment according to the pattern. You can unravel the square and re-use the yarn from it, if you like, although some textured yarns such as mohair and chenille tend to knot together as you knit them and can't be unravelled easily. It's also a good idea to keep the tension square as a reference; for example, when you want to wash the item, you can use the tension square to try out different washing methods (see Chapter 11).

Substituting yarn

It's not always possible to use the yarn recommended by the pattern for a particular project. Perhaps the pattern is a vintage one and the yarn is no longer in production, or you can't get the colour you want in the required quantities. In these cases, it's possible to substitute a different yarn, providing you carefully check your tension and the quantities required.

Try to keep to the same yarn type and weight; for instance, if a pattern calls for a particular brand of 8-ply wool you can easily substitute any other brand of 8-ply wool, and often 8-ply acrylic will be fine too. However, because acrylic yarn is lighter than wool yarn—and some wool yarns are lighter than others—check the quantity required by looking at the number of metres per ball rather than the weight of the ball.

It is not advisable to use yarn of a different weight or ply, even if it is the same type. It is possible to do so, but you'll need to do a lot of complicated recalculating of stitch numbers, needle sizes, measurements and quantities. One option is to knit with two strands of 4-ply yarn to imitate 8-ply, but do check your tension and yarn quantities carefully if you try this.

Using a different yarn type altogether, such as 8-ply cotton instead of 8-ply wool, will give quite different results. The garment will hang differently and may not look the way you intended. In this case, you will probably be better off seeking a pattern designed for yarn similar to the type you intend to use, than trying to adapt a pattern made for another type of yarn.

5

Getting started

* Casting on * Knit stitch

* Purl stitch * Ribbing * Shaping

* Troubleshooting * Knitting in the round

Cast your net

They all paint tables, cover screens, and net purses. I scarcely know anyone who cannot do all this, and I am sure I never heard a young lady spoken of for the first time, without being informed that she was very accomplished. *Jane Austen,* PRIDE AND PREJUDICE

Knitting sometimes used to be known as 'netting', as in making nets of yarn. Whether the nets were used for catching fish or catching a man (as in Jane Austen's example above), the process of linking threads in continuous rows is the same, or similar.

In woven fabric, the yarns travel in two directions: along the length of the fabric (the warp), and across the fabric (the weft), which passes over and under the warp threads to hold them in place. When you are knitting, the fabric you make consists of rows of continuous yarn loops, each one linked to the one below it. The horizontal rows of loops across the fabric are called courses (but are usually referred to as 'rows'), while the vertical rows of linked stitches are called wales.

Casting on

To start knitting, you need to make a row of stitches on your knitting needle: this is called casting on. Someone once told me that there were more than a hundred different methods of casting on! I'm sure this is true: and if you were to read lots of knitting books and search the Internet you could find them all. In my thirty-odd years of knitting I've learned and used five different methods, but I regularly use only two.

The first thing you need to do is make a slip knot.

① Wrap the yarn round your finger to make a loop.

② Pass a loop of yarn through the middle of the first loop.

③ Gently pull the loop through while holding the tails of yarn to form the knot.

④ Place the loop on a knitting needle and pull the working end of the yarn to tighten the loop.

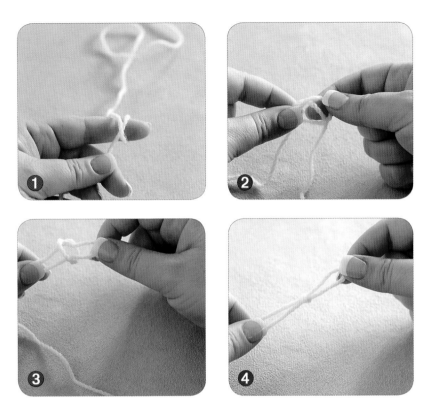

A NOTE ABOUT THROWING AND PICKING

There are two ways of holding the yarn and knitting needles while you knit: these are the throwing (or English) method and the picking (or Continental) method. The English method is called throwing because you hold the working yarn in the right hand and 'throw' it around the point of the needle to make a stitch; the Continental method, which comes originally from Germany, is called picking because you hold the working yarn with the left hand and 'pick' it through the loop on the needle to make a stitch.

It doesn't really matter which knitting style you choose to learn; try both at first and see which is easier for you. Both methods are illustrated here. Once you've mastered the basic knit and purl stitches and techniques in this chapter, the instructions are the same for both styles of knitting.

KNITTING ONTO A NEEDLE

The most basic method of casting on is simply to knit stitches onto a knitting needle. Use the yarn and the needles you are going to start the fabric with.

① Start with a slip knot, leaving a tail about 10 to 20 cm (4 to 8 in) long at the beginning of the yarn. Place the slip knot on the left-hand needle.

② Place the tip of the right-hand needle into the front of the slip-knot stitch, pass the yarn around the right-hand needle and bring it up between the two needles.

③ Use the point of the right-hand needle to bring the yarn from between the two needles through the slip-knot stitch and onto the right-hand needle. So far, this is just like making a regular knitting stitch.

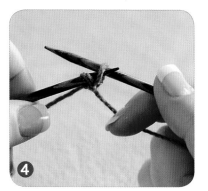
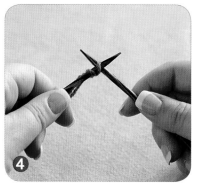

④ Take the loop of yarn from the right-hand needle and place it onto the left-hand needle, by slipping the point of the left-hand needle into the loop and allowing the stitch to slide off the right-hand needle.

⑤ Now you have 2 stitches on the left-hand needle. Repeat the process from step 2, slipping the point of the right-hand needle into the stitch you just made and making another stitch. Continue to do this until you have the correct number of stitches for your project on the left-hand needle.

A variation of this method of casting on is to place the point of the right-hand needle under both sides of each stitch you cast on after the first (see photograph). This is often called 'cable cast on' as it leaves a double loop visible at the edge of the fabric that looks a bit like a chain or cable. Some people prefer the appearance of this method.

THUMB METHOD

This is probably my favourite method of casting on, because I like the neat appearance of the edge that results from using it. The main difficulty of this method is working out how long the tail of yarn needs to be when you begin, as you make the basic stitches with the tail and knit into them with the working yarn. A good rule of thumb (pun intended), which you can also use to estimate yarn use when you are knitting, is to allow at least four times the width of the

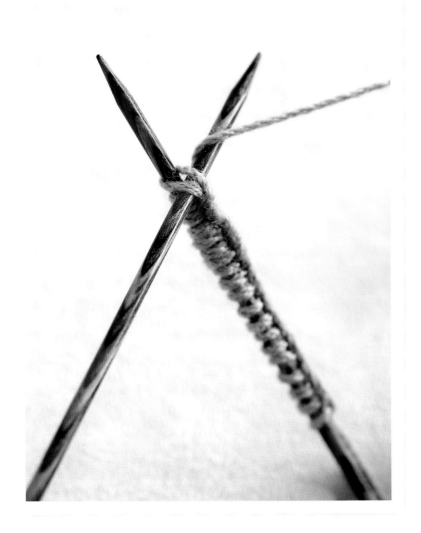

Cable cast on.

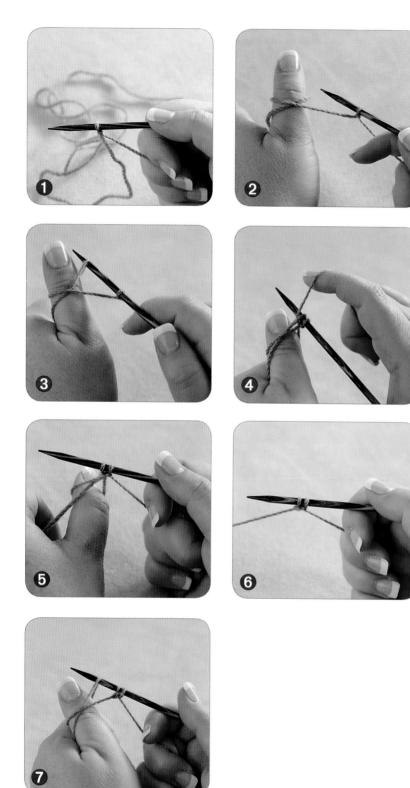

finished project. To work this out, say you are casting on 60 stitches and the recommended tension is 20 stitches to 10 cm; 60 stitches will measure 30 cm when the knitting is done, and so you should allow 120 cm of yarn in the tail of the yarn.

① Make a slip knot, leaving a tail of yarn long enough to knit with. Place the slip knot on the needle, which you will hold in your right hand.
② Take the tail of yarn in your left hand and wrap a loop of yarn around your thumb, ensuring that the yarn crosses itself inside the loop.
③ Insert the point of the needle into the loop.
④ Pass the main part of the yarn (not the tail) between the needle and your thumb.
⑤ Use the needle to pull the loop of yarn from between your thumb and the needle through the loop on your thumb.
⑥ Drop the loop off your thumb and pull the tail to make the new stitch sit firmly (but not too tightly) on the needle.
⑦ Repeat the process from step 2 until you have enough stitches on the needle to begin your knitting.

When you begin knitting, leave the tail of the yarn and make sure you knit with the main part of the yarn only.

Knitting basics

CROCHET CHAIN

If you know how to make a chain in crochet, you can use this technique to begin your knitting. Start with a slip knot on the crochet hook, then wrap the working yarn around the hook and pull it through the loop, slipping the loop off the hook before making the next chain. Ideally, the crochet hook should be the same size as the needles you will use for the project.

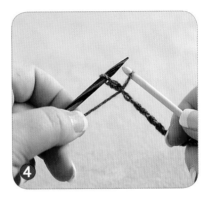

① Make a chain of crochet with the same number of loops as the number of stitches you want to cast on.

② Hold the crochet chain in your left hand along with a knitting needle. Insert the crochet hook through the first chain loop.

③ Hook the yarn with the crochet hook and draw a loop through.

④ Place the hooked loop on the needle.

⑤ Repeat the process from step 2 until you have the required number of stitches for your project.

This casting on method is sometimes known as 'provisional cast on', as the original chain stitches can be easily undone to allow the loops of the first course of stitches to be knitted up and worked in the opposite direction (if you wanted to knit a decorative edge, for example).

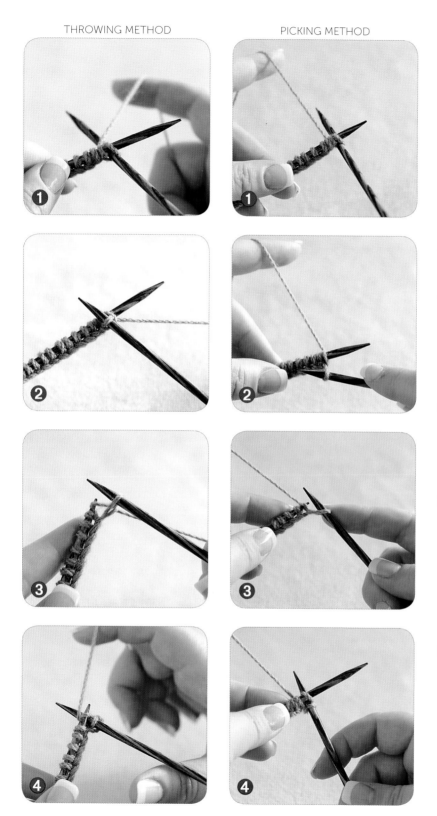

Knit stitch

The basic knitting stitch is sometimes known as right-side stitch, but usually it is described in patterns as knit stitch. All knitting is worked from the left-hand needle to the right-hand needle, and knit stitch makes the 'V' shaped part of the stitch at the front of the fabric (whichever way the fabric is facing at the time) and the top of the loop at the back.

① To make a knit stitch, place the point of the right-hand needle into the first loop on the left-hand needle, and bring the yarn up between the two needles.

② Use the point of the right-hand needle to draw a loop of the yarn through the stitch and bring it to the front of the work.

③ The new loop of yarn makes a stitch on the right-hand needle. Now carefully drop the first loop of yarn off the left-hand needle: it will be held in place under the new stitch on the right-hand needle.

④ Repeat from step 1, placing the point of the right-hand needle into the next loop on the left-hand needle.

GARTER STITCH

When you knit only knit (right-side) stitches in every row, your knitted fabric looks like the example here, with horizontal rows of loops alternating with horizontal rows of interlocking stitches. This type of knitting is called garter stitch, also known as mousse stitch. The rows alternate because you are working the right-side stitch in one direction, and then turning the fabric around and working the right-side stitch from the back of the fabric (making it, effectively, a wrong-side stitch).

Garter stitch is the simplest of all knitting stitches and, because it looks the same on both sides of the fabric, it is great for items like scarves and shawls where you will see both sides of the work.

Garter stitch.

Purl stitch

Also known as wrong-side stitch, purl stitch is basically a knit stitch worked backwards, so that the stitch is made at the back of the work and the loop at the front.

① Bring the working yarn forward to the front of the work, between the two needles. Place the point of the right-hand needle into the front of the stitch on the left-hand needle, in the opposite direction to the angle you would take if you were working a knit stitch.

② Pass the yarn around the needle and draw the loop through the stitch onto the right-hand needle.

③ Allow the original stitch to slip off the left-hand needle. If the next stitch you will make is a purl stitch, keep the yarn at the front of the work. If you will make a knit stitch next, don't forget to return the yarn to the back of the work.

Stocking stitch, front.

Stocking stitch, reverse.

Ribbing.

STOCKING STITCH

Purl stitches, when combined with knit stitches, allow you to make many different fabrics. The majority of knitted fabrics are based on a version of stocking stitch, also known as stockinette stitch and right-side work. This is constructed by knitting 1 row of knit stitch (on the right side of the fabric) and then 1 row of purl stitch (on the wrong side of the fabric). This puts all the loops on the wrong side of the fabric and gives a neat, flat finish to the front of the work—just like a pair of stockings, from which it gets its name.

The wrong side of the fabric can also be used as the right side, in which case the stitch is called reverse stocking stitch, or just reverse stitch.

Ribbing

Alternating knit and purl stitches in the same row makes a stretchier knitted fabric that is called ribbing. Ribbing is usually knitted at the edge of garments—such as around waistbands and cuffs of jumpers—where you want the garment to be slightly more fitted and yet stretchy enough to go over wider areas of the body. However, you can also knit whole garments or accessories in rib stitches: it's not just for borders.

Basic rib stitch is an alternate knit one, purl one pattern. The thing to remember about knitting rib is to make sure that the wales of stitches are all facing the same direction. In the right-side row, you knit one stitch and then purl the next. When you turn the work to knit back across the wrong-side row, you need to purl into the knit stitches and knit into the purl stitches so that the loops of each wale are all facing the same direction, either at the front or the back of the fabric.

The wales of ribbing don't always alternate one stitch at a time. For variations on ribbing patterns, see Chapter 7 (page 117).

When you are knitting fabric, slip the first stitch of each row from the left-hand needle to the right-hand needle without knitting it. This makes the edges of the fabric neater. You can either add two extra stitches to your casting on, or count the slipped stitch as the first stitch of the row.

Hot-water bottle jumper

To prove that you've mastered the basic stitches of knitting, knit this easy project in stocking stitch and ribbing.

YOU WILL NEED:

* Two 50 g balls of silk yarn (about 8- to 10-ply equivalent)
* One pair 5.5 mm (UK 5, US 9) knitting needles
* One pair 4.5 mm (UK 7, US 7) knitting needles
* Wool needle and scissors
* Hot-water bottle 20 cm (8 in) wide and 25 cm (10 in) long (not including the neck)

CONSTRUCTION:

Knit a tension square in stocking stitch using the 5.5 mm needles. The required tension is 20 stitches to 10 cm (4 in).

Using the 5.5 mm needles, cast on 42 stitches. Beginning with a knit row (right side of the fabric), knit in stocking stitch until the fabric is 26 cm (10¼ in) long: approximately 64 rows. Finish with a purl (wrong-side) row.

NEXT ROW: Slip the first stitch onto the right-hand needle, then knit the next two stitches together (K2tog). Knit the rest of the stitches in the row.

FOLLOWING ROW: Slip the first stitch onto the right-hand needle, then purl the next 2 stitches together (P2tog). Purl the rest of the stitches in the row.

Repeat these 2 rows twice more: you should now have 36 stitches.

Cast off 3 stitches knitwise at the beginning of the next row, then cast off 3 stitches purlwise at the beginning of the following row: 30 stitches. (See Chapter 6 for instructions on casting off.)

Change to 4.5 mm needles and ribbing stitch. Continue on these 30 stitches.

Row 1: * K2, P2 *, repeat * to * to last two stitches, K2.
Row 2: * P2, K2 *, repeat * to * to last two stitches, P2.
Repeat these 2 rows until the ribbing is 14 cm (5½ in) long (approximately 32 rows). Cast off loosely in rib.

You have now completed one side of the hot-water bottle cover. Make another piece exactly the same as this one.

Place the two sides of the cover with right sides facing and pin around the sides and bottom edge using knitter's pins. Use a piece of the same yarn and a wool needle to sew right around the sides and across the bottom of the cover using back stitch. Darn the tails of the yarn into the seam allowances (see Chapter 6 for more instructions about sewing up projects). Turn right side out.

Fold the empty hot-water bottle in half and ease it through the ribbing and into the main bag, where you can allow it to flatten out. Fold the top half of the ribbing over like a turtleneck jumper, fill the bottle with hot water and snuggle up.

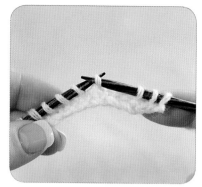

Simple slip stitch.

Shaping

As well as the basic knitting stitches—knit and purl—you will also need to master a few simple knitting techniques if you are going to attempt to knit anything other than a scarf or a square of fabric. To shape your knitting, you'll need to know how to increase and decrease. To make different fabric textures, you might need to know how to slip a stitch, or knit two stitches together. Once you've learned how to do these easy things, you're ready to tackle almost any pattern.

SLIPPING STITCHES

When knitting pattern instructions ask you to slip a stitch, it means you need to move a stitch from the left-hand needle to the right-hand needle without knitting it. The simplest method of slipping a stitch is to slip it directly from one needle to the other without turning the loop, and keeping the yarn at the back of the work. Use this simple slip technique when you are placing stitches on a stitch holder (or taking them off again) to ensure that they don't twist around on the needle.

Slipping knitwise and purlwise

Sometimes pattern instructions will tell you to slip the stitch 'knitwise' or 'purlwise'. This simply

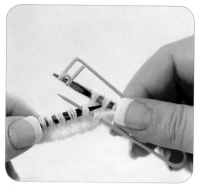

Placing stitches on a stitch holder.

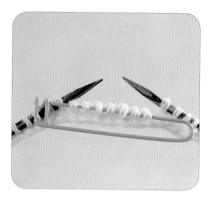

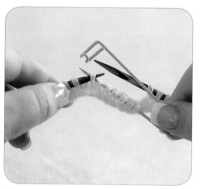

Taking stitches off a stitch holder.

Slipping a stitch knitwise.

Slipping a stitch purlwise.

means that you insert the right-hand needle into the stitch as though you are going to knit or purl it, and lift it off the left-hand needle. Normally, the yarn is held at the back of the work (or in front, if you are knitting a purl row) when slipping a stitch. Occasionally, a pattern will indicate to slip the stitch 'with yarn in front (wyif)' or 'with yarn in back (wyib)'.

Slipping stitches to a cable needle

If you are knitting a cable pattern, you need to slip stitches onto a cable needle to hold them while you knit the twisty part (see Chapter 9, page 159). Simply slip the stitches onto the cable needle without turning the loops and then, when it is time to pick the stitches up again, knit them off the other end of the cable needle, as though they were still on the left-hand needle. Cabling can seem tricky to the uninitiated, but it won't take much practice until you become confident with this technique. Choose a simple cable chain with a loose twist for your first attempt.

① Slip the required number of stitches onto a cable needle.
② Knit the required number of stitches from the left-hand needle.
③ Knit the stitches off the other end of the cable needle.

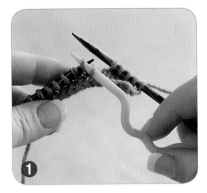

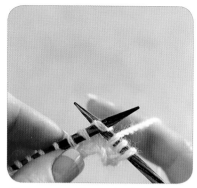

Yarn over needle method.

Yarn over needle method.

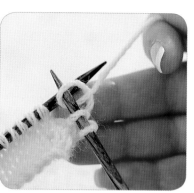

Crossed yarn loop method.

Showing the difference between simple yarn over needle and crossed yarn loop method.

INCREASING

To shape a garment, such as a sleeve that is narrow at the wrist and wide at the shoulder, you may need to increase the number of stitches in each row. This is usually done gradually and at the edges of the garment, although it is occasionally done evenly across the width of the fabric piece. To increase at the edge, slip or knit the first stitch of the row and make your increase in the second stitch of the row.

There are several techniques that knitters like to use to make new stitches and you will soon find your favourite. Three of the most common are shown here.

Yarn over needle

The simplest method of increasing is to wrap an extra loop of yarn around the needle before knitting (or purling) the next stitch. The main drawback of this method is that it creates a small gap in the knitting. This may be fine, as it is usually at the edge of the fabric and will be hidden by the seam when the garment is sewn up. Sometimes, you want to make a hole, as in eyelet stitches (see Chapter 8, page 139).

One way to avoid a large hole is to cross the yarn over itself as you bring it around the needle, so that the tail of the yarn is between the previous stitch and the new loop.

Knit a stitch twice

Another easy method of making an extra stitch is to knit twice into the same stitch.

① Begin by knitting into the next stitch as usual, but don't slip it off the left-hand needle.
② Knit into the back of the same stitch on the left-hand needle.

③ Now that you have two stitches on the right-hand needle you can slip the original stitch off the left-hand needle.

④ You will notice that the second stitch appears as a purl stitch. If you are increasing in a purl row, take the yarn back behind the needle and knit into the front and back of the next stitch, then bring the yarn forward and continue with the purl stitches as before.

Knitting into the row below

My favourite method of making a new stitch is by knitting into the space between stitches in the row below. I prefer this method because it gives a neater look to the fabric, with no holes or stray purl stitches.

① As for other methods of increasing, slip or knit the first stitch in the row, then use the tip of the right-hand needle to pick up the loop of thread between the first and second stitches and place it on the left-hand needle.

② Knit this loop as though it were a stitch and slide it off the left-hand needle.

③ This method makes a nice neat stitch with no hole and works equally well for both knit and purl rows.

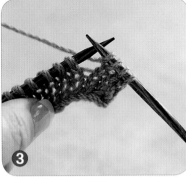

Getting started

Knitting basics

Triangular shawl

Now that you know how to increase, you can make this simple but stunning shawl in garter stitch.

YOU WILL NEED:

* Two 50 g balls of fine mohair yarn (about 2-ply equivalent)
* One pair 7 mm (UK 4, US 10) knitting needles
* Wool needle and scissors

There is no need to knit a tension square for this project.

CONSTRUCTION:

Cast on 3 stitches.

Row 1: Knit all stitches.

Row 2: Knit all stitches.

Row 3: To make a neat edge, slip the first stitch of each row without knitting it. Increase in the next stitch by your preferred method (see pages 80-81). I used the 'knit into the row below' method. Knit all stitches to end.

Row 4 and every following row: Repeat row 3.

Continue knitting and increasing at the beginning of each row until you have 175 stitches. Note, when you need to join the second ball of yarn, do it at the edge of the work (see page 87).

Next row: * K2, increase in next stitch *, repeat * to * to last stitch, K1. (These extra stitches give more elasticity to the cast-off edge.)

Cast off all stitches. Darn in tails of yarn along the side edges of the shawl.

Casting on stitches at the beginning of a row.

Casting on more stitches

If you need to make a large number of new stitches at the edge of the garment, simply cast on the required number of stitches at the beginning of the row (see page 68).

DECREASING

To shape a piece of knitted fabric by decreasing the number of stitches in each row, it's simply a matter of knitting the loops of two stitches as though they were one stitch: you'll see this in patterns as 'knit two together (K2tog)' or sometimes 'purl two together (P2tog)'.

Knit two together

1. Place the tip of the right-hand needle through the loops of the next two stitches as though they were one stitch.
2. Wrap the yarn around the needle and draw it through the loops of both stitches. Slip both stitches off the left-hand needle at once.
3. The second stitch lies over the top of the previous stitch.

Purl two together

① Place the tip of the right-hand needle through the loops of the next two stitches as though they were one stitch.

② Wrap the yarn around the needle and draw it through the loops of both stitches. Slip both stitches off the left-hand needle at once.

③ The second stitch lies over the top of the previous stitch.

Knit two together through the back of the loops

When you knit two stitches together, the second stitch lies over the top of the first stitch on the right side of the work; when you purl stitches together, the second stitch lies over the top of the first stitch on the wrong side of the work.

There will be times when, for decorative reasons, you want the stitches to lie in the opposite direction. If that is the case, and you knit using the throwing (English) method, you can make the second stitch lie over the first by knitting through the back of the loops (K2tog tbl).

If you knit using the picking method, or if you simply find it easier, you can also change the direction of the loops by working a 'slip, slip, knit' stitch combination (SSK) as shown on page 86.

Knit two together through the back of the loops.

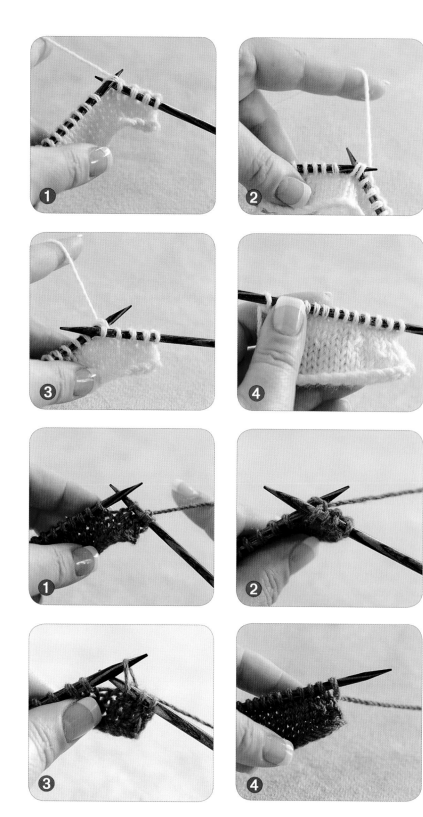

1. Slip a stitch knitwise from the left-hand needle to the right-hand needle and then slip another stitch the same way.

2. Place the tip of the left-hand needle into the two loops on the right-hand needle and slip them back onto the left-hand needle.

3. Knit the two stitches together.

4. The first stitch lies over the second stitch.

Pass a stitch over

Another way of turning two stitches into one is to slip one stitch over the other as you knit. The usual way you will see this written in pattern instructions is as 'slip one, knit one, pass the slipped stitch over (slip 1, K1, psso)'.

1. Simply slip the next stitch from the left-hand needle to the right-hand needle without knitting it.

2. Knit the next stitch and drop it off the left-hand needle as usual.

3. Use the point of the left-hand needle to lift the loop of the slipped stitch over the next stitch on the right-hand needle and drop the slipped stitch off the needle.

4. The slipped stitch lies over the knitted stitch.

To decrease a larger number of stitches at the same time, such as for a buttonhole or neck edge, simply cast off the required number of stitches (see page 94).

Troubleshooting

JOINING NEW YARN

When you finish a ball of yarn part way through a piece of knitting, or if you are knitting in multiple colours, you will need to join in a new length of yarn. Generally, you should do this at the edge of the fabric. If you run out of yarn halfway along a row, un-knit the row (see page 89) back to the beginning and join the new yarn there. If you think you might run out of yarn before you finish the next row, remember the rule of thumb: you will use a length of yarn approximately four times the width of the finished row. So measure the yarn you have left and only begin knitting the next row if you are sure there will be enough.

The only exception to the rule of starting new yarn at the edge of the work is if you are introducing a new colour in an intarsia pattern (intarsia is when you knit coloured areas into a design to make a motif or picture). In that case, join the yarn in the same way as shown here, wherever you need to join it in the row. You may not need to finish off the previous colour of yarn as you can carry it across the back of the work: see Chapter 10 (page 185) for more information about knitting with different coloured yarns.

1. Trim the tail of the old yarn to about 15 cm (6 in) and lay the new yarn alongside the tail.
2. Begin knitting the row with the new yarn. Don't be too concerned about the tension of the first few stitches at this stage.
3. After you've knitted several stitches, you can stop and tie the two yarn tails in a loose knot. You will want to undo this knot later to sew in the ends of the yarn (see page 103), so make sure it's not too tight.

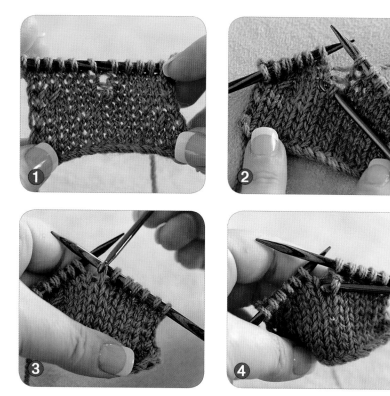

PICKING UP A DROPPED STITCH

Every knitter drops stitches now and then. It's not the end of the world. The easiest way to pick up a dropped stitch is to use a crochet hook.

① Knit across to the wale where the dropped stitch should be. Lay the fabric out as flat as possible and find the loop of the dropped stitch.

② Place the crochet hook through the loop and pick up the yarn from the next row. Put the crochet hook through from the front for a knit stitch. If it's a purl stitch, you need to bring the hook through the loop from behind.

③ Pull the yarn from the next row through the loop.

④ Repeat the process until you reach the last row you knitted.

⑤ Place the loop on the left-hand needle and continue with your knitting.

Don't be too concerned about the tension of this wale; it will seem a little tight for now but it will soon even up with the rest of the knitting work.

UNRAVELLING

If you find you need to undo some of your work because you've made a mistake, it's simply a matter of un-knitting.

1. Hold the work with the stitches to be un-knitted on the left-hand needle. Slip the point of the right-hand needle into the stitch below the working stitch on the left-hand needle.

2. Slide the working stitch off the left-hand needle and gently pull out the loop of yarn, leaving the stitch on the right-hand needle.

3. Continue un-knitting until you reach the point where you made the mistake, then begin reknitting.

If you have a large number of rows to unravel, it will be easier to take the knitting off the needles.

1. Find the row you want to return to.

2. Lay the work out flat on a table and slip a needle into one side of each loop in this row. It may help to use a smaller gauge needle than the size you are knitting with. Gently tug the yarn so that the stitches come undone.

3. When you reach the needle, wind the unravelled yarn loosely back onto the ball so that it doesn't become tangled while you reknit.

4. Carefully pick up the knitting and check that the loops of all the stitches are sitting in the correct orientation on the knitting needle. Reknit the unravelled work.

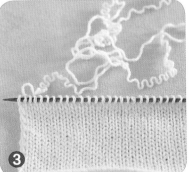

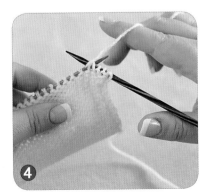

Stitch and row markers in knitted fabric.

LOSING COUNT

It's important to keep track of the number of stitches you're knitting—particularly if you're knitting a complicated pattern—as well as the number of rows you've completed. It's usually pretty easy to count the number of loops on your needles, but if there are a lot of stitches it can be tedious and repetitive to count them again every few rows. To help keep track, use a stitch marker on your needle to mark out, say, every twenty stitches, or every pattern repeat.

To help you count the number of rows you have knitted, use a row marker every 10 rows (or every pattern repeat). Simply clip the row marker to the yarn; it stays in the same place as you knit so that you can easily see how many rows you've completed. If you lose count, don't despair: lay the knitting out as flat as possible and, starting from the cast-on row, count 10 (or 20) rows and insert a row marker.

Stitch and row markers like the ones shown here are inexpensive; however, you can easily substitute a loop of contrasting coloured yarn, a paperclip, an odd earring or even a plastic bread tie, for example. Just try to avoid items that are too heavy or have sharp edges that might catch on the yarn.

Knitting in the round

For some types of knitted work, it is preferable to knit in the round; that is, in one continuous spiral of knitting on circular needles or double-pointed needles (DPNs). Socks, hats and some jumpers can be knitted this way. There are a few important techniques for knitting in the round that you'll need to learn.

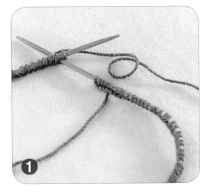

Casting on in the round

On a circular needle, cast on the required number of stitches using your preferred technique. On DPNs, divide the total number of stitches by three (if you're using four needles) or four (if you're using five needles) and cast them onto the DPNs. The tricky part is joining the last cast-on stitch to the first, to begin the first round of knitting. It's important to make sure that you don't have any twists in your stitching when you join the ends together.

1. Cast on the required number of stitches.
2. Make sure there are no twists in the work.
3. Knit into the first cast-on stitch.

Counting rows

When knitting in the round, all rows are knitted as right-side rows. Use a stitch marker to mark the beginning of the round. The stitch marker slips from one needle to another as you knit, always staying in the same wale of the work, so that you can tell each time you have completed a row when working in the round.

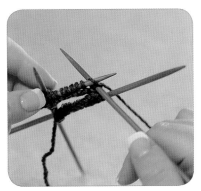

Holding DPNs to knit.

Double-pointed needles

DPNs can seem scary to a beginner: you'll drop enough stitches when there's a head on the needle to hold them in place! But they aren't as difficult to manage as they look, and if you make sure that you don't have too many stitches on each needle, you'll be fine.

The stitches should be evenly divided between the needles, with one needle spare to use as the working needle. With the working needle in your right hand, knit stitches off the left-hand needle. When all the stitches have been knitted onto the right-hand needle, the left-hand needle that is now free of stitches becomes the working needle as you knit around the circle.

6

Finishing touches

* Casting off

* Preparing the finished fabric * Sewing up seams

* Knitting up on an edge * Decorations

Make it up

When we retired, she took from her work-drawer an enormous interminable piece of knitting; the young ladies began to play at cribbage with a dirty pack of cards.

William Makepeace Thackeray, VANITY FAIR

Quite unlike the interminable piece of knitting worked by the chaperone in Thackeray's *Vanity Fair*, it's intended that your efforts at knitting will eventually come to an end. Once you come to the end of the pattern, you need to take the stitches off the needles and make the various sections into a complete garment.

Casting off

The process of taking the working loops off the needle is known as casting off or, sometimes, binding off. Basically, you pass each stitch over the next as you knit, ensuring that the loop of the previous stitch is bound to the next one so that the work can't come undone. When you're casting off, it is best to knit the stitches according to the pattern you're following: if you're knitting stocking stitch, the stitches will be all knit or all purl. If you're knitting a pattern, such as ribbing, you should knit the knit stitches and purl the purl stitches before you pass them over.

> When you're casting off and have knitted a purl stitch, you might find it easier to take the yarn back behind the needle before passing the loop over, even if the next stitch is to be another purl stitch.

SIMPLE CAST OFF

① Knit the first two stitches of the next row.

② Pick up the first stitch from the right-hand needle with the point of the left-hand needle.

③ Pass the first stitch over the second one and drop it off the needle.

④ Knit the next stitch off the left-hand needle.

⑤ Pass the previous stitch over the new one and drop it off.

⑥ When you reach the last stitch, break off the yarn with a short tail and pull the tail right through the final loop.

Tension

The cast-off row of knitting tends to be less stretchy than the rows in the fabric, and so it's important not to knit the stitches too tightly. Make a conscious effort to knit loosely and, if you find your cast-off edge is still too tight, try using a larger gauge needle for the casting off.

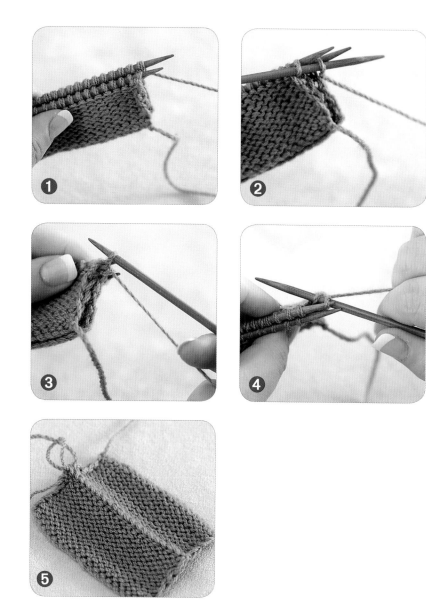

THREE-NEEDLE CAST OFF

If you have two pieces of knitting with the same number of stitches that need to be joined with a seam, you can use the three-needle cast-off method to save yourself the trouble of sewing up.

① Place the stitches to be cast off on two needles side by side, with the right sides of the fabric facing each other.

② Put the point of the right-hand needle into the first stitch on the front left-hand needle, and then into the first stitch on the back left-hand needle.

③ Knit the two stitches together and drop them both off the needles.

④ Knit the next two stitches and then pass the first loop from the right-hand needle over the second. Continue to the end and finish off as for simple cast off.

⑤ Darn in the tails of yarn from both pieces of fabric.

DECORATIVE EDGES

The edges of knitted fabrics are usually finished in some way. Many items begin with a section of ribbing, which is a way of finishing the bottom or top edge of a garment even though it is knitted at the start of the project. The top or cast-off edge of a project also usually needs to be finished in some way. The only exception is a straight edge worked in stocking stitch, which will naturally roll itself up. Some people like this finish and prefer to leave the edge otherwise unfinished when possible.

Crochet cast off

Use a crochet hook the same gauge as the knitting needles you have been using. This method makes a neat, slightly raised edge.

① With the left-hand needle holding the stitches in your left hand as though you were knitting, use the crochet hook to knit two stitches.

② Wrap the yarn around the hook and pull a loop through the two stitches on the crochet hook, dropping them off the hook. There will be one loop on the crochet hook. Knit another stitch with the crochet hook, then repeat step 2.

③ Repeat to the end of the row, and then finish off by pulling the tail of yarn right through the last loop, as for simple cast off.

Knitting basics

Striped beanie

Knit this beanie in colourful stripes and add a giant tassel. The edge of the stocking stitch fabric will roll up naturally for a fun effect.

YOU WILL NEED:

* One 50 g ball of 8-ply wool yarn in each of three colours
* One small 4 mm (UK 8, US 6) circular needle (21 cm or 8 in cable)
* One set of 4 mm (UK 8, US 6) double-pointed needles OR one pair of 4 mm (UK 8, US 6) knitting needles (see To knit flat, page 100)
* Wool needle and scissors
* Piece of corrugated cardboard 15 cm (6 in) wide for tassel

One size fits most teens and adults. Tension is 22 stitches to 10 cm (4 in).

CONSTRUCTION:

Using the circular needle, cast on 112 stitches in the first colour. This is the colour that will show at the brim of the hat.

Knit all stitches in the round, forming a stocking stitch fabric. After 6 rounds in the first colour, join the second colour (see page 87) and knit 5 rounds. Join the third colour and continue knitting in stocking stitch, working in random stripes. Twist the three yarns together at the back of the fabric as you go past the end of the row—make sure you stop every few rows and untangle the yarns.

Continue until the work is 18 cm (7 in) long. Change to DPNs as you knit the next row, distributing the stitches evenly on the needles.

DECREASE FOR CROWN:

ROUND 1: * K2, K2tog *, repeat * to * to end.
ROUND 2: Knit all stitches.
ROUND 3: * K1, K2tog *, repeat * to * to end.
ROUND 4: Knit all stitches.
ROUND 5: * K2tog *, repeat * to * to end.
ROUND 6: Knit all stitches.
ROUNDS 7 AND 8: * K2tog *, repeat * to * to end (7 stitches).

Break off the yarn, leaving a tail about 15 cm (6 in) long. Thread the tail into the wool needle and pass it through the remaining stitches, dropping them off the needles as you go. Draw the stitches together, make a back stitch through the fabric on the wrong side to fasten them and darn the tail into the fabric.

Darn in the yarn tails where you joined the yarn in the beginning.

MAKING THE TASSEL:

See page 111 for step-by-step photographs of making a tassel. Wrap one strand of each yarn colour several times around the cardboard until you have sufficient wraps to make a tassel: this one used about thirty full wraps of each yarn. Slip a doubled length of yarn under the fold of the yarn at the top of the tassel and knot it firmly. Now use sharp scissors to cut the other fold of the yarn.

Hold the knotted yarn in one hand and smooth the other hand over the tassel, from the knot downwards, holding it tightly in a bunch just below the point you want to wrap with yarn. Take about 2 m (6 ft) of yarn, double it and wrap it tightly around the tassel. When you're happy with the wrap, thread the end of the yarn into the wool needle and push the needle into the centre of the tassel, bringing it out at the end.

Trim the ends of the wrapping yarn along with any stray ends of yarn at the end of the tassel.

Use the wool needle to pass the ends of the knotted yarn at the top of the tassel through the crown of the beanie and knot them together on the wrong side. Darn the ends of the yarn into the fabric.

TO KNIT FLAT:
Cast on 112 stitches and knit stocking stitch (odd rows knit, even rows purl). When the work is 18 cm (7 in) long, decrease as for in-the-round, remembering to purl the even rows rather than knit them. When you reach the 7 stitches at the crown, leave a longer tail of yarn (about 40 cm or 15 in). Pass the yarn through the 7 stitches and draw them together, making a small back stitch at the seam. Use the same yarn to sew the two edges of the beanie together, and then darn in the yarn ends as for the in-the-round version.

FOR A CHILD:
For younger children, measure the child's head circumference. You need 5 stitches for every 2 cm (¾ in), but make sure that the number of stitches you cast on is a multiple of 4. For example, if the child's head measures 42 cm (16½ in), 5 x 21 is 105. 105 is not divisible by 4, so cast on 104 stitches. Knit 12 cm (4½ in) of fabric and begin decreasing. Decrease in the same manner as for the adult beanie, stopping when you have fewer than 8 stitches on the needles.

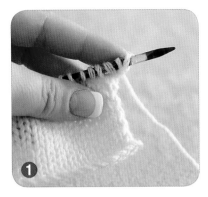

Picot cast off

Picots are tiny little points knitted into the cast-off edge, giving a slightly lacy look to the fabric edge. You can make the picots as small or large as you like: the only rule is to cast off double the number of stitches you cast on for each picot—cast on two, cast off four, as in the example below, or cast on three, cast off six, and so on.

1. Cast on two stitches, using the cable cast-on method (see page 69).
2. Cast off four stitches using the simple cast-off method.
3. Slip the loop that's still on the right-hand needle back onto the left-hand needle.
4. Repeat the process from step 1. Continue to the end of the row and then finish off by pulling the tail of yarn through the last loop.

Preparing the finished fabric

BLOCKING

Blocking is a way of stretching and shaping a piece of knitted work. It flattens out any little lumps and bumps in your knitting and can help with fitting pieces of a garment together (see 'Easing', on page 102). It is important not to overstretch the fabric; pull it gently into the desired shape.

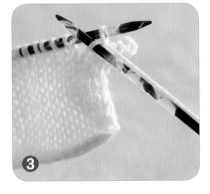

You'll need a blocking surface. An ironing board is ideal if the piece is small enough; if it's larger, a blanket wrapped and fastened over a board or on a table can be used. Take the knitted fabric and lay it flat on the blocking surface. Use pins to gently stretch it into shape, vertically and horizontally. When you're satisfied with the pinned-out shape and size, use a steam iron on a wool setting to just warm and dampen the fabric. Allow it to dry and cool completely on the blocking surface before removing the pins.

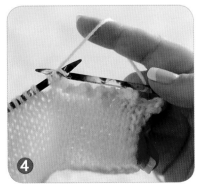

If you prefer, you can block your fabric by wetting it (use a spray bottle and tepid water to just dampen it—you don't want to soak it) before pinning it out and leaving it to dry completely.

Blocking of wool fabric is sometimes desirable but it's not compulsory, and it's not advisable for novelty and synthetic yarns. A light press with a steam iron on the appropriate setting is usually enough for most yarns.

EASING

If the two edges to be sewn together are not quite the same length, you need to ease the longer edge evenly across the shorter edge. This is quite often necessary when sewing a shaped sleeve into an armhole of a garment, for example.

① Pin the two pieces together (with right sides facing) at both ends of the seam.

② Find the halfway point of both edges and pin them together at this point.

③ Now divide the halves in half and pin these points together. Continue halving the distances until the longer edge is pinned to the shorter edge evenly. When sewing the pieces together, use back stitch and work from the shorter side to keep the stitches even.

In a shaped sleeve, you can usually do most of the easing near the top of the sleeve (around the shoulder seam). Pin the edges together from the underarm edge towards the halfway point. When you get near the top, pin the extra fabric evenly between the last few pins without stretching the armhole edge.

Sewing up seams

One of my friends once admitted that, although she loves knitting, she dislikes sewing up so much that she gives the completed fabric pieces to her mother, who finishes all her projects for her. I confess that sewing up is the least favourite part of the process for me, too, but my mother lives too far away for me to rely on her skills. Besides, she knits as much as I do and has all her own sewing up to do.

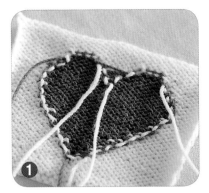

TYING UP LOOSE ENDS

The first thing you need to do is neaten the edges of your knitted fabric by sewing in all of the loose ends of yarn where you have joined new balls or new colours. You should have left tails of yarn about 15 cm (6 in) long at the beginning and end of the yarn.

① On the wrong side of the knitted fabric, untie any knots and lay the fabric flat.

② Thread one tail into a wool needle and weave the needle over and under the back of several stitches.

③ Pull the yarn through firmly, being careful not to tighten up the stitches, and then trim off the tail close to the fabric.

④ If you've used different coloured yarns, try to weave the tail only through stitches of the same colour.

You can weave the yarn ends along a row or along the wale. If the edge is to be sewn into a seam, weaving the ends along the edge is a good idea.

SEWING SEAMS

There are several ways of sewing seams in knitted projects. Three easy stitches are shown on the following pages, as well as the crochet method. You can also use the three-needle cast-off to join seams with the same number of stitches (see page 96).

It is preferable to sew up using the same yarn as you used to knit the fabric, unless you've used a novelty yarn with lots of texture. If that's the case, choose a plain yarn of a similar colour, weight and fibre composition to do the sewing up; for example, use a synthetic 8-ply yarn if you've knitted with a synthetic fur or ribbon yarn, or use a bulky wool yarn if you've knitted with wool rovings. (In our examples on the following pages, we've used a contrasting yarn for sewing up, so that you can see the stitches easily).

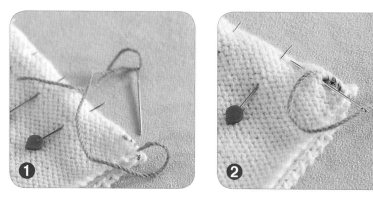

Back stitch

One of the easiest of sewing stitches, back stitch (above) is often used to join seams in knitted fabric.

① Place the two pieces of knitted fabric with their right sides together and use pins to hold them in place. Thread the sewing yarn into a wool needle and darn the end into the fabric at the beginning of the seam.

② Starting with a single short stitch 1 row (or wale) long, bring the needle and yarn up 1 row (or wale) from the entry point and take the needle back down at the end of the first stitch.

③ Continue stitching until the seam is complete. Knot the end of the sewing yarn and weave the end of the yarn back into the fabric along the seam edge.

Whip stitch

This over-and-over stitch (below) is also very easy, but it can be visible on the right side of the garment, so make sure you use the same yarn for sewing up as you used for knitting.

① Place the two pieces of knitted fabric with their right sides together and use pins to hold them in place. Thread the sewing yarn into a wool needle and darn the end into the fabric at the beginning of the seam.

② Holding the fabric upright with the edges towards you, pass the needle through both layers of the fabric, taking in 1 row or wale with each stitch.

③ Finish by knotting the sewing yarn into the last stitch and weaving the tail into the seam.

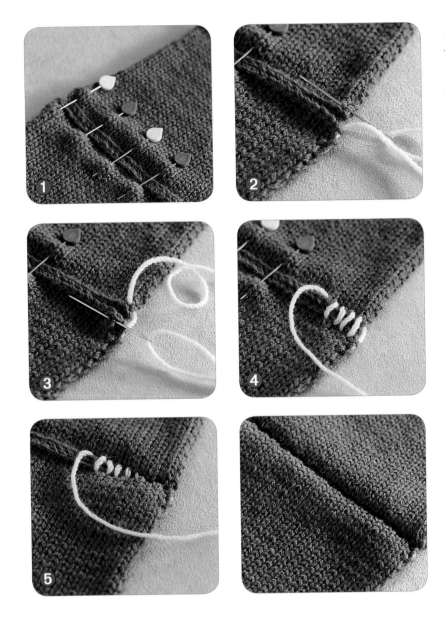

Ladder stitch

This stitch is a little more difficult to master but gives a nice, flat, invisible finish.

1. Lay the two pieces to be joined on a flat surface, right side up, with the edges together. Use pins to hold them close together. Thread the sewing yarn into a wool needle and darn the end into the fabric at the beginning of the seam.

2. Take the first stitch by carrying the yarn across the gap and passing the needle under 1 row (or wale) on the other piece of fabric. You've made one rung and one side bar of the 'ladder'.

3. Now carry the yarn back across the gap and under the next row (or wale) on the first piece of fabric. This is the next rung and side bar of the 'ladder'.

4. Work several stitches loosely, before drawing the yarn up firmly to close the gap and hide the 'ladder'.

5. Continue stitching in the same way to the end of the seam. Finish by knotting the sewing yarn into the last stitch and weaving the tail into the seam.

Knitting up on an edge

Sometimes it's necessary to knit up stitches in finished fabric to add the final touches to a project. For example, if you've cast off stitches and decreased to shape the neckline of a jumper, you need to knit up stitches around the neckline to make the ribbed collar. You might also want to knit up stitches around the cuffs or hem of a garment to add a frill, or along the front of a cardigan to make a button band. There are also knitting patterns in which stitches are knitted up to make an interesting design in the fabric.

The knitting pattern you're using will usually indicate how many stitches you need to knit up, and you need to knit them up evenly across or around the edge. If you're lucky, you'll knit up one stitch in each row or wale of the edge, but this isn't always the case. If the number of stitches isn't the same as the number of rows or wales in the edge, you'll need to work out how you're going to knit the stitches evenly. For example, if there are 40 rows of knitting and you need to knit up thirty stitches, you can miss a row every 4 rows to make the correct number of stitches; however, to make sure you don't end up with a missed stitch at the end, start by knitting two stitches and missing 1 row, then knit four, miss 1 row, and so on, until you get to the end and knit two stitches after the last missed row.

Generally, when you are knitting up stitches, you will knit them up on a smaller gauge needle than the needle you used to create the fabric, particularly if you are knitting up for a ribbed collar around the neckline of a jumper.

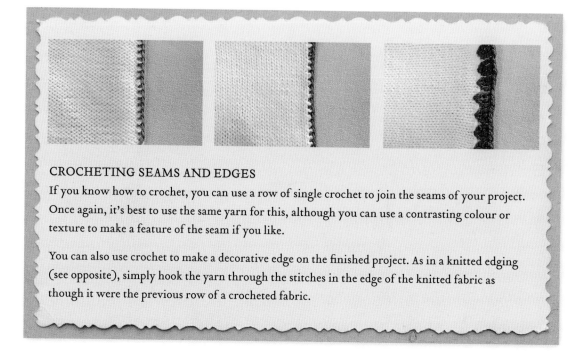

CROCHETING SEAMS AND EDGES

If you know how to crochet, you can use a row of single crochet to join the seams of your project. Once again, it's best to use the same yarn for this, although you can use a contrasting colour or texture to make a feature of the seam if you like.

You can also use crochet to make a decorative edge on the finished project. As in a knitted edging (see opposite), simply hook the yarn through the stitches in the edge of the knitted fabric as though it were the previous row of a crocheted fabric.

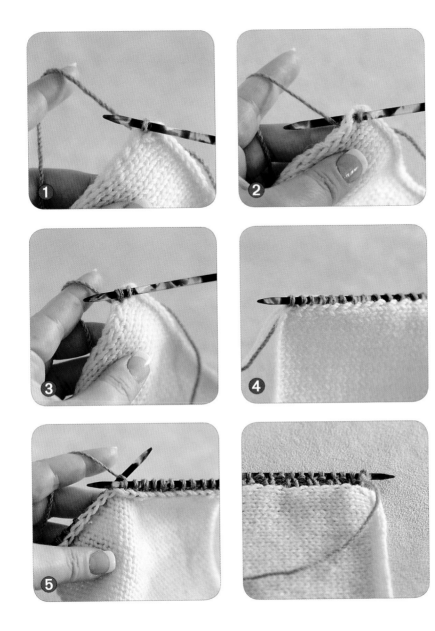

1. Leave a tail of yarn about 15 cm (6 in) long at the beginning of the work. Hold the knitted fabric in your left hand and place the point of the needle into the first row or wale on the fabric, close to the edge.

2. Wrap the yarn around the needle as though you were knitting a stitch and draw the loop through the knitted fabric.

3. Move along to the next row or wale and make another stitch in the same way.

4. Continue knitting stitches evenly across the edge until you reach the end.

5. Turn the work and pass the needle to your left hand. Take up the other needle in your right hand and knit on these stitches according to the pattern.

MAKING BUTTONHOLES

When making a cardigan or other garment with button fastenings, buttonholes can be knitted into the fabric of the garment, or button loops can be added when finishing the garment. You will need to know the size of the buttons you'll be using when you make the buttonholes. Generally, the chunkier the yarn, the larger the buttons should be, as small buttons won't hold thick fabric with large stitches. The pattern you're using might recommend the size of buttons and the number of stitches to make the buttonhole.

To work out buttonhole placement on the front of a cardigan, mark the position of the top buttonhole and the bottom one. They should sit about 2 or 4 rows from the top and bottom edges of the button tab respectively. Now divide the space between the two by the number of buttons remaining. When you're knitting the band, count the number of stitches or rows over this distance and place the buttonholes accordingly.

Small buttonholes

Small buttonholes can be made simply by creating eyelets in the fabric.

1. When you reach the row in which you want to make a buttonhole, knit across to the first buttonhole position.
2. Bring the yarn around the right-hand needle to make an extra loop and then knit the next two stitches together (yon, K2tog). Knit across to the next buttonhole position, and repeat.
3. When you knit the next row, simply knit according to the pattern, knitting the yarn loop as though it were the missing stitch.
4. This creates a small hole in the fabric. Check that the button you want to use will pass through this hole.

Large buttonholes

For large buttons, you will need to make larger holes. This involves casting off and casting on stitches. Measure your button against the knitted fabric to work out the number of stitches to cast off. Remember that the button will generally sit with the shank at the top of a vertical buttonhole, so position your buttons and buttonholes accordingly.

① When you reach the position for the buttonhole, cast off the required number of stitches and continue knitting according to the pattern.

② In the next row, when you reach the cast-off stitches, turn the work and cast on the same number of stitches as you cast off, using the knitting on method (see Chapter 5, page 65).

③ Turn the work again and continue knitting the same row.

④ Check that the button fits through the hole.

ZIPPERS

Zippers are not generally used in knitted projects because they don't allow for the stretch of the knitted fabric; however, they are occasionally required. Inserting a zipper in a knitted garment is basically the same as putting one in a garment made of woven fabric. If the pattern calls for a zipper, you will usually knit some extra stitches for a wider seam allowance at the zipped edge. Turn over the allowance and pin it to the zipper tape, being careful not to stretch the knitted fabric as you work. Sew the knit to the tape with a sewing machine, or by hand using sewing cotton and a sewing needle.

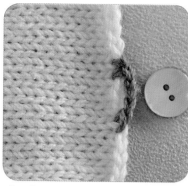

Crocheted button loop.

Stitched button loop.

Button loops

Decorative button loops can be sewn or crocheted along an edge or on top of a piece of knitted fabric, to save you knitting buttonholes into your work.

Crocheted button loops can be worked either as part of a decorative crocheted edge or simply crocheted into the fabric. Make a crocheted stitch through the fabric, work a short chain of crochet (long enough to fit over the button) and then make another crochet stitch through the fabric at the end of the buttonhole. If you like, work a row of single crochet back across the chain to strengthen it. Finish off the ends of the yarn on the wrong side of the work by darning them in.

To stitch a button loop, thread a wool needle with doubled yarn and knot it into the knitted fabric at one end of the buttonhole placement. Make a stitch the full length of the buttonhole and knot the yarn so that the stitch sits loosely on top of the fabric. Now work buttonhole stitch over the yarn, pushing the stitches tightly together as you go. When you have finished, weave the yarn ends in on the wrong side of the work.

Decorations

The right finish will make all the difference to a knitted project. Pompoms, tassels, fringes and embroidery can add a decorative touch signifying that the project is really your creation. In Chapter 2 there are instructions for making and attaching pompoms to a project. You can make tassels and fringes in a similar way.

TASSELS AND FRINGES

A tassel is like a one-sided pompom and it looks great hanging from the end of a knitted tie or on the top of a beanie. Fringed edges on scarves and around the hem of a tunic can also be effective.

Making a tassel

1. Decide on the length of the tassel: about 6 or 7 cm (2½ or 3 in) is a good size for 8-ply yarn. Cut a strip of corrugated cardboard the same width as your tassel's length and wrap the yarn firmly but loosely around the cardboard.

2. Cut two lengths of yarn about 30 cm (12 in) long. Use a wool needle to pass both pieces of yarn under the wraps on the cardboard, then draw the two ends up and knot them tightly around the wraps of yarn.

3. Cut the loops of yarn at the opposite edge of the cardboard from the knot.

4. Hold the tassel in one hand and wrap some more yarn tightly around the top, about a centimetre or two from the knot.

5. Finish the tassel by knotting the ends of the wrapping yarn and sewing them into the tassel.

6. Trim the ends of the tassel so that they are even.

7. Use the ends of the knotted yarn at the top to sew the tassel to your project.

Finishing touches

Making a fringe

① Decide on the length of the fringe: about 10–15 cm (4–6 in) is a good size for a scarf. Allow a little extra for trimming. Cut a strip of corrugated cardboard as wide as your fringe is long and wrap the yarn loosely around the cardboard.

② Cut the loops of yarn along one edge of the cardboard so that you have lots of pieces of fringing double the desired length.

③ Fold a piece of fringe in half and use a crochet hook to draw the loop through the edge of the knitted fabric. (You can work with two pieces of fringe at a time for a thicker fringe.)

④ Pass the ends of the fringe through the loop and pull them tight. Continue until the fringe is complete.

⑤ To make the fringe more secure, sew each loop in place with a whip stitch if you like. Lay the fringe out flat and trim the ends of the yarn straight.

CORDS

Cords made of the same yarn as the knitted fabric can be very useful and decorative as well. You can use them to tie things up: attach one to each side of a beanie or the front opening of a cardigan and simply tie them in a bow. You can use them as loops for hanging things from, or as handles for small bags (see the iPod holder project on pages 134–135). You can even sew them onto the surface of a knitted fabric as decorations.

There are three ways of making a cord: twisting yarn together, French knitting or knitting on double-pointed needles.

Twisted cord

① Decide on the length of cord you need and multiply the measurement by three. Cut at least two lengths of yarn twice that length (the more lengths of yarn you use, the thicker the cord will be). Hold all the ends together and knot them tightly.

② Have a helper hold the knot securely, or hook it onto something firm and stable. Place a knitting needle through the loops of yarn and stretch them out tightly.

③ Turn the knitting needle, keeping the yarn taut, until the cord is twice the length you want. Bring the end with the knitting needle up to the knotted end without letting go of the yarn. The cord will twist on itself.

④ Tie a firm knot in the ends of the cord, or wrap some more yarn tightly around the loose ends to hold the twist.

Finishing touches

French knitting

Bobbins for French knitting are easy to find at craft stores; they consist of a wooden bobbin with a hole in the centre and a number of nails spaced evenly around the top. I recently bought a little contraption with a handle on one side that does French knitting very quickly, but it's only useful for very fine yarns so you'll probably find the traditional kind more versatile and less expensive.

① Pass the tail of the yarn down through the centre of the bobbin until about 15 cm (6 in) is hanging below the bobbin. Wrap the yarn firmly but not tightly around the outside of the nails at the top.

② Wrap the yarn around again, just above the first wrap.

③ Use a crochet hook to pick up the bottom loop of yarn from the first nail and pull it up over the second loop of yarn and off the nail. Continue around the circle of nails, wrapping more yarn and lifting the bottom loop over the top of each nail.

④ As you knit, the cord will fall through the bottom of the bobbin. It can help to attach something with a little bit of weight to the end of the cord to encourage it through—a heavy wooden bead or a bulldog clip would do.

⑤ To finish, cut the yarn and thread the end onto a wool needle. Pick up the last loop from each nail with the needle and pull the yarn through. Knot the yarn into the cord.

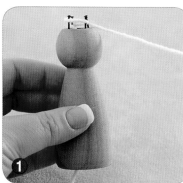

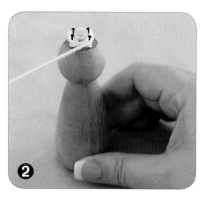

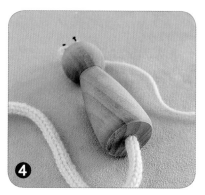

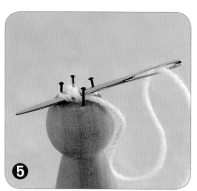

I-cord

Cord knitted on double-pointed needles is often called I-cord. You need two DPNs, in a gauge a couple of sizes smaller than you would normally use with the yarn; for example, for 8-ply yarn, you would choose 3.25 mm (UK 10, US 3) needles.

① Cast on four stitches and knit 1 row.
② Instead of turning the work, push the stitches to the other end of the needle and knit another row in the same direction, pulling the yarn as firmly as possible when you start to knit.
③ Continue swapping the needles in this way until the cord is the desired length. Cast off the stitches using the simple cast-off method and darn in the tail of the yarn.

EMBROIDERY

If you know some embroidery stitches, you can use them to decorate your knitted project. Blanket stitch (or buttonhole stitch) is great for making a feature of edges, particularly if it's worked in a contrasting colour. Running stitch and back stitch make graphic decorative lines, while lazy daisy (detached chain), chain stitches and grub roses (bullion roses) can bring a garden to life on your woollens. Cross stitch and herringbone stitch can be used for borders.

Use contrasting wool of the same ply as your project, or use tapestry wool or embroidery cotton if you prefer. The main thing to remember is that, if you are going to launder the project, you should stick to the same or similar fibres—wool with wool, cotton with cotton, synthetic with synthetic—and make sure the yarn is colourfast by washing it before you use it.

There is a method of embroidering on knitted fabric that uses a contrasting yarn to follow the rows and wales of knitted stitches. This is known as Swiss darning or overstitching, and there are instructions and examples in Chapter 12 (page 221).

7
Knit and purl

* Pattern repeats * Ribbing
* Simple textures * Stripes * Diamonds and other shapes
* Dynamic shapes * All-over patterns
* More textures * Gansey stitch patterns

Plain plus purl

Once you've mastered the basics, the variety of different fabric textures and patterns you can create using only plain knit and purl stitches is almost limitless. Here are just a few to get you started.

The knitted fabrics you create with different combinations of the two basic stitches that you've already learned (in Chapter 5, page 65) can vary not only in appearance but also in size and shape. In a ribbed pattern the fabric will be drawn in more than in stocking stitch, while stitches like garter stitch (page 73) and moss stitch (page 121) tend to make a more open fabric. Thus the same number of stitches will result in pieces of fabric of vastly different sizes.

This is why it's so important to knit a tension square (see page 62) before you start a project. Make sure you knit the tension square using the stitch pattern that you intend to follow, and adjust the needle size or number of stitches accordingly.

Pattern repeats

Most stitch patterns consist of a series of different basic stitches that are repeated across the rows of knitting to fill the entire fabric. Some patterns cover a number of rows that are repeated until the fabric is complete. These are called 'pattern repeats'.

At the beginning of the instructions for the stitch patterns in this chapter you will see a note of the pattern repeat. This is the number of stitches you will need to cast on to work the pattern in full. For example, if a pattern is 4 stitches wide, you will need to work on a multiple of 4 stitches to complete the whole pattern a number of times. So, if your fabric is 64 stitches wide, you will repeat the 4-stitch pattern 16 times across the row.

In most cases it is useful to have an extra stitch at each end of every row to provide a neat edge to the fabric. If the pattern repeat is a multiple of 4, add 2 stitches to your cast on and simply slip the first stitch of each row and knit the last stitch. In the example above, you would need to cast on 66 stitches to complete 16 pattern repeats across the row with a slipped stitch at the beginning of each row and a knit stitch at the end.

Some more complicated stitch patterns require more extra stitches at the end of each row to ensure that the centre of the design falls in the centre of the fabric. This is also the case if stitches are twisted, looped or knitted together at the edge of a repeat, as in the following chapters. Follow the instructions carefully at the beginning and end of the rows for these patterns, and factor in a slipped stitch if necessary.

LEFTOVER STITCHES

What can you do if the required number of stitches for the item you want to knit isn't divisible by the pattern repeat number? First work out how many stitches you'll have left over by dividing your number of stitches by the pattern repeat. If you have 70 stitches across your fabric, and the pattern repeat is 6 stitches, you will be able to knit 11 repeats (6 x 11 = 66) with 4 stitches left over. Divide the remainder in two and knit half of the spare stitches at the start of the row and half at the end. In the example, this means you will have 2 spare stitches at each end of every row. You can simply knit or purl these 2 stitches to form a non-patterned edge on your fabric. This will often be in the seam allowance anyway, and it forms a sort of selvedge for the fabric.

If you have a larger number of leftover stitches, such as if the pattern repeat is 14 stitches and you have 12 left over, you should still divide the remainder in half (6 spare at each end of the row). For this many stitches, it's best to knit them as if they were part of

a pattern repeat (knit the first 6 stitches of the row as though they were the last 6 stitches of a pattern repeat, and knit the last 6 stitches of the row as though they were the first 6 stitches of a new pattern repeat). You can still start and finish with one or two plain stitches to make a selvedge, as well.

VERTICAL PATTERN REPEATS

Stitch patterns also repeat vertically, over a set number of rows. If it's a simple pattern, the number of vertical pattern repeats may not be particularly important. For a more complex pattern, which repeats over a large number of rows (such as the 3D box design on page 130), you might want to work out in advance the number of vertical repeats so that you can, for example, line up the top of a row of boxes below the neckline of a jumper.

KNIT (AND PURL) AWAY

All of the stitch patterns in this chapter use only knit and purl stitches. They can be combined to create visual interest in your fabric by playing lines and textures against one another. You'll be surprised and amazed at how clever you can be with just two simple knitting stitches. Remember to slip the first stitch of every row for a neater finish.

Double ribbing

Ribbing

Ribbing is usually knitted on smaller needles than is recommended for the yarn weight, because it is such a stretchy pattern. For example, for 8-ply yarn, 3.25 mm (UK 10, US 3) needles—two sizes smaller than the 4 mm (No 8) needles usually recommended—are often used. The samples shown here have been knitted in 8-ply yarn on 4 mm needles.

DOUBLE RIBBING

I like to work double ribbing with an extra two stitches so that I can start and end the fabric with wales on the same side of the fabric; for example, if I begin with K2 (a double rib on the right side of the fabric), I add an extra two stitches so that I can end with a K2 rib on the right side. You can also start by knitting one—K1, * P2, K2 *, repeat * to * to last stitch, K1—to start and end with half a double wale in every row.

Pattern repeat: 4 stitches
Row 1: * K2, P2 *, repeat to end.
Row 2: * P2, K2 *, repeat to end.
Repeat these 2 rows until you have the required length of fabric.

Chunky ribbing

CHUNKY RIBBING

This rib pattern is a particular favourite of mine: it's funkier than just a plain rib. This pattern splits one repeat at the beginning and end to ensure that it is balanced.

Pattern repeat: 10 stitches
Row 1: K2, P2, K2, P2, * K4, P2, K2, P2 *, repeat to last two stitches, K2.
Row 2: P2, * K2, P2, K2, P4 *, repeat to last eight stitches, K2, P2, K2, P2.
Repeat these 2 rows until you have the required length of fabric.

Mistake ribbing

MISTAKE RIBBING

It's not really a mistake; it's deliberate. The ribbed pattern is formed by knitting the wrong-side rows of a double ribbing stitch one stitch out of step with the right-side rows. It's super easy to knit, because the stitch pattern is the same for every row.

Pattern repeat: 4 stitches + 3 extras
Row 1: * K2, P2 *, repeat to last three stitches, K2, P1.
Row 2: Repeat row 1.
Continue knitting every row the same until you have the required length of fabric.

Simple textures

MOSS STITCH

Moss stitch produces a very simple flat but textured fabric, created by alternating knit and purl stitches across the row and in each wale.

Pattern repeat: 2 stitches (any even number)
Row 1: * K1, P1 *, repeat to end.
Row 2: * P1, K1 *, repeat to end.
Repeat these 2 rows until you have the required length of fabric.

Moss stitch

DOUBLE MOSS STITCH

Sometimes known as wheat stitch (I imagine because it looks like ears of wheat in a field), this pattern is created by working moss stitch 2 rows at a time.

Pattern repeat: 2 stitches (any even number)
Row 1: * K1, P1 *, repeat * to * to end.
Row 2: * K1, P1 *, repeat * to * to end.
Row 3: * P1, K1 *, repeat * to * to end.
Row 4: * P1, K1 *, repeat * to * to end.
Repeat these 4 rows until you have the required length of fabric.

Double moss stitch

BASKETWEAVE STITCH

This fabric gives the appearance of woven strips of stocking stitch and reverse stocking stitch. The first 4 rows establish the pattern, which moves across by half a repeat in the second 4 rows to make the woven effect.

Pattern repeat: 8 stitches + 5 extras
Row 1: Knit.
Row 2: * K5, P3 *, repeat * to * to last 5 stitches, K5.
Row 3: * P5, K3 *, repeat * to * to last 5 stitches, P5.
Row 4: Repeat row 2.
Row 5: Knit.
Row 6: K1, P3, * K5, P3 *, repeat * to * to last stitch, K1.
Row 7: P1, * K3, P5 *, repeat * to * to last 4 stitches, K3, P1.
Row 8: Repeat row 6.
Repeat these 8 rows until you have the required length of fabric.

Basketweave stitch

Knit and purl

Knitting basics

Ribbed legwarmers

These eighties classics, once restricted to dance studios, are making a fashion comeback. Choose your favourite colour and knit them in a chunky rib.

YOU WILL NEED:
* Six 50 g balls of 8-ply woollen yarn
* One set of four 3.25 mm (No 10) DPNs (or 1 pair 3.25 mm needles)
* Wool needle and scissors

CONSTRUCTION:
Cast on 88 stitches evenly on three needles—I put 32 stitches on each of two needles and 24 on the third needle (see page 91 for tips on casting on for DPNs). Begin knitting in the round, in a pattern of K3, P2, K1, P2 (8 stitch repeat). Remember that when knitting in the round all rows are right-side rows; just continue knitting in pattern around and around the work. Join a new ball of yarn at the beginning of a pattern repeat, but don't worry if it's not at the beginning of a row. Each legwarmer will use three full balls of the yarn. When you have about a metre of yarn left, cast off in pattern. Carefully darn in the ends of the yarn (see page 98), and one legwarmer is complete. Repeat the process to make the second legwarmer.

If you prefer to knit on straight needles, cast on 90 stitches, slip the first stitch and work 1 row of the ribbing pattern (K3, P2, K1, P2), then knit the last stitch. Work the wrong-side row: slip 1, * K2, P1, K2, P3 * and repeat from * to * to the end, and then knit the last stitch. Continue until you have used three balls of the yarn, joining the new balls at the side of the work. Cast off, and sew the side edges of the fabric together using ladder stitch to make a flat seam (see page 105). Darn the yarn ends into the seam. Repeat the process to make the second legwarmer.

These legwarmers are quite stretchy and will fit most teens and adults, but if you want to make them for a child or someone with very skinny legs, reduce the number of stitches you cast on by 8 or 16 (one or two pattern repeats). For a child, use just two balls of yarn per legwarmer; for a thin adult, stop knitting when the legwarmer is about 50 cm (20 in) long.

Horizontal garter stitch stripes

Stripes

HORIZONTAL GARTER STITCH STRIPES

A single row of purl stitches on the right side of the fabric makes a fine horizontal stripe on a stocking stitch background.

Pattern repeat: any number of stitches
Row 1 and all odd rows: Knit all stitches.
Rows 2 and 4: Purl all stitches.
Row 6: Knit all stitches.
Repeat these 6 rows until you have the required length of fabric.

WIDE HORIZONTAL STRIPES

Bands of 6 rows of stocking stitch and reverse stocking stitch create this simple pattern.

Pattern repeat: any number of stitches
Knit 6 rows of stocking stitch (odd rows knit, even rows purl).
Knit 6 rows reverse stocking stitch (odd rows purl, even rows knit).
Repeat these 12 rows until you have the required length of fabric.

Wide horizontal stripes

HORIZONTAL MOSS STITCH STRIPES

Horizontal stripes of moss stitch alternate with stocking stitch bands to make this pattern.

Pattern repeat: any even number of stitches
Knit 6 rows of stocking stitch (odd rows knit, even rows purl).
Row 7: * K1, P1 *, repeat * to * to end.
Row 8: * P1, K1 *, repeat * to * to end.
Repeat these 8 rows until you have the required length if fabric.

Horizontal moss stitch stripes

VERTICAL PINSTRIPES

Fine vertical stripes of knit stitches appear against a background of reverse stocking stitch. One repeat is split over the beginning and end of the rows to centre the stripes.

Pattern repeat: 6 stitches
Row 1: P2, * K1, P5 *, repeat * to * to last 4 stitches, K1, P3.
Row 2: K3, * P1, K5 *, repeat * to * to last 3 stitches, P1, K2.
Repeat these 2 rows until you have the required length of fabric.

Vertical pinstripes

WIDE VERTICAL STRIPES

Alternating stripes of stocking stitch and reverse stocking stitch form this pattern.

Pattern repeat: 10 stitches
Row 1: * K5, P5 *, repeat * to * to end.
Row 2: Work the same as row 1 (all rows the same).
Continue knitting in pattern until you have the required length of fabric.

VERTICAL MOSS STITCH STRIPES

Five wales of stocking stitch alternate with three wales of moss stitch. One repeat is split over the beginning and end of the rows to centre the stripes.

Pattern repeat: 8 stitches
Row 1: K2, * P1, K1, P1, K5 *, repeat * to * to last 6 stitches, P1, K1, P1, K3.
Row 2: P3, * P1, K1, P1, P5 *, repeat to last 5 stitches, P1, K1, P1, P2.
Repeat these 2 rows until you have the required length of fabric.

Wide vertical stripes

Vertical moss stitch stripes

Knit and purl

Diagonal pinstripes

DIAGONAL PINSTRIPES

Fine stripes of purl stitches on a stocking stitch background slope across the knitted fabric. The pattern repeat is moved along by one stitch in every row.

Pattern repeat: 6 stitches
Row 1: * K5, P1 *, repeat * to * to end.
Row 2: * P5, K1 *, repeat * to * to end.
Row 3: K1, * P1, K5 *, repeat to last 5 stitches, P1, K4.
Row 4: P3, * K1, P5 *, repeat to last 3 stitches, K1, P2.
Row 5: K3, * P1, K5 *, repeat to last 3 stitches, P1, K2.
Row 6: P1, * K1, P5 *, repeat to last 5 stitches, K1, P4.
Repeat these 6 rows until you have the required length of fabric.

To reverse the direction of the stripes:
Row 1: * P1, K5 *, repeat * to * to end.
Row 2: * K1, P5 *, repeat * to * to end.
Row 3: K4, * P1, K5 *, repeat * to * to last 2 stitches, P1, K1.
Row 4: P2, * K1, P5 *, repeat * to * to last 4 stitches, K1, P3.
Row 5: K2, * P1, K5 *, repeat * to * to last 4 stitches, P1, K3.
Row 6: P4, * K1, P5 *, repeat * to * to last 2 stitches, K1, P1.
Repeat these 6 rows until you have the required length of fabric.

WIDE DIAGONAL STRIPES

Stripes of stocking stitch alternate with stripes of reverse stocking stitch in this pattern.

Wide diagonal stripes

Pattern repeat: 6 stitches
Row 1: * P3, K3 *, repeat * to * to end.
Row 2: * P3, K3 *, repeat * to * to end.
Row 3: K1, * P3, K3 *, repeat * to * to last 5 stitches, P3, K2.
Row 4: P2, * K3, P3 *, repeat * to * to last 4 stitches, K3, P1.
Row 5: K2, * P3, K3 *, repeat * to * to last 4 stitches, P3, K1.
Row 6: P1, * K3, P3 *, repeat * to * to last 5 stitches, K3, P2.
Row 7: * K3, P3 *, repeat * to * to end.
Row 8: * K3, P3 *, repeat * to * to end.
Row 9: P1, * K3, P3 *, repeat * to * to last 5 stitches, K3, P2.
Row 10: K2, * P3, K3 *, repeat * to * to last 4 stitches, P3, K1.
Row 11: P2, * K3, P3 *, repeat * to * to last 4 stitches, K3, P1.
Row 12: K1, * P3, K3 *, repeat * to * to last 5 stitches, P3, K2.
Repeat these 12 rows until you have the required length of fabric.

To reverse the direction of the stripes:

Row 1: * K3, P3 *, repeat * to * to end.
Row 2: * K3, P3 *, repeat * to * to end.
Row 3: K2, * P3, K3 *, repeat * to * to last 4 stitches, P3, K1.
Row 4: P1, * K3, P3 *, repeat * to * to last 5 stitches, K3, P2.
Row 5: K1, * P3, K3 *, repeat * to * to last 5 stitches, P3, K2.
Row 6: P2, * K3, P3 *, repeat * to * to last 4 stitches, K3, P1.
Row 7: * P3, K3 *, repeat * to * to end.
Row 8: * P3, K3 *, repeat * to * to end.
Row 9: P2, * K3, P3 *, repeat * to * to last 4 stitches, K3, P1.
Row 10: K1, * P3, K3 *, repeat * to * to last 5 stitches, P3, K2.
Row 11: P1, * K3, P3 *, repeat * to * to last 5 stitches, K3, P2.
Row 12: K2, * P3, K3 *, repeat * to * to last 4 stitches, P3, K1.
Repeat these 12 rows until you have the required length of fabric.

DIAGONAL MOSS STITCH STRIPES

These stripes look like a double row of pinstripes.

Pattern repeat: 8 stitches
Row 1: * K5, P1, K1, P1 *, repeat * to * to end.
Row 2: * P1, K1, P5, K1 *, repeat * to * to end.
Row 3: * K1, P1, K5, P1 *, repeat * to * to end.
Row 4: * P5, K1, P1, K1 *, repeat * to * to end.
Row 5: * K1, P1, K1, P1, K4 *, repeat * to * to end.
Row 6: * P3, K1, P1, K1, P2 *, repeat * to * to end.
Row 7: * K3, P1, K1, P1, K2 *, repeat * to * to end.
Row 8: * P1, K1, P1, K1, P4 *, repeat * to * to end.
Repeat these 8 rows until you have the required length of fabric.

To reverse the direction of the stripes:
Row 1: * K5, P1, K1, P1 *, repeat * to * to end.
Row 2: * P1, K1, P1, K1, P4 *, repeat * to * to end.
Row 3: * K3, P1, K1, P1, K2 *, repeat * to * to end.
Row 4: * P3, K1, P1, K1, P2 *, repeat * to * to end.
Row 5: * K1, P1, K1, P1, K4 *, repeat * to * to end.
Row 6: * P5, K1, P1, K1 *, repeat * to * to end.
Row 7: * K1, P1, K5, P1 *, repeat * to * to end.
Row 8: * P1, K1, P5, K1 *, repeat * to * to end.
Repeat these 8 rows until you have the required length of fabric.

Diagonal moss stitch stripes

Simple diamonds

Diamonds and other shapes

SIMPLE DIAMONDS

Crossing lines of purl stitches in both directions make a simple diamond patterned fabric.

Pattern repeat: 6 stitches
Row 1: * K5, P1 *, repeat * to * to end.
Row 2: * P1, K1, P3, K1 *, repeat * to * to end.
Row 3: * K1, P1, K1, P1, K2 *, repeat * to * to end.
Row 4: * P3, K1, P2 *, repeat * to * to end.
Row 5: Repeat row 3.
Row 6: Repeat row 2.
Repeat these 6 rows until you have the required length of fabric.

KING CHARLES BROCADE

The royal connections of this traditional pattern might add a regal texture to a man's jumper or scarf.

Pattern repeat: 12 stitches + 1 extra
Row 1: * K5, P1, K1, P1, K4 *, repeat * to * to last stitch, K1.
Row 2: * P4, K1, P1, K1, P1, K1, P3 *, repeat * to * to last stitch, P1.
Row 3: * K3, P1, K1, P1, K1, P1, K1, P1, K2 *, repeat * to * to last stitch, K1.
Row 4: * P2, K1, P1, K1, P3, K1, P1, K1, P1 *, repeat * to * to last stitch, P1.
Row 5: * K1, P1, K1, P1, K5, P1, K1, P1 *, repeat * to * to last stitch, K1.
Row 6: * K1, P1, K1, P7, K1, P1 *, repeat * to * to last stitch, K1.
Row 7: * K1, P1, K9, P1 *, repeat * to * to last stitch, K1.
Row 8: Repeat row 6.
Row 9: Repeat row 5.
Row 10: Repeat row 4.
Row 11: Repeat row 3.
Row 12: Repeat row 2.
Repeat these 12 rows until you have the required length of fabric.

King Charles brocade

BROCADE DIAMONDS

After you've had a bit of practice, you could experiment with repeating these brocade diamonds in horizontal or vertical rows.

Pattern repeat: 14 stitches
Row 1: * K4, P1, K1, P1, K1, P1, K1, P1, K3 *, repeat * to * to end.
Row 2 and all even rows: Purl all stitches.
Row 3: * P1, K4, P1, K1, P1, K1, P1, K4 *, repeat * to * to end.

Brocade diamonds

Row 5: * K1, P1, K4, P1, K1, P1, K4, P1 *, repeat * to * to end.

Row 7: * P1, K1, P1, K4, P1, K4, P1, K1 *, repeat * to * to end.

Row 9: * K1, P1, K1, P1, K7, P1, K1, P1 *, repeat * to * to end.

Row 11: Repeat row 7.

Row 13: Repeat row 5.

Row 15: Repeat row 3.

Repeat these 16 rows until you have the required length of fabric.

CHEQUERBOARD

This chequerboard is made up of stocking stitch and reverse stocking stitch squares. You could also replace the reverse stocking stitch squares with moss stitch ones.

Pattern repeat: 10 stitches

Rows 1 to 6: * K5, P5 *, repeat * to * to end.

Rows 7 to 12: * P5, K5 *, repeat * to * to end.

Repeat these 12 rows until you have the required length of fabric.

Chequerboard

TRIANGLES

Like mountains reflected in lakes, these pairs of triangles draw the eye.

Pattern repeat: 10 stitches + 1 extra

Row 1: K1, * P9, K1 *, repeat from * to * to end.

Row 2: * P2, K7 *, repeat from * to * to last stitch, P1.

Row 3: K1, * K2, P5, K3 *, repeat from * to * to end.

Row 4: * P4, K3, P3 *, repeat from * to * to last stitch, P1.

Row 5: K1, * K4, P1, K5 *, repeat from * to * to end.

Row 6: * K5, P1, K4 *, repeat from * to * to last stitch, K1.

Row 7: P1, * P2, K3, P5 *, repeat from * to * to end.

Row 8: * K4, P3, K3 *, repeat from * to * to last stitch, K1.

Row 9: P1, * P2, K5, P3 *, repeat from * to * to end.

Row 10: * K5, P1, K4 *, repeat from * to * to last stitch, K1.

Repeat these 10 rows until you have the required length of fabric.

Triangles

Knit and purl

3D boxes

Parallelograms

Dynamic shapes

3D BOXES

Here's a little optical illusion you can create using just three basic stitch patterns: stocking stitch, reverse stocking stitch and moss stitch.

Pattern repeat: 10 stitches
Row 1: * K1, P1 *, repeat * to * to end.
Row 2: * P1, K1, P1, K2, P2, K1, P1, K1 *, repeat * to * to end.
Row 3: * K1, P1, K3, P3, K1, P1 *, repeat * to * to end.
Row 4: * P1, K4, P4, K1 *, repeat * to * to end.
Row 5: * K5, P5 *, repeat * to * to end.
Rows 6 to 8: Repeat row 5 three more times.
Row 9: * K4, P1, K1, P4 *, repeat * to * to end.
Row 10: * K3, P1, K1, P1, K1, P3 *, repeat * to * to end.
Row 11: * K2, P1, K1, P1, K1, P1, K1, P2 *, repeat * to * to end.
Row 12: * K1, P1 *, repeat * to * to end.
Row 13: * P1, K1 *, repeat * to * to end.
Row 14: * P2, K1, P1, K1, P1, K1, P1, K2 *, repeat * to * to end.
Row 15: * P3, K1, P1, K1, P1, K3 *, repeat * to * to end.
Row 16: * P4, K1, P1, K4 *, repeat * to * to end.
Row 17: * P5, K5 *, repeat * to * to end.
Rows 18 to 20: Repeat row 17 three more times.
Row 21: * K1, P4, K4, P1 *, repeat * to * to end.
Row 22: * P1, K1, P3, K3, P1, K1 *, repeat * to * to end.
Row 23: * K1, P1, K1, P2, K2, P1, K1, P1 *, repeat * to * to end.
Row 24: * P1, K1 *, repeat * to * to end.
Repeat these 24 rows until you have the required length of fabric.
If you need to stop part-way through a vertical repeat, try to stop at row 4, 8, 12, 16 or 20 if you can.

PARALLELOGRAMS

These lozenges zigzag across the fabric to make a dynamic pattern.

Pattern repeat: 10 stitches
Row 1: * K5, P5 *, repeat * to * to end.
Row 2: K4, * P5, K5 *, repeat * to * to last 6 stitches, P5, K1.
Row 3: P2, * K5, P5 *, repeat * to * to last 8 stitches, K5, P3.
Row 4: K2, * P5, K5 *, repeat * to * to last 8 stitches, P5, K3.
Row 5: P4, * K5, P5 *, repeat * to * to last 6 stitches, K5, P1.
Row 6: Repeat row 1.
Repeat these 6 rows until you have the required length of fabric.

STAR MOTIF

This large star in moss stitch can be included as a motif on stocking stitch fabric.

Pattern repeat: 30 stitches
Row 1: K8, P1, K13, P1, K8.
Row 2: P9, K1, P11, K1, P9.
Row 3: K8, P1, K1, P1, K9, P1, K1, P1, K8.
Row 4: P9, K1, P1, K1, P7, K1, P1, K1, P9.
Row 5: K8, P1, K1, P1, K1, P1, K5, P1, K1, P1, K1, P1, K8.
Row 6: P9, K1, P1, K1, P1, K1, P3, K1, P1, K1, P1, K1, P9.
Row 7: K8, (P1, K1) 7 times, P1, K8.
Row 8: P9, (K1, P1) 6 times, K1, P9.
Row 9: K2, (P1, K1) 14 times, K1.
Row 10: P3, (K1, P1) 13 times, P2.
Row 11: K4, (P1, K1) 12 times, K3.
Row 12: P5, (K1, P1) 11 times, P4.
Row 13: K6, (P1, K1) 10 times, K5.
Row 14: P7, (K1, P1) 9 times, P6.
Row 15: K8, (P1, K1) 8 times, K7.
Row 16: P9, (K1, P1) 7 times, P8.
Row 17: Repeat row 15.
Row 18: Repeat row 14.
Row 19: Repeat row 13.
Row 20: Repeat row 12.
Row 21: Repeat row 11.
Row 22: Repeat row 10.
Row 23: Repeat row 9.
Row 24: Repeat row 8.
Row 25: Repeat row 7.
Row 26: Repeat row 6.
Row 27: Repeat row 5.
Row 28: Repeat row 4.
Row 29: Repeat row 3.
Row 30: Repeat row 2.
Row 31: Repeat row 1.

HEARTS

These little hearts can be worked as an all-over pattern (as in our sample), across a row or as a single motif. The instructions are for one heart motif.

Pattern repeat: 11 stitches
Row 1: K5, P1, K5.
Row 2: P4, K3, P4.
Row 3: K3, P5, K3.
Row 4: P2, K7, P2.
Row 5: K1, P9, K1.
Row 6: Knit all stitches.
Row 7: Purl all stitches.
Row 8: Knit all stitches.
Row 9: K1, P4, K1, P4, K1.
Row 10: P2, K2, P3, K2, P2.

To repeat in a row horizontally, allow two wales of stocking stitch between each motif (13 stitch repeat). To repeat as a row vertically, work 2 rows of stocking stitch between motifs (see the iPod holder project on page 135). To repeat as an overall pattern, as in our sample, leave nine wales of stocking stitch between the motifs (20 stitch repeat), starting a new motif with a purl stitch in the centre of this gap when you reach row 6 of the first set of motifs.

Star motif

Hearts

Hailspots

All-over patterns

HAILSPOTS

A scattering of purl stitches over a stocking stitch background creates the impression of a shower of rain falling softly.

Pattern repeat: 4 stitches
Row 1: Knit all stitches.
Row 2 and all even rows: Purl all stitches.
Row 3: * K3, P1 *, repeat * to * to end.
Row 5: Knit all stitches.
Row 7: K1, * P1, K3 *, repeat * to * to last 3 stitches, P1, K2.
Repeat these 8 rows until you have the required length of fabric.

Caterpillars crawling

CATERPILLARS CRAWLING

Sometimes known as dash stitch because of the punctuation mark it resembles, this pattern uses short rows of purl stitches.

Pattern repeat: 8 stitches
Row 1 and all odd rows: Knit all stitches.
Row 2: Purl all stitches.
Row 4: * K5, P3 *, repeat * to * to end.
Row 6: Purl all stitches.
Row 8: K1, * P3, K5 *, repeat * to * to last 7 stitches, P3, K4.
Repeat these 8 rows until you have the required length of fabric.

CATERPILLARS CLIMBING

Vertical lines of knit stitches sitting on reverse stocking stitch.

Pattern repeat: 6 stitches
Row 1: * K1, P5 *, repeat * to * to end.
Row 2: * K5, P1 *, repeat * to * to end.
Rows 3 to 6: Repeat rows 1 and 2 twice more.
Row 7: P3, * K1, P5 *, repeat * to * to last 3 stitches, K1, P2.
Row 8: K2, * P1, K5 *, repeat * to * to last 4 stitches, P1, K3.
Rows 9 to 12: Repeat rows 7 and 8 twice more.
Repeat these 12 rows until you have the required length of fabric.

Caterpillars climbing

BLOCKS AND RIBBONS

Ribbons of reverse stocking stitch draw stocking stitch 'cobblestones' together in this optical illusion.

Pattern repeat: 16 stitches
Row 1: Knit all stitches.
Row 2: Purl all stitches.
Row 3: K6, * P4, K12 *, repeat * to * to last 10 stitches, P4, K6.
Row 4: P6, * K4, P12 *, repeat * to * to last 10 stitches, K4, P6.
Row 5: Repeat row 3.
Row 6: Repeat row 4.
Rows 7 to 10: Repeat rows 1 and 2 twice.
Row 11: P2, * K12, P4 *, repeat * to * to last 14 stitches, K12, P2.
Row 12: K2, * P12, K4 *, repeat * to * to last 14 stitches, P12, K2.
Row 13: Repeat row 11.
Row 14: Repeat row 12.
Row 15: Knit all stitches.
Row 16: Purl all stitches.
Repeat these 16 rows until you have the required length of fabric.

Blocks and ribbons

RIBBONS WOVEN HORIZONTALLY

Interlacing reverse stocking stitch with stocking stitch gives a horizontally woven appearance.

Pattern repeat: 6 stitches
Row 1: Knit all stitches.
Row 2: Purl all stitches.
Row 3: * K1, P4, K1 *, repeat * to * to end.
Row 4: * P1, K4, P1 *, repeat * to * to end.
Row 5: Repeat row 3.
Row 6: Repeat row 4.
Row 7: Knit all stitches.
Row 8: Purl all stitches.
Repeat these 8 rows until you have the required length of fabric.

Ribbons woven horizontally

RIBBONS WOVEN VERTICALLY

Stocking stitch ribbons weave their way up the garter stitch fabric.

Pattern repeat: 6 stitches
Row 1 and all odd rows: Knit all stitches.
Rows 2, 4, 6, 8, 10: * K3, P3 *, repeat * to * to end.
Row 12, 14, 16, 18, 20: * P3, K3 *, repeat * to * to end.
Repeat these 20 rows until you have the required length of fabric.

Ribbons woven vertically

Knit and purl

Knitting basics

iPod holder

Slip your iPod or MP3 player—or your mobile phone—into this cute pouch and sling it around your neck for easy access while you're out and about.

YOU WILL NEED:
* One 50 g ball of 8-ply woollen yarn
* One pair of 4 mm (UK 8, US 6) knitting needles
* One French knitting bobbin and crochet hook, or a pair of 3.25 mm (UK 10, US 3) DPNs
* Wool needle, scissors and pins for sewing up

CONSTRUCTION:

FRONT: Using the 4 mm needles, cast on 19 stitches. Work 6 rows of stocking stitch.

BEGIN MOTIF:

Row 1: K9, P1, K9.

Row 2: P8, K1, P1, K1, P8.

Row 3: K7, P1, K1, P1, K1, P1, K7.

Row 4: P6, (K1, P1) 3 times, K1, P6.

Row 5: K5, (P1, K1) 4 times, P1, K5.

Row 6: P4, (K1, P1) 5 times, K1, P4.

Row 7: Repeat row 5.

Row 8: Repeat row 6.

Row 9: Repeat row 5.

Row 10: Repeat row 6.

Row 11: K5, P1, K1, P1, K3, P1, K1, P1, K5.

Row 12: P6, K1, P5, K1, P6.

Work 2 rows of stocking stitch and then repeat the motif (rows 1 to 12).

When you've finished the second motif, work a further 6 rows of stocking stitch. Cast off.

BACK: Using 4 mm needles, cast on 19 stitches. Work 38 rows of stocking stitch. Cast off.

HANDLE:

Use a French knitting bobbin or 3.25 mm DPNs to make a cord (see page 114) about 90 cm (3 ft) long, or your preferred length.

ASSEMBLY:

Pin the back and front pieces together with right sides facing and sew around the sides and cast-on edge with backstitch. Weave the tails of yarn into the seams. Use the tails of yarn from the ends of the cord to stitch each end securely into the top of a side seam. Sling the holder around your body, pop in your iPod and set off on a walk.

Andalusian stitch

Seersucker stitch

Knotted ribbons

More textures

ANDALUSIAN STITCH

This pretty textured stitch is called Andalusian stitch: perhaps because it looks like the crenellations of the Alhambra, a famous medieval castle in Granada.

Pattern repeat: any number
Row 1: Knit all stitches.
Row 2: Purl all stitches.
Row 3: Knit all stitches.
Row 4: * K1, P1 *, repeat * to * to end. If there's an odd number of stitches, simply end with a K1. Repeat these 4 rows until you have the required length of fabric.

SEERSUCKER STITCH

Seersucker is that bubbly cotton fabric that was vary popular for tablecloths (and clothing) in the seventies. This knitting stitch has a similar bubbly texture.

Pattern repeat: 4 stitches
Row 1: * K1, P1, K1, P1 *, repeat * to * to end.
Row 2: * K1, P1, K1, P1 *, repeat * to * to end.
Row 3: * P1, K3 *, repeat * to * to end.
Row 4: * P3, K1 *, repeat * to * to end.
Row 5: Repeat row 1.
Row 6: Repeat row 2.
Row 7: * K2, P1, K1 *, repeat * to * to end.
Row 8: * P1, K1, P2 *, repeat * to * to end.

Repeat these 8 rows until you have the required length of fabric.

KNOTTED RIBBONS

Vertical ribbons of stocking stitch are caught up in knots of moss stitch every 8 rows.

Pattern repeat: 8 stitches
Row 1: Knit all stitches.
Row 2: Purl all stitches.
Row 3: * K3, P2, K1, P2 *, repeat * to * to end.
Row 4: * K1, P1, K1, P1, K1, P3 *, repeat * to * to end.
Row 5: Repeat row 3.
Row 6: Repeat row 4.
Row 7: Repeat row 1.
Row 8: Repeat row 2.
Row 9: * P1, K1, P2, K3, P1 *, repeat * to * to end.
Row 10: * K1, P3, K1, P1, K1, P1 *, repeat * to * to end.
Row 11: Repeat row 9.
Row 12: Repeat row 10.
Repeat these 12 rows until you have the required length of fabric. It will look better if you can finish at either row 2 or row 8.

Gansey stitch patterns

Ganseys are traditional patterned fisherman's jumpers. Chapter 9 (page 163) has more information and stitch instructions.

MOCK CABLES

If you're not ready to tackle the twisted stitches of a true cable design (see Chapter 9), this stitch gives a similar rope-like effect.

Pattern repeat: 10 stitches
Row 1: * P4, K1, P1, K4 *, repeat * to * to end.
Row 2: * P3, K2, P2, K3 *, repeat * to * to end.
Row 3: * P2, K2, P1, K1, P2, K2 *, repeat * to * to end.
Row 4: * P1, K2, P2, K2, P2, K1 *, repeat * to * to end.
Row 5: * K2, P3, K3, P2 *, repeat * to * to end.
Row 6: * K1, P4, K4, P1 *, repeat * to * to end.
Repeat these 6 rows until you have the required length of fabric.

GANSEY LADDERS

Ladders, like ropes represented by cables, are essential shipboard equipment. On a gansey, ladders can be wide or narrow.

Pattern repeat: 12 stitch panel set in a stocking stitch fabric. Instructions are for the panel only.
Row 1: P1, K1, P1, K6, P1, K1, P1.
Row 2: K1, P1, K1, P6, K1, P1, K1.
Row 3: Repeat row 1.

Row 4: Repeat row 2.
Row 5: P1, K1, P8, K1, P1.
Row 6: K1, P1, K8, P1, K1.
Repeat these 6 rows until you have the required length of fabric. If you are knitting in the round, as for a traditional gansey, even numbered rows should be an exact repeat of the previous row.

GANSEY MARRIAGE LINES

Ganseys were often knitted for a fisherman by his prospective bride, perhaps as a way of showing off her housekeeping ability. This zigzag pattern is thought to represent the course of a marriage (for richer, for poorer) or the sailor's life of going out to sea and then returning to his wife on shore.

Pattern repeat: 14 stitch panel set in a stocking stitch fabric. Instructions are for the panel only.
Row 1: P1, K1, P1, K1, P1, K8, P1.
Row 2: K1, P7, K1, P1, K1, P2, K1.
Row 3: P1, K3, P1, K1, P1, K6, P1.
Row 4: K1, P5, K1, P1, K1, P4, K1.
Row 5: P1, K5, P1, K1, P1, K4, P1.
Row 6: K1, P3, K1, P1, K1, P6, K1.
Row 7: P1, K7, P1, K1, P1, K2, P1.
Row 8: K1, P1, K1, P1, K1, P8, K1.
Row 9: Repeat row 7.
Row 10: Repeat row 6.
Row 11: Repeat row 5.
Row 12: Repeat row 4.
Row 13: Repeat row 3.
Row 14: Repeat row 2.
Repeat these 14 rows until you have the required length of fabric.

Mock cables

Gansey ladders

Gansey marriage lines

Knit and purl

8

Lacy looks

* Making a lacy hole

* Eyelets * Openwork * Organic forms

* Trellis and mesh patterns * Seaside patterns

* Architectural motifs * Wide open spaces

* Feathers and fronds * Lacy edgings

An open case

The stitch patterns in this chapter involve creating deliberate holes in your work, by slipping or knitting stitches together and then making new stitches with loops of yarn.

Most stitch patterns consist of a series of instructions that are repeated across the rows of knitting to fill the entire fabric. They may also have a number of rows that are repeated until the fabric is complete. These are called 'pattern repeats'. For more information about working out the number of horizontal and vertical pattern repeats for your project, see pages 118–19.

It's still important to knit a tension square (see page 62) before you start a project. Make sure you knit the tension square using the stitch pattern that you intend to follow, and adjust the needle size or number of stitches accordingly.

Making a lacy hole

To make a basic lacy hole, you need to reduce the number of stitches in the row by one (knit two stitches together) and loop the yarn around the needle to re-create the correct number of stitches for the following row.

1. Pass the yarn around the needle and knit two stitches together.
2. In the next row, knit the loop of yarn as though it were a normal stitch.
3. If you are working with purl stitches, make sure the yarn goes right around the needle.

MAKE A HOLE IN IT

All of the stitch patterns in this chapter create lacy holes in the knitted fabric. They range in difficulty from simple eyelets to clusters of lacy branches, but none of them is very difficult to master, particularly if you practise by knitting a tension square first. Remember to slip the first stitch of every row for a neater finish.

1

1

2

2

3

3

Lacy looks

Hailspot eyelets

Eyelets

HAILSPOT EYELETS

This pattern produces a scattering of simple eyelets over the whole surface of stocking stitch fabric.

Pattern repeat: 6 stitches + 1 extra
Row 1: Knit all stitches.
Row 2 and all even rows: Purl all stitches.
Row 3: * K2, yon, K2tog, K2 *, repeat * to * to last stitch, K1.
Row 5: Knit all stitches.
Row 7: K1, *K4, yon, K2tog *, repeat * to * to end.
Repeat these 8 rows until you have the required length of fabric.

LACY BUTTERFLY STITCH

A group of four eyelets looks like a butterfly.

Pattern repeat: 8 stitches + 1 extra
Row 1: K1 * K1, K2tog, yon, K1, yon, slip 1, K1, psso, K2 *, repeat * to * to end.
Row 2: * P4, slip 1 purlwise, P3 *, repeat * to * to last stitch, P1.
Row 3: Repeat row 1.
Row 4: Repeat row 2.
Row 5: K1, * yon, slip 1, K1, psso, K3, K2tog, yon, K1 *, repeat * to * to end.
Row 6: * Slip 1 purlwise, P7, * repeat pattern to last stitch, P1.
Row 7: Repeat row 5.
Row 8: Repeat row 6.
Repeat these 8 rows until you have the required length of fabric.

Lacy butterfly stitch

FLOWER EYELETS

Groups of six eyelets make a pattern like a field of flowers in bloom.

Pattern repeat: 12 stitches + 1 extra
Row 1: Knit all stitches.
Row 2 and all even rows: Purl all stitches.
Row 3: * K2, yon, slip 1, K2tog, psso, yon, K7 *, repeat * to * to last stitch, K1.
Row 5: * K2tog, yon, K3, yon, K2tog tbl, K5 *, repeat * to * to last stitch, K1.
Row 7: Repeat row 3.
Row 9: * K9, yon, slip 1, K2tog, psso, yon *, repeat * to * to last stitch, K1.
Row 11: K6, * K2tog, yon, K3, yon, K2tog tbl, K5 *, repeat * to * to last 7 stitches, K7.
Row 13: Repeat row 9.
Repeat these 14 rows until you have the required length of fabric.

Flower eyelets

Openwork

ROWS OF EYELETS

One horizontal row of eyelets can be used as a feature. You can also weave a pretty ribbon through the eyelets to draw up the knitted fabric.

Pattern repeat: any odd number of stitches
Row 1: K1, * yon, K2tog *, repeat * to * to end.
Row 2: Purl.
These 2 rows make the eyelets and can be placed anywhere in a stocking-stitch fabric and repeated as many times as you like.

Rows of eyelets

OPENWORK LADDERS

A wale of eyelets climbs stocking stitch fabric in this pattern. Change the number of stitches between repeats to vary the width of the stripes.

Pattern repeat: 7 stitches (or any odd number you like, if you want the ladders closer together or further apart)
Row 1: * K3, K2tog, yon, K2tog tbl *, repeat * to * to end. (NOTE that you finish with only six stitches on the needle for each repeat, including the loop of yarn, even though you started with seven.)
Row 2: * P1 tbl, yon, drop the yon loop from the previous row, P1 tbl, P3 *, repeat * to * to end.
Row 3: * K3, K1 tbl, yon, drop the yon loop from the previous row, K1 tbl *, repeat * to * to end.
Row 4: Repeat row 2.
Repeat rows 3 and 4 until you have the required length of fabric.

Openwork ladders

DIAGONAL OPENWORK

Use a slip, slip, knit (SSK) stitch combination (see page 86) to create the strong diagonal lines with these eyelet chains.

Pattern repeat: 4 stitches + 1 extra
Row 1: * K3, yon, SSK *, repeat * to * to end.
Row 2 and all even rows: Purl all stitches (including the yon loop).
Row 3: K1, * K3, yon, SSK *, repeat * to * to last 4 stitches, K4.
Row 5: K2, * K3, yon, SSK *, repeat * to * to last 3 stitches, K3.
Row 7: K1, yon, SSK, * K3, yon, SSK *, repeat * to * to last 2 stitches, K2.
Row 9: K2, yon, SSK, * K3, yon, SSK *, repeat * to * to last stitch, K1.
Repeat these 10 rows until you have the required length of fabric.

Diagonal openwork

Lacy looks

Horizontal chevrons

Vertical chevrons

HORIZONTAL CHEVRONS

Chevrons are zigzag patterns; these are on a background of stocking stitch. You can work single chevrons or group them together (see the triple chevron border on page 157).

Pattern repeat: 8 stitches + 2 extra
Row 1: K1, * K6, K2tog, yon *, repeat * to * to last stitch, K1.
Row 2 and all even rows: Purl all stitches (including the yon loop).
Row 3: K1, * yon, K2tog tbl, K3, K2tog, yon, K1 *, repeat * to * to last stitch, K1.
Row 5: K1, * K1, yon, K2tog tbl, K1, K2tog, yon, K2 *, repeat * to * to last stitch, K1.
Row 7: K1, * K2, yon, S1, K2tog, psso, yon, K3 *, repeat * to * to last stitch, K1.
Row 9: K1, * K3, yon, K2tog tbl, K3 *, repeat * to * to last stitch, K1.
These 10 rows form the single chevron pattern. Repeat as often as desired in a stocking stitch fabric.

VERTICAL CHEVRONS

Vertical chevrons form zigzags that draw the eye up the fabric.

Pattern repeat: 7 stitches
Row 1: * K5, yon, K2tog tbl *, repeat * to * to end.
Row 2 and all even rows: Purl all stitches (including the yon loop).
Row 3: * K4, yon, K2tog tbl, K1 *, repeat * to * to end.
Row 5: * K3, yon, K2tog tbl, K2 *, repeat * to * to end.
Row 7: * K2, yon, K2tog tbl, K3 *, repeat * to * to end.
Row 9: * K1, yon, K2tog tbl, K4 *, repeat * to * to end.
Row 11: Repeat row 7.
Row 13: Repeat row 5.
Row 15: Repeat row 3.
Repeat these 16 rows until you have the required length of fabric.

Organic forms

CATERPILLAR'S LUNCH

The little caterpillars from Chapter 7 (page 117) appear to have eaten their way through the stocking stitch fabric.

Pattern repeat: 8 stitches + 2 extras

Row 1: K1, * yon, K2tog tbl, K6 *, repeat * to * to last stitch, K1.

Row 2 and all even rows: Purl all stitches (including yon loop).

Row 3: K2, * yon, K2tog tbl, K6 *, repeat * to * to end.

Row 5: K3, * yon, K2tog tbl, K6 *, repeat * to * to last 7 stitches, yon, K2tog tbl, K5.

Row 7: K4, * yon, K2tog tbl, K6 *, repeat * to * to last 6 stitches, yon, K2tog tbl, K4.

Row 9: K7, * K2tog, yon, K6 *, repeat * to * to last 3 stitches, K3.

Row 11: K6, * K2tog, yon, K6 *, repeat * to * to last 4 stitches, K4.

Row 13: K5, * K2tog, yon, K6 *, repeat * to * to last 5 stitches, K5.

Row 15: K4, * K2tog, yon, K6 *, repeat * to * to last 6 stitches, K6.

Repeat these 16 rows until you have the required length of fabric.

Caterpillar's lunch

LACY DIAMONDS

These diamonds make a pattern that will add brilliance to your knitting.

Pattern repeat: 10 stitches + 1 extra

Row 1: * K1, yon, K2tog tbl, K5, K2tog, yon *, repeat * to * to last stitch, K1.

Row 2 and all even rows: Purl all stitches (including yon loops).

Row 3: * K2, yon, K2tog tbl, K3, K2tog, yon, K1 *, repeat * to * to last stitch, K1.

Row 5: * K3, yon, K2tog tbl, K1, K2tog, yon, K2 *, repeat * to * to last stitch, K1.

Row 7: * K4, yon, slip 1, K2tog, psso, yon, K3 *, repeat * to * to last stitch, K1.

Row 9: * K3, K2tog, yon, K1, yon, K2tog tbl, K2 *, repeat * to * to last stitch, K1.

Row 11: * K2, K2tog, yon, K3, yon, K2tog tbl, K1 *, repeat * to * to last stitch, K1.

Row 13: * K1, K2tog, yon, K5, yon, K2tog tbl *, repeat * to * to last stitch, K1.

Row 15: K2tog, * yon, K7, yon, slip 1, K2tog, psso *, repeat * to * to last 9 stitches, yon, K7, yon, K2tog.

Repeat these 16 rows until you have the required length of fabric.

Lacy diamonds

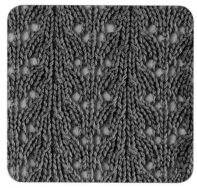

Branches

BRANCHES

By decreasing and making new stitches in different places, you can create subtle curved lines in your lacy knitting.

Pattern repeat: 9 stitches
Row 1: Knit all stitches.
Row 2 and all even rows: Purl all stitches, including yon loops.
Row 3: * K2tog, K2, yon, K1, yon, K2, K2tog tbl *, repeat * to * to end.
Row 5: * K1, K2tog, yon, K3, yon, K2tog tbl, K1 *, repeat * to * to end.
Repeat these 6 rows until you have the required length of fabric.

LEAVES

This pretty all-over lace design looks like leaves falling down the fabric.

Leaves

Pattern repeat: 8 stitches + 1 extra
Row 1: * K1, yon, K2, slip 1, K2tog, psso, K2, yon *, repeat * to * to last stitch, K1.
Row 2 and all even rows: Purl all stitches, including yon loops.
Row 3: * K2, yon, K1, slip 1, K2tog, psso, K1, yon, K1 *, repeat * to * to last stitch, K1.
Row 5: * K3, yon, slip 1, K2tog, psso, yon, K2 *, repeat * to * to last stitch, K1.
Row 7: * K2tog, psso, K2, yon, K1, yon, K2 *, repeat * to * to last stitch, SSK.
Rows 9 and 11: Repeat row 7.
Row 13: * Slip 1, K2tog, psso, K1, yon, K3, yon, K1 *, repeat * to * to last stitch, K1.
Row 15: * Slip 1, K2tog, psso, yon, K5, yon *, repeat * to * to last stitch, K1.
Rows 17 and 19: Repeat row 1.
Repeat these 20 rows until you have the required length of fabric.

FERNS

Double sprays of eyelets cover this lacy fabric like fronds of bracken.

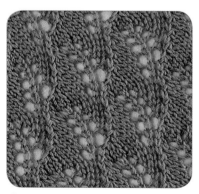

Ferns

Pattern repeat: 8 stitches + 1 extra
Row 1: K1, * K1, yon, K5, K2tog *, repeat * to * to end.
Row 2 and all even rows: Purl all stitches, including yon loop.
Row 3: K1, * yon, K1, yon, K4, K3tog *, repeat * to * to end.
Row 5: K1, * K1, yon, K1, yon, K3, K3tog *, repeat * to * to end.
Row 7: K1, * K2, yon, K1, yon, K2, K3tog *, repeat * to * to end.
Row 9: K1, * K3, yon, K1, yon, K1, K3tog *, repeat * to * to end.
Repeat these 10 rows until you have the required length of fabric.

LILIES

Work one pattern for a lovely vertical garden of lilies on your knitted fabric, or repeat it as many times as you like for an overall effect.

Pattern repeat: 18 stitches (Repeat these 18 stitches as many times as required across the row.)

NOTE: in each row, you can replace the K2tog tbl with SSK, if you prefer.

Row 1: K4, K2tog, K2, yon, K5, yon, K2, K2tog tbl, K1.

Row 2 and all even rows: Purl all stitches, including yon loops.

Row 3: K3, K2tog, K2, yon, K1, yon, K2, K2tog tbl, K6.

Row 5: K2, K2tog, K2, yon, K3, yon, K2, K2tog tbl, K5.

Row 7: K1, K2tog, K2, yon, K5, yon, K2, K2tog tbl, K4.

Row 9: K6, K2tog, K2, yon, K1, yon, K2, K2tog tbl, K3.

Row 11: K5, K2tog, K2, yon, K3, yon, K2, K2tog tbl, K2.

Repeat these 12 rows until you have the required length of fabric.

Lilies

Trellis and mesh patterns

MOORISH SCREEN

This trellis of open lace looks a bit like a carved and painted screen in a North African mosque.

Pattern repeat: 3 stitches + 1 extra

Row 1: * K1, yon, K2tog *, repeat * to * to last stitch, K1.

Row 2: P1, * P1, K1, P1 *, repeat * to * to end (knit into loops, purl into stitches).

Row 3: * K1, K2tog, yon *, repeat to last stitch, K1.

Row 4: P1, * K1, P2 *, repeat * to * to end (knit into loops, purl into stitches).

Repeat these 4 rows until you have the required length of fabric.

Moorish screen

TURKISH STITCH

Peer into the seraglio through this lattice of lacy knitting. This stitch is completely reversible: it looks the same on both sides of the fabric.

Pattern repeat: any even number of stitches

Row 1: K1, * yon, K2tog *, repeat * to * to last stitch, K1.

All rows are the same, so continue knitting the pattern until you have the required length of fabric.

Turkish stitch

Lacy looks

Knitting basics

Lacy socks

Socks are not difficult to knit once you've mastered the technique of knitting in the round on DPNs. As practice, start with a tiny pair for a toddler until you get the hang of it.

YOU WILL NEED:
* 50 g ball of 4-ply baby wool or sock yarn
* One set of four 2.25 mm (UK 13, US 1) DPNs
* Wool needle and scissors

These instructions make a pair of socks that will fit a 14 cm (5 in) foot, measured heel to toe. You can vary the length of the foot while knitting the instep.

CONSTRUCTION:

Cast on 50 stitches, dividing them over three needles: 16 stitches on the first needle and 17 stitches on the next two needles.

KNIT IN THE ROUND: * K1, P1 *, repeat * to * for 10 rounds (about 2.5 cm or 1 in).

Begin the double chevron lace pattern. NOTE: when the pattern calls for a yon at the changeover point for the next needle, be extra careful to ensure that it stays on the needle. If you have one stitch left on the needle and the pattern says K2tog, slip the last stitch onto the next needle before you K2tog. It doesn't matter if the number of stitches on each needle changes at this stage.

ROUND 1: Knit all stitches.
ROUND 2: * K8, K2tog, yon *, repeat * to * four more times.
ROUND 3 AND ALL ODD ROUNDS: Knit all stitches.
ROUND 4: * yon, K2tog tbl, K5, K2tog, yon, K1 *, repeat * to * four more times.
ROUND 6: * K1, yon, K2tog tbl, K3, K2tog, yon *, repeat * to * four more times.

ROUND 8: * yon, K2tog tbl, yon, K2tog tbl, K1, K2tog, yon, K2tog, yon, K1 *, repeat * to * four more times.
ROUND 10: * K1, yon, K2tog tbl, yon, slip 1, K2tog, psso, yon, K2tog, yon, K2 *, repeat * to * four more times.
ROUND 12: * K2, yon, slip 1, K2tog tbl, psso, yon, K2tog, yon, K3 *, repeat * to * four more times.
ROUND 14: * K3, yon, slip 1, K2tog, psso, yon, K4 *, repeat * to * four more times.
ROUND 16: * K3, K2tog, yon, K5 *, repeat * to * four more times.
Knit all stitches for 6 more rounds.

MAKING THE HEEL:

The beginning of the next round will be the centre back of the heel. K12, K2tog and then stop. Slip the last 13 stitches of the previous round onto the other end of the same needle, so that you have 26 stitches with the working yarn at one end.

Divide the remaining 23 stitches evenly over two needles and leave them for the instep.

Working on the 26 stitches for the heel, use two DPNs to continue in stocking stitch (alternating purl and knit rows and beginning with a purl row). Slip the first stitch of every row knitwise and knit the last stitch of every row, even the purl rows. Knit 15 rows stocking stitch in this manner, ending on a purl row.

SHAPE THE HEEL:

Row 16: K15, K2tog, K1, turn work.
Row 17: Slip 1, P5, P2tog, P1, turn work.

(Note that in each row you knit across to the last stitch you worked in the previous row, then knit that stitch together with the next unworked stitch.)

Row 18: Slip 1, K6, K2tog, K1, turn work.

Row 19: Slip 1, P7, P2tog, P1, turn work.

Row 20: Slip 1, K8, K2tog, K1, turn work.

Row 21: Slip 1, P9, P2tog, P1, turn work.

Row 22: Slip 1, K10, K2tog, K1, turn work.

Row 23: Slip 1, P11, P2tog, P1, turn work.

Row 24: Slip 1, K12, K2tog, K1, turn work.

Row 25: Slip 1, P13, P2tog, P1. You should now have 16 stitches on one needle. Knit 8 stitches to bring the yarn back to the centre of the heel.

WORKING THE INSTEP:

Slip all 23 instep stitches onto one needle. You should now have 8 stitches on the first needle, 23 on the second needle and 8 on the third needle (39 stitches in total). Use the fourth needle to begin knitting in the round again as follows:

K8 stitches from first needle, then knit up 10 stitches along the side edge of the heel onto the same needle (see page 106 for instructions on knitting up stitches); K23 on the second needle; then use the spare needle to knit up 10 stitches along the side of the heel, then K8 stitches from the remaining needle (you should now have 59 stitches: 18, 23, 18 on three needles).

Round 1: Knit all stitches in the round.

Round 2: On the first needle, knit to last 3 stitches, K2tog, K1; K23 on the second needle; on the third needle, K1, K2tog tbl, knit to end.

Repeat these 2 rounds five more times, until 47 stitches remain.

Continue working in stocking stitch without shaping for 22 rounds. If you want to shorten or lengthen the foot of the sock slightly, work a few rounds more or less, allowing approximately 4 rows for each centimetre (5 rows for half an inch).

Decrease 1 stitch at the beginning of the third needle in the last round (46 stitches).

SHAPING THE TOE:

Round 1: On the first needle, knit to last 3 stitches, K2tog, K1; on the second needle, K1, K2tog tbl, knit to last 3 stitches, K2tog, K1; on the third needle, K1, K2tog tbl, knit to end.

Round 2: Knit all stitches.

Repeat these 2 rounds until there are 6 stitches on the first needle, 11 stitches on the second needle and 5 stitches on the third needle.

FINISHING:

Cast off using the three-needle method (see page 96), which creates a nice flat seam at the toe. Alternatively, cast off as usual and stitch the toe seam using a wool needle and the knitting yarn.

Darn in the tails of yarn. Work a second sock to match the first.

Note: The sample socks in the photograph were knitted in 2 ply yarn on 2.25 mm needles, with the foot shortened to fit the teddy bear.

LAYETTE STITCH

Although this stitch is not truly reversible, it looks good from both sides.

Pattern repeat: 8 stitches + 2 extra
Row 1: K1, * P1, K3, P1, K3 *, repeat * to * to last stitch, K1.
Row 2: P1, * P3, K1, P3, K1 *, repeat * to * to last stitch, P1.
Row 3: Repeat row 1.
Row 4: P1, * yon, P3tog, yon, K1, yon, P3tog, yon, K1 *, repeat * to * to last stitch, P1. NOTE: When you loop the yarn around the needle before purling the three stitches together, make sure it goes right around the needle, from the front to the back of the work and then to the front again (see the step-by-step instructions on page 85).
Row 5: K1, * K2, P1, K3, P1, K1 *, repeat * to * to last stitch, K1.
Row 6: P1, * P1, K1, P3, K1, P2 *, repeat * to * to last stitch, P1.
Row 7: Repeat row 5.
Row 8: P1, * yon, K1, yon, P3tog, yon, K1, yon, P3tog *, repeat * to * to last stitch, P1.
Repeat these 8 rows until you have the required length of fabric.

Layette stitch

CHEQUERBOARD

A lacy variation on the chequerboard pattern in the last chapter.

Pattern repeat: 16 stitches + 1 extra
Row 1: K1, * K8, (yon, K2tog) four times *, repeat * to * to end.
Row 2: * (P1, K1) four times, P8 *, repeat * to * to last stitch, P1.
Rows 3 to 8: Repeat rows 1 and 2 three more times.
Row 9: K1, * (yon, K2tog) four times, K8 *, repeat * to * to end.
Row 10: * P8, (P1, K1) four times *, repeat * to * to last stitch, P1.
Rows 11 to 16: Repeat rows 9 and 10 three more times.
Repeat these 16 rows until you have the required length of fabric.

Chequerboard

STARRY MESH

This is not a true reversible stitch but the fabric looks good from both sides, and so this stitch could be used to make a lacy shawl or scarf.

Pattern repeat: 4 stitches + 1 extra
Rows 1 and 3: Purl all stitches. (This is the wrong side of the fabric.)
Row 2: * K1, yon, slip 2 knitwise, K1, pass 2 slipped stitches over, yon *, repeat from * to * to last stitch, K1.
Row 4: SSK, yon, * K1, yon, slip2 knitwise, K1, p2sso, yon, *, repeat from * to * to last three stitches, K2tog, K1.
Repeat these 4 rows until you have the required length of fabric.

Starry mesh

Waves

Seaside patterns

WAVES

This is a variation on a traditional feather-and-fan stitch pattern.

Pattern repeat: 18 stitches
Row 1: Knit all stitches.
Row 2 and all even rows: Purl all stitches.
Row 3: Knit all stitches.
Row 5: * (P2tog) 3 times, (K1, yon) 6 times, (P2tog) 3 times *, repeat * to * to end.

Repeat these 6 rows until you have the required length of fabric.

NORFOLK ISLAND PINES

A row of pine trees along the esplanade on the beach front.

Pattern repeat: 13 stitches
NOTE: in each row you can replace the K2tog tbl with SSK, if you prefer.
Rows 1 to 4: Knit all stitches (garter stitch).
Row 5: * K1, K2tog, K2tog, (yon, K1) three times, yon, K2tog tbl, K2 tog tbl, K1 *, repeat * to * to end.
Row 6: * P3, (K1, P1) three times, K1, P3 *, repeat * to * to end.
Rows 7 to 12: Repeat rows 5 and 6 three more times.

Repeat these 12 rows until you have the required length of fabric.

Norfolk Island pines

CLAMSHELLS

Shell-like eyelet curves are clustered like mussels in a rock pool.

Pattern repeat: 10 stitches + 2 extras
NOTE: in row 1 you can replace the K2tog tbl with SSK, if you prefer.
Row 1: K1, * K1, yon, K3, K2tog tbl, K4 *, repeat * to * to last stitch, K1.
Row 2 and all even rows: Purl all stitches.
Row 3: K1, * yon, K1, yon, K2, slip 1, K2tog, psso, K4 *, repeat * to * to last stitch, K1.
Row 5: K1, * K3, yon, K1, slip 1, K2tog, psso, K3, yon *, repeat * to * to last stitch, K1.
Row 7: K1, * K4, yon, slip 1, K2tog, psso, K2, yon, K1 *, repeat * to * to last stitch, K1.
Row 9: K1, * K5, slip 1, K2tog, psso, K1, yon, K1, yon *, repeat * to * to last stitch, K1.
Row 11: K1, * yon, K4, slip 1, K2tog, psso, yon, K3 *, repeat * to * to last stitch, K1.

Repeat these 12 rows until you have the required length of fabric.

Clamshells

Architectural motifs

ROMAN STRIPE STITCH

The stripes of this fancy mesh look a little like the colonnades around the Roman Coliseum.

Pattern repeat: any even number

Row 1: Knit all stitches.

Row 2: Knit all stitches.

Row 3: K1, * yon, K1 *, repeat * to * to last stitch, K1. (NOTE that you will have almost doubled the number of stitches you started with.)

Row 4: K1, purl to last stitch, K1.

Row 5: K1, * K2tog *, repeat * to * to last stitch, K1.

Row 6: K1, * yon, K2tog *, repeat * to * to last stitch, K1.

Row 7: Repeat row 6.

Row 8: Knit all stitches.

Repeat these 8 rows until you have the required length of fabric.

Roman stripe stitch

GOTHIC ARCHES

You could work a single row of arches as a pretty border, or cover the whole fabric in them.

Pattern repeat: 10 stitches + 2 extras

NOTE: in row 1 you can replace the K2tog tbl with SSK, if you prefer.

Row 1: K1, * yon, K2tog, K5, K2tog tbl, yon, K1 *, repeat * to * to last stitch, K1.

Row 2 and all even rows: Purl all stitches.

Row 3: Repeat row 1.

Row 5: K1, * yon, K3, slip 1, K2tog, psso, K3, yon, K1 *, repeat * to * to last stitch, K1.

Row 7: K1, * K1, yon, K2, slip 1, K2tog, psso, K2, yon, K2 *, repeat * to * to last stitch, K1.

Row 9: K1, * K2, yon, K1, slip 1, K2tog, psso, K1, yon, K3 *, repeat * to * to last stitch, K1.

Row 11: K1, * K3, yon, slip 1, K2tog, psso, yon, K4 *, repeat * to * to last stitch, K1.

Repeat these 12 rows until you have the required length of fabric.

Gothic arches

Cottages

COTTAGES

If you knit these cute little cottages with chimneys all over the fabric, the pattern looks the same from the top as from the bottom.

Pattern repeat: 10 stitches + 1 extra

Row 1: * (K1, yon, K2tog tbl, K2 tog, yon) twice *, repeat * to * to last stitch, K1.

Row 2 and all even rows: Purl all stitches.

Row 3: Repeat row 1.

Row 5: * K1, yon, K2tog tbl, K5, K2 tog, yon *, repeat * to * to last stitch, K1.

Row 7: * K2, yon, K2tog tbl, K3, K2tog, yon, K1 *, repeat * to * to last stitch, K1.

Row 9: * K3, yon, K2tog tbl, K1, K2tog, yon, K2 *, repeat * to * to last stitch, K1.

Row 11: * K4, yon, slip 1, K2tog, psso, yon, K3 *, repeat * to * to last stitch, K1.

Repeat these 12 rows until you have the required length of fabric.

Wide open spaces

DOUBLE ROWS

By looping the yarn around the needle between stitches and then dropping the extra loop on the return row, you can create wide, open rows of stitches in stripes across the fabric. A double-height row of stitches works in any plain fabric, so choose stocking stitch, garter stitch or reverse stocking stitch.

Make sure you work the first row of the pattern on the right side of the fabric.

Pattern repeat: any odd number of stitches

Row 1: * K1, yon twice *, repeat * to * to last stitch, K1.

Row 2: Purl all knitted stitches and let the loops of yarn drop off the left-hand needle as you knit.

Knit the plain fabric pattern you began with (stocking stitch in our example) for the desired number of rows then repeat the pattern.

Double rows

SEAFOAM STITCH

This is a variation on the double row created with extra loops of yarn around the needle. In this version, different numbers of extra loops create a wavy effect on a garter stitch ground.

Pattern repeat: 8 stitches

Row 1: * K3, yon, K1, yon twice, K1, yon twice, K1, yon, K2 *, repeat * to * to end.

Row 2: Knit all knitted stitches and let the loops of yarn drop off the left-hand needle as you knit.

Rows 3 and 4: Knit all stitches (garter stitch).

Row 5: * K1, yon twice, K1, yon, K5, yon, K1, yon twice *, repeat * to * to end.

Row 6: Repeat row 2.

Rows 7 and 8: Knit all stitches (garter stitch).

Repeat these 8 rows until you have the required length of fabric.

Seafoam stitch

Feathers and fronds

FEATHER-AND-FAN STITCH

Put a feather in your cap when you successfully tackle this lacy pattern.

Pattern repeat: 11 stitches

Row 1: Knit all stitches.

Row 2: Purl all stitches.

Row 3: * P2tog, P2tog, (yon, K1) three times, yon, P2tog, P2tog *, repeat * to * to end.

Row 4: Purl all stitches.

Repeat these 4 rows until you have the required length of fabric.

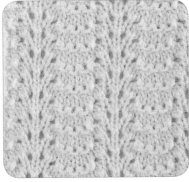

Feather stitch

PALM FRONDS

This stitch pattern will challenge your lace-knitting skills.

Pattern repeat: 12 stitches

Row 1: P4, K2, * K3, P7, K2 *, repeat * to * to last six stitches, K3, P3.

Row 2 and all even rows: Purl all stitches.

Row 3: P2tog, P2, K2, yon, * K1, yon, K2, P2, slip 1, K2tog, psso, P2, K2, yon *, repeat * to * to last 6 stitches, K1, yon, K2, P1, P2tog.

Row 5: P2tog, P1, K2, yon, K1, * K2, yon, K2, P1, slip 1, K2tog, psso, P1, K2, yon, K1 *, repeat * to * to last 6 stitches, K2, yon, K2, P2tog.

Row 7: P2tog, K2, yon, K2, * K3, yon, K2, slip 1, K2tog, psso, K2, yon, K2 *, repeat * to * to last 6 stitches, K3, yon, K1, K2tog.

Repeat these 8 rows until you have the required length of fabric.

Palm fronds

Lacy looks

Lace ribbing

Lacy edgings

The following stitches are designed to be used as borders on the edge of a plain fabric, such as stocking stitch, garter stitch, reverse stitch or moss stitch.

LACE RIBBING

This lacy ribbing is not quite as stretchy as traditional ribbing but it makes a pretty border.

Pattern repeat: 7 stitches + 2 extras
NOTE: in row 3 you can replace the K2tog tbl with SSK, if you prefer.

Row 1: * P2, K5 *, repeat * to * to last 2 stitches, P2.

Row 2: * K2, P5 *, repeat * to * to last 2 stitches, K2.

Row 3: * P2, K2tog, yon, K1, yon, K2tog tbl *, repeat * to * to last 2 stitches, P2.

Row 4: Repeat row 2.

Repeat rows 1 to 4 another three times, or until the desired length of ribbing is reached, and then change to plain fabric.

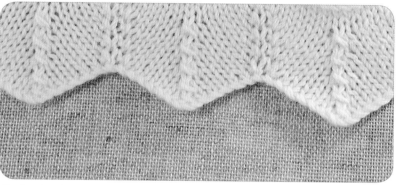

Scallop border

SCALLOP BORDER

This pattern adds a scalloped edge to stocking stitch fabric.

Pattern repeat: 15 stitches + 2 extras

Row 1: K1, * K2 in next stitch, K5, slip 1, K2 tog, psso, K5, K2 in next stitch *, repeat * to * to last stitch, K1.

Row 2: Purl all stitches.

Triple chevron border

Repeat these two rows four more times, then change to stocking stitch and continue until you have the required length of fabric.

TRIPLE CHEVRON BORDER

This lacy variation on the scalloped border above has a triple row of chevron eyelets at the edge.

Pattern repeat: 24 stitches + 2 extras

Row 1: K1, (K2tog, yon) 6 times, * K1, (yon, K2tog tbl) 5 times, yon, slip 1, K2tog, psso, yon, (K2tog, yon) 5 times *, repeat from * to * to last 13 stitches, K1, (yon, K2tog tbl) 6 times.

Row 2 and all even rows: Purl all stitches.

Rows 3 and 5: Repeat row 1.

Row 7: K1, K2tog, * K10, make 1 by knitting into the space between the stitches of the row below, K1, make 1, K10, slip 1, K2tog, psso *, repeat * to * to last 23 stitches, K10, make 1, K1, make 1, K10, K2tog, K1.

Rows 9 and 11: Repeat row 7.

Row 12: Purl all stitches.

Change to the plain fabric of your choice, such as stocking stitch, and continue knitting until you have the required length of fabric.

9

Twisted stitches

* Gansey cables ✳ Gansey braids

✳ All-over patterns ✳ Knots and bobbles

✳ Twisted ribbing ✳ Cable variations

✳ Diagonal cord patterns ✳ Slipped loops

✳ More cable variations ✳ Borders

Cables and curls

Beginning with basic cables, in this chapter you'll learn how to twist your stitches into new and amazing patterns and shapes.

Most stitch patterns consist of a series of instructions that are repeated across the rows of knitting to fill the entire fabric. They may also have a number of rows that are repeated until the fabric is complete. These are called 'pattern repeats'. For more information about working out the number of horizontal and vertical pattern repeats for your project, see pages 118–19.

It's still important to knit a tension square (see page 62) before you start a project. Make sure you knit the tension square using the stitch pattern that you intend to follow, and adjust the needle size or number of stitches accordingly.

TWIST AWAY

The textured stitches in this chapter are slipped, twisted, doubled and looped. Try a simple cable first, or a chunky fisherman's rib, and then tackle some of the more complex designs. Before you know it, you'll be ready to knit your first traditional gansey!

MAKING A CABLE

To make a basic cable, you need a cable needle to hold the stitches for a short time. The cable needle should be a similar size to the needles you're using to knit with, but it doesn't matter if it's a little smaller or larger. The important thing to remember is that you should slip the stitches onto the cable needle without twisting them, and then knit them off the other end of the cable needle. Don't allow the cable needle to turn around so that you knit them in the wrong order! The example shown on the following page is a four-stitch cable.

TIP
Pass the cable needle through a few stitches near the edge of your work when you are not using it, so that you won't need to search for it behind the sofa cushions or in the folds of your clothing the next time you want it.

① A cable is usually knitted in stocking stitch on a background of reverse stocking stitch.

② At the beginning of the cable stitches, slip the required number (2, in this case) of stitches onto a cable needle (abbreviated as CN in stitch instructions) and hold it in front of the work for a twist to the left.

③ Ignore the stitches on the cable needle and knit the next 2 stitches from the left-hand needle.

④ Now bring up the cable needle in front of the left-hand needle and knit the stitches off as though they were next in line on the left-hand needle. This makes the cable twist to the left. Continue knitting as usual.

⑤ For a twist to the right, slip the stitches onto the cable needle and move it to the back of the work. Knit the next 2 stitches from the left-hand needle.

⑥ Bring the cable needle up behind the left-hand needle and knit the stitches off as though they were next in line on the left-hand needle. Continue knitting.

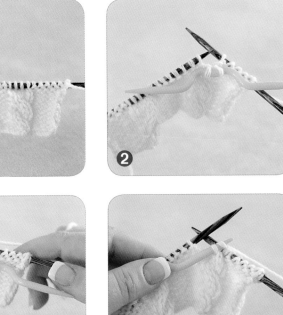

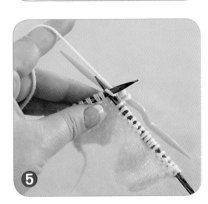

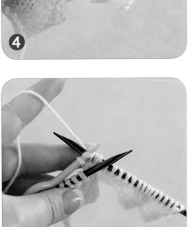

Twisted stitches

Six-by-six cables

Six-by-six cables, reverse twist

Gansey cables

SIX-BY-SIX CABLES

Cables are usually knitted in stocking stitch on a background of reverse stocking stitch. The number of stitches in the cable and the number of rows between twists make the chains look different.

Pattern repeat: 12 stitches (6 stitches for the cable only)

Row 1: P3, K6, P3.

Row 2: K3, P6, K3.

Row 3: Repeat row 1.

Row 4: Repeat row 2.

Row 5: P3, slip next three stitches onto cable needle in front of work, K3, K3 from CN, P3.

Row 6: Repeat row 2.

Repeat these instructions for each cable. You can change the number of stitches between each cable to make the spacing as wide or as narrow as you like. Repeat these 6 rows until you have the required length of fabric.

SIX-BY-SIX CABLES, REVERSE TWIST

The cables in this example are the same as the ones above. By placing the cable needle behind the fabric instead of in front, you can reverse the direction of the twist.

Pattern repeat: 12 stitches (6 stitches for the cable only)

Row 1: P3, K6, P3.

Row 2: K3, P6, K3.

Row 3: Repeat row 1.

Row 4: Repeat row 2.

Row 5: P3, slip 3 to CN behind the work, K3, K3 from CN, P3.

Row 6: Repeat row 2.

Repeat these instructions for each cable. You can change the number of stitches between each cable to make the spacing as wide or as narrow as you like. Repeat these 6 rows until you have the required length of fabric.

SIX-BY-EIGHT CABLES

These cables are longer and slimmer than the previous examples because there are two extra rows between twists. The cables have a twist to the left, but you can make them twist to the right by holding the cable needle behind the work.

Pattern repeat: 12 stitches (6 stitches for the cable only)
Rows 1 and 3: P3, K6, P3.
Row 2 and all even rows: K3, P6, K3.
Row 5: P3, slip 3 to CN in front, K3, K3 from CN, P3.
Row 7: Repeat row 1.
Repeat these instructions for each cable. You can change the number of stitches between each cable to make the spacing as wide or as narrow as you like. Repeat these 8 rows until you have the required length of fabric.

Six-by-eight cables

EIGHT-BY-TEN CABLES

Eight stitches wide and twisting every 10 rows, these chunky cables are a little more challenging.

Pattern repeat: 16 stitches (8 stitches for the cable only)
Rows 1 and 3: P4, K8, P4.
Row 2 and all even rows: K4, P8, K4.
Row 5: P4, slip 4 to CN*, K4, K4 from CN, P4.
* Hold the cable needle in front of the work for the twist to the left, or behind the work for the twist to the right.
Rows 7 and 9: Repeat row 1.
Repeat these instructions for each cable. You can change the number of stitches between each cable to make the spacing as wide or as narrow as you like. Repeat these 10 rows until you have the required length of fabric.

Eight-by-ten cables

GANSEYS

Traditional fisherman's ganseys (also known as guernseys or jerseys after the islands where they were made) were originally knitted by the women of the fishing community for their seagoing menfolk. The fancy stitches that were knitted into the seamless pullovers were often distinctive to the village where they were knitted, and they incorporated the initials or personal symbols of the wearer. (This sometimes made the gruesome task of identifying drowned sailors easier.) The gansey stitches (see page 137 as well as this chapter) were inspired by sailing and the sea: ropes, ladders, waves, nets and sand—as well as family relationships on shore—are represented. These gansey stitches can be easily combined to make a fun and interesting design, such as our scoodie on page 164.

Twisted stitches

Knitting basics

Scoodie

A cross between a hood and a scarf, this type of cable-knitted circular garment has recently featured in designer collections. Now you can make your own.

YOU WILL NEED:
* Six 50 g balls of 8-ply wool
* 5.5 mm (UK 5, US 9) circular needle, at least 40 cm (15¾ in) long
* Cable needle
* Stitch and row markers
* Wool needle and scissors

CONSTRUCTION:

Cast on 220 stitches. You might find it helpful to place a stitch marker every 55 stitches, as the pattern repeats four times around the scarf. Place a different stitch marker at the beginning of the work so that it's easy to see when you've completed a row.

Knit in the round, following this pattern: moss stitch panel; K2; small cable—left twist; K1, P1, K1; large cable; K1, P1, K1; small cable—right twist; K2; repeat from beginning (four repeats in total).

Continue knitting until you have completed the large cable three times (108 rows). Cast off loosely in pattern. Darn in the tails of the yarn.

MOSS STITCH PANEL (5 STITCHES)
ODD ROWS: P1, K1, P1, K1, P1; EVEN ROWS: K1, P1, K1, P1, K1.

SMALL CABLE—LEFT TWIST (8 STITCHES)
Row 1: P2, K4, P2.
ROW 2 AND ALL EVEN ROWS: P2, K4, P2.
ROW 3: P2, slip next 2 sts to CN in front, K2, K2 from CN, P2.
Repeat these 4 rows.

SMALL CABLE—RIGHT TWIST (8 STITCHES)
Row 1: P2, K4, P2.
ROW 2 AND ALL EVEN ROWS: P2, K4, P2.
Row 3: P2, slip next 2 sts to CN behind, K2, K2 from CN, P2.
Repeat these 4 rows.

LARGE CABLE (24 STITCHES)
Row 1: P7, K4, P2, K4, P7.
Row 2: P7, K4, P2, K4, P7.
Row 3. P7, slip next 4 sts to CN in front, P1, K4 from CN, slip next st to CN behind, K4, P1 from CN, P7.
Row 4: P8, K8, P8.
Row 5: P8, slip next 4 sts to CN in front, K4, K4 from CN, P8.
Row 6: P8, K8, P8.
Row 7: P7, slip next st to CN behind, K4, P1 from CN, slip next 4 sts to CN in front, P1, K4 from CN, P7.
(PATTERN CONTINUED OVER PAGE)

Twisted stitches

Row 8: P7, K4, P2, K4, P7.

Row 9: P6, slip next st to CN behind, K4, P1 from CN, P2, slip next 4 sts to CN in front, P1, K4 from CN, P6.

Row 10: P6, K4, P4, K4, P6.

Row 11: P5, slip next st to CN behind, K4, P1 from CN, P4, slip next 4 sts to CN in front, P1, K4 from CN, P5.

Row 12: P5, K4, P6, K4, P5.

Row 13: P4, slip next st to CN behind, K4, P1 from CN, P6, slip next 4 sts to CN in front, P1, K4 from CN, P4.

Row 14: P4, K4, P8, K4, P4.

Row 15: P3, slip next st to CN behind, K4, P1 from CN, P8, slip next 4 sts to CN in front, P1, K4 from CN, P3.

Row 16: P3, K4, P10, K4, P3.

Row 17: P2, slip next st to CN behind, K4, P1 from CN, P10, slip next 4 sts to CN in front, P1, K4 from CN, P2.

Row 18: P2, K4, P12, K4, P2.

Rows 19 and 20: Repeat row 18.

Row 21: P2, slip next 4 sts to CN in front, P1, K4 from CN, P10, slip next st to CN behind, K4, P1 from CN, P2.

Row 22: P3, K4, P10, K4, P3.

Row 23: P3, slip next 4 sts to CN in front, P1, K4 from CN, P8, slip next st to CN behind, K4, P1 from CN, P3.

Row 24: P4, K4, P8, K4, P4.

Row 25: P4, slip next 4 sts to CN in front, P1, K4 from CN, P6, slip next st to CN behind, K4,

P1 from CN, P4.

Row 26: P5, K4, P6, K4, P5.

Row 27: P5, slip next 4 sts to CN in front, P1, K4 from CN, P4, slip next st to CN behind, K4, P1 from CN, P5.

Row 28: P6, K4, P4, K4, P6.

Row 29: P6, slip next 4 sts to CN in front, P1, K4 from CN, P2, slip next st to CN behind, K4, P1 from CN, P6.

Row 30: P7, K4, P2, K4, P7.

Row 31: P7, slip next 4 sts to CN in front, P1, K4 from CN, slip next st to CN behind, K4, P1 from CN, P7.

Row 32: P8, K8, P8.

Row 33: P8, slip next 4 sts to CN behind, K4, K4 from CN, P8.

Row 34: P8, K8, P8.

Row 35: P7, slip next st to CN behind, K4, P1 from CN, slip next 4 sts to CN in front, P1, K4 from CN, P7.

Row 36: P7, K4, P2, K4, P7.

Repeat these 36 rows.

Gansey braids

ENSIGN'S BRAID

An ensign is a lowly officer in the navy, and so he has only four strands in the braid on his gansey.

Pattern repeat: 20 stitches (braid only)

Row 1: K3, P4, slip 3 to CN at back, K3, K3 from CN, P4, K3.

Row 2 and following even rows to Row 22: Knit all stitches as they are presented on the needle (for example, in row 2: P3, K4, P6, K4, P3).

Row 3: * Slip 3 to CN in front, P1, K3 from CN, P2, slip 1 to CN at back, K3, P1 from CN *, repeat * to *.

Row 5: * P1, slip 3 to CN in front, P1, K3 from CN, slip 1 to CN at back, K3, P1 from CN, P1 *, repeat * to *.

Row 7: P2, slip 3 to CN in front, K3, K3 from CN, P4, slip 3 to CN at back, K3, K3 from CN, P2.

Row 9: * P1, slip 1 to CN at back, K3, P1 from CN, slip 3 to CN at front, P1, K3 from CN, P1 *, repeat * to *.

Row 11: * Slip 1 to CN at back, K3, P1 from CN, P2, slip 3 to CN at front, P1, K3 from CN *, repeat * to *.

Row 13: K3, P4, slip 3 to CN at front, K3, K3 from CN, P4, K3.

Row 15: Repeat row 3.

Row 17: Repeat row 5.

Row 19: P2, slip 3 to CN at back, K3, K3 from CN, P4, slip 3 to CN at front, K3, K3 from CN, P2.

Row 21: Repeat row 9.

Row 23: Repeat row 11.

Row 24: * P3, K4, P3 *, repeat * to *.

Repeat these 24 rows until you have a braid of the required length.

Ensign's braid

CELTIC PRINCESS BRAID

The garments of a Celtic princess are decorated with five interwoven strands of braid.

Pattern repeat: 14 stitches (braid only)

Row 1: (K2, P1) four times, K2.

Row 2 and all even rows: (P2, K1) four times, P2.

Row 3: K2, * P1, slip 3 to CN in front, K2, slip purl stitch from CN to left-hand needle and P1, K2 from CN *, repeat * to *.

Row 5: Repeat row 1.

(Pattern continued over page)

Celtic princess braid

Twisted stitches

Row 7: * Slip 3 to CN at back, K2, slip purl stitch from CN to left-hand needle and P1, K2 from CN, P1 *, repeat * to *.

Repeat these 8 rows until you have the required length of braid.

SAXON BRAID

This six-strand braid is a decoration worthy of a Saxon warrior.

Pattern repeat: 22 stitches (braid only)

Cable A: slip 2 to CN in front, K2, K2 from CN.

Cable B: slip 1 to CN at back, K2, P1 from CN.

Cable C: slip 2 to CN in front, P1, K2 from CN.

Cable D: slip 2 to CN at back, K2, K2 from CN.

Row 1: P3, (Cable A), P2, (Cable A), P2, (Cable A), P3.

Row 2 and all even rows: Work all stitches as they are presented on the left-hand needle.

Row 3: P2, (Cable B), (Cable C), repeat Cable B and Cable C twice more, P2.

Row 5: P2, K2, P2, (Cable D), P2, (Cable D), P2, K2, P2.

Row 7: P1, (Cable B), P1, (Cable B), (Cable C), (Cable B), (Cable C), P1, (Cable C), P1.

Row 9: P1, K2, P2, K2, P2, (Cable A), P2, K2, P2, K2, P1.

Row 11: P1, (Cable C), P1, (Cable C), (Cable B), (Cable C), (Cable B), P1, (Cable B), P1.

Row 13: P2, K2, P2, (Cable D), P2, (Cable D), P2, K2, P2.

Row 15: P2, (Cable C), (Cable B), (Cable C), (Cable B), (Cable C), (Cable B), P2.

Repeat these 16 rows until you have the required length of braid.

Saxon braid

All-over patterns

HONEYCOMB

In this three-dimensional fabric, the cells of the honeycomb help trap air and make a jumper look and feel warmer.

Pattern repeat: 8 stitches

Row 1: Knit all stitches.

Row 2 and all even rows: Purl all stitches.

Row 3: * Slip 2 to CN at back, K2, K2 from CN, slip 2 to CN in front, K2, K2 from CN *, repeat * to * to end.

Row 5: Knit all stitches.

Honeycomb

Row 7: * Slip 2 to CN in front, K2, K2 from CN, slip 2 to CN at back, K2, K2 from CN *, repeat * to * to end.

Repeat these 8 rows until you have the required length of fabric.

REVERSE HONEYCOMB

In this fabric the honeycomb cells are surrounded by walls of reverse stocking stitch. Rather than using a cable needle, the links are created by slipping stitches over several rows.

Pattern repeat: 8 stitches

Row 1: Purl all stitches (this is the right side of the work).

Row 2: Knit all stitches.

Row 3: * K3, slip 2, K3 *, repeat * to * to end.

Row 4: * P3, slip 2 with yarn in front, P3 *, repeat * to * to end.

Rows 5 to 8: Repeat rows 3 and 4 twice more.

Row 9: Purl all stitches.

Row 10: Knit all stitches.

Row 11: * Slip 1, K6, slip 1 *, repeat * to * to end.

Row 12: * Slip 1, P6, slip 1 *, repeat * to * to end.

Rows 13 to 16: Repeat rows 11 and 12 twice more.

Repeat these 16 rows until you have the required length of fabric.

LATTICE

In this pattern, straight lines criss-cross over the fabric.

Pattern repeat: 12 stitches

The pattern uses these cabling abbreviations:

Right cable (RC): slip 2 to CN at back, K2, P2 from CN.

Left cable (LC): slip 2 to CN in front, P2, K2 from CN.

Row 1: * P2, RC, LC, P2 *, repeat * to * to end.

Row 2 and all even rows: Work all stitches as they are presented on the left-hand needle.

Row 3: * RC, P4, LC *, repeat * to * to end.

Row 5: K2, * P8, slip 2 to CN at back, K2, K2 from CN *, repeat * to * to last 10 stitches, P8, K2.

Row 7: * LC, P4, RC *, repeat * to * to end.

Row 9: * P2, LC, RC, P2 *, repeat * to * to end.

Row 11: * P4, slip 2 to CN in front, K2, K2 from CN, P4 *, repeat * to * to end.

Repeat these 12 rows until you have the required length of fabric.

Reverse honeycomb

Lattice

Twisted stitches

Basketweave

BASKETWEAVE

A cable needle is used to create this dense knitted fabric with a tightly woven appearance.

Pattern repeat: 4 stitches

Row 1: K2, * slip 2 to CN at back, K2, K2 from CN *, repeat * to * to last 2 stitches, K2.

Row 2: Purl all stitches.

Row 3: * Slip 2 to CN in front, K2, K2 from CN *, repeat * to * to end.

Row 4: Purl all stitches.

Repeat these 4 rows until you have the required length of fabric.

Leaves

LEAVES

A two-stitch cable pattern packed closely together gives the appearance of leaves.

Pattern repeat: 4 stitches

Row 1: * K2, P2 *, repeat * to * to end.

Rows 2 to 4: Repeat row 1 three more times (four rows in total).

Row 5: * Slip 1 to CN in front, K1, K1 from CN, P2 *, repeat * to * to end.

Row 6: * P2, K2 *, repeat * to * to end.

Rows 7 to 10: Repeat row 6 four more times.

Row 11: * P2, slip 1 to CN in front, K1, K1 from CN *, repeat * to * to end.

Row 12: * K2, P2 *, repeat * to * to end.

Repeat these 12 rows until you have the required length of fabric.

Star stitch

STAR STITCH

A galaxy of sparkling stars are sprinkled over this fabric.

Pattern repeat: 4 stitches + 1 extra

Row 1: Knit all stitches.

Row 2: K1, * (P3tog but don't drop them off the left-hand needle, yon, purl same 3 stitches tog again and drop off the needle), K1 *, repeat * to * to end.

Row 3: Knit all stitches.

Row 4: K1, P1, K1, * (P3tog but don't drop them off the needle, yon, purl same 3 stitches tog again and drop off the needle), K1 *, repeat * to * to last two stitches, P1, K1.

Repeat these 4 rows until you have the required length of fabric.

TULIP STITCH

A field of tulips is represented by these pairs of slipped stitches on a background of reverse stocking stitch.

Pattern repeat: 4 stitches

Make a petal: insert the right-hand needle into the next wale, 3 rows below next stitch and draw a loop of yarn through the fabric. Don't drop any stitches off the left-hand needle but continue knitting as instructed.

Row 1: Purl all stitches.

Row 2: Knit all stitches.

Rows 3 and 4: Repeat rows 1 and 2.

Row 5: * P2, take yarn to back of work, make a petal, K1, make a petal, P1 *, repeat * to * to end.

Row 6: * K1, P3, K2 *, repeat * to * to end. (Note that you purl the two petals and the stitch between them. There are two extra stitches in every repeat in this row.)

Row 7: * P1, P2tog, P1, slip 1, P1, psso *, repeat * to * to end.

Row 8: Knit all stitches.

Repeat these 8 rows until you have the required length of fabric.

Tulip stitch

BEETLE STITCH

These six-legged crawlies look like little bow ties creeping all over the stocking stitch fabric.

Pattern repeat: 10 stitches + 2 extras (Note: each pattern repeat is two beetles and so you can work this pattern with multiples of five stitches by leaving out half a repeat.)

Row 1: K1, * slip 5 with yarn in front of work, K5 *, repeat * to * to last stitch, K1.

Row 2 and all even rows: Purl all stitches.

Row 3: Repeat row 1.

Row 5: K1, * slip 2 wyif, (take yarn to back of work, insert the right-hand needle under the strands from the previous rows and K1 in next stitch on left-hand needle, bringing the loop out over the strands), slip 2 wyif, K5 *, repeat * to * to last stitch, K1.

Row 7: K1, * K5, slip 5 wyif *, repeat * to * to last stitch, K1.

Row 9: Repeat row 7.

Row 11: K1, * K5, slip 2 wyif, (take yarn to back of work, insert the right-hand needle under the strands from the previous rows and K1 in next stitch on left-hand needle, bringing the loop out over the strands), slip 2 wyif *, repeat * to * to last stitch, K1.

Repeat these 12 rows until you have the required length of fabric.

Beetle stitch

Twisted stitches

Knot stitch

Knots and bobbles

KNOT STITCH

Knitting the same stitch over and over again makes a small knot on the surface of the fabric.

Pattern repeat: 6 stitches

Make a knot (MK): knit into the next stitch on the left-hand needle, but don't drop the loop off the needle. Slip the new stitch onto the left-hand needle, and then knit it off. Knit into the same stitch as before and repeat the process. Repeat again, so that you have three new stitches on the right-hand needle. Drop the original stitch off the left-hand needle and then pass the loops of the first two new stitches over the third one.

Row 1: Knit all stitches.

Row 2 and all even rows: Purl all stitches.

Row 3: * K5, MK *, repeat * to * to end.

Row 5: Knit all stitches.

Row 7: * K2, MK, K3 *, repeat * to * to end.

Repeat these 8 rows until you have the required length of fabric.

Bobble stitch

BOBBLE STITCH

This is a highly textured fabric. The purl rows are the right side.

Pattern repeat: 4 stitches

Row 1: Purl all stitches.

Row 2: * (In first stitch: K1, P1, K1), P3tog *, repeat * to * to end.

Row 3: Purl all stitches.

Row 4: * P3tog, (in next stitch: K1, P1, K1) *, repeat * to * to end.

Repeat these 4 rows until you have the required length of fabric.

Bobble grapes

BOBBLE GRAPES

This pattern produces large bobbles that appear to hang from a single stitch like bunches of grapes.

Pattern repeat: 11 stitches (bunch of grapes only)

Make a bobble (MB): K5 in next stitch, turn the work, P5, turn the work, K5, turn the work, P5, turn the work, K5 tog.

Left twist (LT): Slip 1 to CN in front, P1, K1 from CN.

Right twist (RT): Slip 1 to CN at back, K1, P1 from CN.

Row 1: Purl all stitches (this is the right side of the fabric).

Row 2: Knit all stitches.

Row 3: P5, MB, P5.

Row 4: K5, P1, K5.

Row 5: P2, MB, P2, K1, P2, MB, P2.

Row 6: Repeat row 4.

Row 7: MB, P4, K1, P4, MB.

Row 8: P1, K2, P1, K1, P1, K1, P1, K2, P1.

Row 9: LT, P1, LT, K1, RT, P1, RT.

Row 10: K1, LT, K1, P3, K1, RT, K1.

Row 11: P2, LT, make a stitch by purling into the space between stitches in the row below, slip 1, K2tog, psso, make a stitch as before, RT, P2.

Row 12: K3, LT, P1, RT, K3.

Row 13: P4, make a stitch, slip 1, K2tog, psso, make a stitch, P4.

Row 14: K5, P1, K5.

Repeat these 14 rows until you have the required length of fabric.

Twisted ribbing

FISHERMAN'S RIB

This chunky ribbing stitch is probably called fisherman's rib because it looks like an old-fashioned fishing basket, but it also makes a cosy jumper to keep a fisherman warm on a chilly morning.

Pattern repeat: any even number of stitches

Row 1: Purl all stitches (this is the foundation row).

Row 2: K1, * P1, K1 into row below *, repeat * to * to last stitch, K1.

Repeat row 2 (every row the same) until you have the required length of fabric.

Fisherman's rib

KNITTING INTO ROW BELOW
In this pattern, instead of knitting into the working loop on the left-hand needle, you knit into the loop directly below it in the same wale. This catches both loops so that you won't drop any stitches.

Quilted purse

This gorgeous little coin or makeup purse has a satin lining and a button to keep it closed.

YOU WILL NEED

* 50 g ball of 8-ply wool yarn
* 4 mm (UK 8, US 6) knitting needles
* 10 x 22 cm (4 x 8⅝ in) satin fabric
* Sewing needle and matching thread
* Wool needle and scissors
* 40 mm diameter button

CONSTRUCTION:

CATCH STITCH: insert right-hand needle under the looped yarn in the earlier row and knit the next stitch on the left-hand needle, allowing the looped yarn to drop behind the stitch.

Cast on 27 stitches.
Row 1: K2, * slip 5 wyif, K1 *, repeat * to * to last stitch, K1.
Row 2 AND ALL EVEN ROWS: Purl all stitches.
Row 3: K4, * (catch stitch), K5 *, repeat to last 5 stitches, (catch stitch), K4.
Row 5: K1, slip 3 wyif, * K1, slip 5 wyif *, repeat * to * to last 5 stitches, K1, slip 3 wyif, K1.
Row 7: K1, * (catch stitch), K5 *, repeat * to * to last 2 stitches, (catch stitch), K1.
Repeat these 8 rows nine more times (ten vertical repeats).

Begin ribbing.
Row 1: * K1, P1 *, repeat * to * to last stitch, K1.
Row 2: K1, * K1, P1 *, repeat * to * to last 2 stitches, K2.
Rows 3 AND 5: Repeat row 1.
Rows 4 AND 6: Repeat row 2.
Row 7: (K1, P1) five times, cast off next 7 stitches in rib, (P1, K1) five times.

Row 8: K1, (K1, P1) four times, K1. Turn work and cast on 7 stitches using cable method (see page 69), then turn work again and continue in rib on the remaining 10 stitches.
Rows 9 AND 11: Repeat row 1.
Rows 10 AND 12: Repeat row 2.
Cast off in rib.

LINING AND SEWING UP:

Lay the knitted fabric right side down on a flat surface. Press a small hem (about 5 mm or a quarter inch) around all edges of the satin and lay it right side up on top of the knitted fabric. Note that the lining only extends to the beginning of the ribbing. Pin the lining to the knitted fabric around all the edges, just inside the edge of the knitted fabric.

Use matching sewing thread to slip stitch the satin lining to the wrong side of the knitted fabric, just inside the edge stitches.

When the lining is attached, fold the cast-on edge up in front to form the purse, so that four pattern repeats are visible on the front. Use the same yarn as the knitted fabric and a wool needle to stitch up both sides of the purse with ladder stitch (see page 105).

Fold the top flap forward to check the position of the button. Stitch the button in place on the front of the purse through both the knitted fabric and the lining using sewing thread, and then use the yarn and wool needle to place one decorative stitch over the sewing thread to hide it.

Now button up and go!

Brioche stitch

BRIOCHE STITCH

This double-sided ribbing stitch looks great worked in just one colour; when you're feeling confident about knitting it, turn to page 190 to see how to knit it in two colours at once.

Pattern repeat: any even number of stitches
Row 1: K1, * yon, slip 1 purlwise with yarn at the back of the work, K1 *, repeat * to * to last stitch, K1 (this is the foundation row).
Row 2: K1, * yon, slip 1 purlwise wyib, K2tog *, repeat * to * to last stitch, K1. (Note: you are knitting the slipped stitch and the yarn over the needle together.)
Repeat row 2 (every row the same) until you have the required length of fabric.

Rickrack ribbing

RICKRACK RIBBING

Pattern repeat: 5 stitches + 2 extras
Ktwist: skip 1 stitch, K1 into back of next stitch but leave both stitches on left-hand needle, K1 in the skipped stitch, slip both stitches off left-hand needle.
Ptwist: with yarn in front of work, skip the next stitch and P1 in next stitch but leave both stitches on left-hand needle, P1 in the skipped stitch, slip both stitches off left-hand needle.
Row 1: K1, * P1, (Ktwist), P1, K1 *, repeat * to * to last stitch, K1.
Row 2: K1, * P1, K1, (Ptwist), K1 *, repeat * to * to last stitch, K1.
Repeat these 2 rows until you have the required length of fabric.

Cable variations

TWISTED CABLE

This stitch uses a slipped stitch to give a cabled appearance to a simple column of stocking stitch worked on a background of reverse stitch.

Pattern repeat: 3 stitches (cable only). In the example, the cable is worked with four stitches of reverse stocking stitch between each repeat.

Row 1: K3.

Row 2: P3.

Row 3: Slip 1 knitwise, K2, yon, pass the slipped stitch over all three loops.

Row 4: P3.

Repeat these 4 rows until you have the required length of fabric.

Twisted cable

TWISTED CORD

This pattern is really just a six-by-four cable: because it's wide and short, it looks like a twisted cord.

Pattern repeat: 6 stitches (cable only). In the example, the cable is worked with three stitches of reverse stocking stitch between each repeat.

Row 1: K6.

Row 2: P6.

Row 3: Slip 3 to CN in front of work, K3, K3 from CN.

Row 4: Repeat row 2.

Repeat these 4 rows until you have the required length of fabric.

Twisted cord

INVISIBLE CABLE

By working the cable twist on a stocking stitch background, you leave only a hint of ghostly cables behind.

Pattern repeat: 14 stitches (Note: you can work in multiples of seven stitches by leaving out half a repeat.)

Row 1: Knit all stitches.

Row 2 and all even rows: Purl all stitches.

Row 3: Repeat row 1.

Row 5: * K1, slip 3 to CN in front, K3, K3 from CN, K7 *, repeat * to * to end.

Rows 7 and 9: Repeat row 1.

Row 11: * K8, slip 3 to CN in front, K3, K3 from CN *, repeat * to * to end.

Repeat these 12 rows until you have the required length of fabric.

Invisible cable

Twisted stitches

Diagonal cords

Diagonal cord patterns

DIAGONAL CORDS

Pattern repeat: 6 stitches + 2 extras

To work the cords slanting to the left:

Row 1: * Slip 2 to CN in front, P1, K2 from CN, P3 *, repeat * to * to last 2 stitches, K2.

Row 2 and all even rows: Work all stitches as they are presented on the left-hand needle.

Row 3: P1, * slip 2 to CN in front, P1, K2 from CN, P3 *, repeat * to * to last stitch, K1.

Row 5: P2, * slip 2 to CN in front, P1, K2 from CN, P3 *, repeat * to * to end.

Row 7: P3, * slip 2 to CN in front, P1, K2 from CN, P3 *, repeat * to * to last 5 stitches, slip 2 to CN in front, P1, K2 from CN, P2.

Row 9: K1, P3, * slip 2 to CN in front, P1, K2 from CN, P3 *, repeat * to * to last 4 stitches, slip 2 to CN in front, P1, K2 from CN, P1.

Row 11: K2, P3, * slip 2 to CN in front, P1, K2 from CN, P3 *, repeat * to * to last 3 stitches, slip 2 from CN in front, P1, K2 from CN.

Repeat these 12 rows until you have the required length of fabric.

To work the cords slanting to the right:

Row 1: K2, * P3, slip 1 to CN at back, K2, P1 from CN *, repeat * to * to end.

Row 2 and all even rows: Work all stitches as they are presented on the left-hand needle.

Row 3: K1, P1, * P2, slip 1 to CN at back, K2, P1 from CN, P1 *, repeat * to * to end.

Row 5: P2, * P1, slip 1 to CN at back, K2, P1 from CN, P2 *, repeat * to * to end.

Row 7: P2, * slip 1 to CN at back, K2, P1 from CN, P3 *, repeat * to * to end.

Row 9: P1, * slip 1 to CN at back, K2, P1 from CN, P3 *, repeat * to * to last stitch, K1.

Row 11: * Slip 1 to CN at back, K2, P1 from CN, P3 *, repeat * to * to last 2 stitches, K2.

Repeat these 12 rows until you have the required length of fabric.

ZIGZAG CORDS

Pattern repeat: 6 stitches

Right cable (RC): slip 1 to CN at back, K2, P1 from CN

Left cable (LC): slip 2 to CN in front, P1, K2 from CN

Row 1: * P3, RC *, repeat * to * to end.

Row 2: * K1, P2, K3 *, repeat * to * to end.

Row 3: * P2, RC, P1 *, repeat * to * to end.

Row 4: * K2, P2, K2 *, repeat * to * to end.

Row 5: * P1, RC, P2 *, repeat * to * to end.

Row 6: * K3, P2, K1 *, repeat * to * to end.

Row 7: * RC, P3 *, repeat * to * to end.

Row 8: * K4, P2 *, repeat * to * to end.

Row 9: * LC, P3 *, repeat * to * to end.

Row 10: Repeat row 6.

Row 11: * P1, LC, P2 *, repeat * to * to end.

Row 12: Repeat row 4.

Row 13: * P2, LC, P1 *, repeat * to * to end.

Row 14: Repeat row 2.

Row 15: * P3, LC *, repeat * to * to end.

Row 16: * P2, K4 *, repeat * to * to end.

Repeat these 16 rows until you have the required length of fabric.

Zigzag cords

CORDED DIAMONDS

Pattern repeat: 13 stitches (diamonds only: work reverse stocking stitch panel either side)

Right cable (RC): slip 1 to CN at back, K2, P1 from CN

Left cable (LC): slip 2 to CN in front, P1, K2 from CN

Row 1: LC, P1, K1, P1, K1, P1, K1, P1, RC.

Row 2 and all even rows: Work all stitches as they are presented on the left-hand needle (purl or knit as per the stitch below).

Row 3: P1, LC, P1, K1, P1, K1, P1, RC, P1.

Row 5: P2, LC, P1, K1, P1, RC, P2.

Row 7: P3, LC, P1, RC, P3.

Row 9: P4, slip 3 to CN at back, K2, slip the third stitch from the CN back to left-hand needle and knit it off behind the two stitches on the CN, K2 from CN, P4.

Row 11: P3, RC, P1, LC, P3.

Row 13: P2, RC, P1, K1, P1, LC, P2.

Row 15: P1, RC, P1, K1, P1, K1, P1, LC, P1.

Row 17: RC, P1, K1, P1, K1, P1, K1, P1, LC.

Row 19: K2, P1, K1, P1, K1, P1, K1, P1, K1, P1, K2.

Repeat these 20 rows until you have the required length of fabric.

Corded diamonds

Ears of wheat

Winged seeds

Slipped loops

EARS OF WHEAT

This stitch reminds me of grains of wheat growing on their stalks, ready for harvest.

Pattern repeat: 7 stitches + 1

Start with two rows of stocking stitch and then begin the pattern.

Row 1: * K3, slip 2, K2 *, repeat * to * to last stitch, K1.

Row 2: * P2, slip 2 with yarn in front, P3 *, repeat * to * to last stitch, K1.

Row 3: Repeat row 1.

Row 4: Repeat row 2.

Row 5: * K1, slip 2 to CN at back, K1 (slipped stitch), K2 from CN, slip 1 (slipped stitch) to CN in front, K2, K1 from CN *, repeat * to * to last stitch, K1.

Repeat these 6 rows until you have the required length of fabric.

WINGED SEEDS

Like seeds from a pinecone fluttering to the ground, these slipped loops make a delicate pattern on the knitted fabric.

Pattern repeat: 4 stitches + 2 extras

Row 1: Knit all stitches.

Row 2: Purl all stitches.

Row 3: K2, * slip 1, K3 *, repeat * to * to end.

Row 4: * P3, slip 1 *, repeat * to * to last 2 stitches, P2.

Row 5: K2, * slip 1 (slipped stitch) to CN in front, K2, K1 from CN, K1 *, repeat * to * to end.

Row 6: Purl all stitches.

Row 7: Knit all stitches.

Row 8: Purl all stitches.

Row 9: Repeat row 3.

Row 10: Repeat row 4.

Row 11: * Slip 2 to CN at back, K1 (slipped stitch), K2 from CN, K1 *, repeat * to * to last 2 stitches, K2.

Row 12: Purl all stitches.

Repeat these 12 rows until you have the required length of fabric.

More cable variations

LITTLE TWISTS

Pairs of small cables twisting in opposite directions.

Pattern repeat: 10 stitches

Row 1: * P3, slip 1, K2, P1, K2, slip 1 *, repeat * to * to end.

Row 2: * Slip 1, P2, K1, P2, slip 1, K3 *, repeat * to * to end.

Row 3: * P3, slip 1 to CN in front, K2, K1 from CN, P1, slip 2 to CN at back, K1, K2 from CN *, repeat * to * to end.

Row 4: * P3, K1, P3, K3 *, repeat * to * to end.

Repeat these 4 rows until you have the required length of fabric.

Little twists

WISHBONE CABLES

These cables are also known as horseshoe cables.

Pattern repeat: 12 stitches (cable only). Work the cable as many times as you like on a background of reverse stocking stitch.

Row 1: K12.

Row 2 and all even rows: P12.

Row 3: Slip 3 to CN at back, K3, K3 from CN, slip 3 to CN in front, K3, K3 from CN.

Row 5: K12.

Repeat these 6 rows until you have the required length of fabric.

Wishbone cables

KISSES AND HUGS

Alternating Os and Xs mean this cable is sometimes called OXO cable.

Pattern repeat: 8 stitches (cable only). Work the cable on a background of reverse stocking stitch.

Right cable (RC): slip 2 to CN at back, K2, K2 from CN

Left cable (LC): slip 2 to CN in front, K2, K2 from CN

Row 1: K8.

Row 2 and all even rows: P8.

Row 3: RC, LC.

Row 5: K8.

Row 7: Repeat row 3: RC, LC.

Row 9: K8.

Row 11: LC, RC.

Row 13: K8.

Row 15: LC, RC.

Repeat these 16 rows until you have the required length of fabric.

Kisses and hugs

Cable border

Borders

CABLE BORDER

This edging is worked lengthwise and has a 2-stitch seam allowance on one side so you can sew it onto a horizontal edge; if you're knitting it vertically as part of a project, leave these stitches out.

Cast on 8 stitches.

Row 1: Knit all stitches.

Row 2 and all even rows: K2, purl to end.

Row 3: Knit all stitches.

Row 5: Slip 3 to CN in front, K3, K3 from CN, K2.

Row 7: Knit all stitches.

Repeat these 8 rows until you have the required length of fabric.

Cable feather edging

CABLE FEATHER EDGING

This pretty lace edging adds a feathery finish to your knitting.

Pattern repeat: 18 stitches (You need to knit at least two repeats to get the effect.)

Row 1: Purl all stitches (this is the wrong side of the fabric).

Row 2: * K2tog three times, (yon, K1) six times, K2tog three times *, repeat * to * to end.

Row 3: K15, * P6, K12 *, repeat * to * to last 3 stitches, K3.

Row 4: K15, * slip 3 to CN at back, K3, K3 from CN, K12 *, repeat * to * to last 3 stitches, K3.

Repeat these 4 rows twice more. Purl 1 row and then cast off or begin knitting your plain fabric.

Loop stitch

LOOP STITCH

Loopy fabric makes funky cuffs and collars, or you can knit it all over for a faux-fur appearance. Every stitch in a right-side row is a loop stitch, and so you can work on any number of stitches. Start and finish the row with a plain knit stitch to make a seam allowance or selvedge. The wrong-side rows are all knit stitches.

1. Begin with a foundation row by knitting all stitches. Keep the tension loose as you'll need a bit of give to make the loop stitches.

2. Place the point of the right-hand needle into the stitch as though to knit, and bring the yarn up between the two needles.

3. Wrap the yarn around your left thumb and take it back between the two needles.

4. Without dropping the stitch off either needle, bring the point of the right-hand needle around the stitch and insert it again as though to knit.

5. Knit the stitch and drop it off the left-hand needle.

6. There are two loops of yarn on the right-hand needle. Pass the first loop over the second one. You have made your first loop stitch.

The example shows 7 rows of loop stitch (14 rows of knitting) and then a change to stocking stitch fabric.

Twisted stitches

10

Changing colours

* Joining coloured yarn

* Stripes * Blocks of colour * Geometrics

* Fair Isle knitting * Intarsia

Classic and modern

Knitting with multiple colours in one fabric is the next step in your knitting adventure.

Some coloured patterns, such as the traditional Fair Isle, consist of a series of instructions that are repeated across the rows of knitting to fill the entire fabric. They may also have a certain number of rows that are repeated until the fabric is complete. These are called 'pattern repeats'. For more information about working out the number of horizontal and vertical pattern repeats for your project, see pages 118–19. If the colours form a motif or pictorial design—this is often called intarsia—there will probably be only one block of stitches, which is usually not repeated.

It's still important to knit a tension square (see page 62) before you start a project. Make sure you knit the tension square using the stitch pattern that you intend to follow, and adjust the needle size or number of stitches accordingly. Multicolour knitting is often—but not always—worked in stocking stitch, which gives a flat finish that doesn't draw attention away from the coloured pattern.

TIP
When working with multiple colours, it's a good idea to stop knitting every few rows and untangle the yarns. At the same time, you could darn in any tails. This will save you the tedium of darning in multiple yarn tails at the end of the project, when you're impatient to sew the item up and wear it! See pages 102–103 for step-by-step instructions on how to darn the tails of yarn in.

Joining coloured yarn

There are two ways of joining a new yarn colour: in stripes and horizontal patterns, such as Fair Isle, the yarn is joined at the side edge of the fabric. See page 87 for step-by-step instructions on how to join yarn.

JOINING YARN IN THE MIDDLE OF FABRIC

In patterns that have multiple blocks of colour in the middle of the fabric, you will find it easier to work with the different yarns if you wind working amounts onto small, lightweight bobbins. You can purchase plastic yarn bobbins at your knitting supplies store, or make your own from heavy cardboard. Cut a piece of cardboard approximately 3 x 5 cm (1¼ x 2 in) and cut a slit about a centimetre (³⁄₈ in) long in one end to hold the yarn. You can estimate the amount of yarn to wind on for each area of colour by using the formula of four times the width of the row.

① When you get to the beginning of the area of coloured knitting, join the yarn as you would at the side by holding the new yarn alongside the old yarn and knitting the next stitch in colour.

② Continue in the new colour for the number of stitches required.

③ You can tie a loose knot in the yarn to help hold the tension while you knit, but you will need to untie the knot when you come to darn in the tails after you've finished.

④ In subsequent rows, twist the two yarns around each other once at the back of the work when you reach the changeover point.

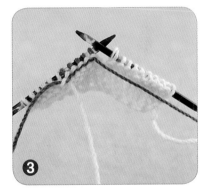

Changing colours

CARRYING YARN ACROSS

In intarsia designs and motifs, each area of colour should have its own bobbin of yarn, even if two or more areas use the same colour. In Fair Isle designs, the colours you are not using can be carried across the back of the work. Getting the tension of the carried yarns right is important: too tight, and the design will pucker and the fabric will be too small; too loose, and not only will the pattern not hold together nicely, but the loops of yarn will catch on fingers and toes and on buttons and belts of the garments worn underneath.

① Join the colours you need for each row at the side edge of the fabric.

② Allow the yarn you are not using to drop at the back of the work while you knit the first colour stitches. Alternatively, hold both yarns loosely in your hand, but only knit with the active yarn.

③ When it's time to change colour, drop the first yarn at the back of the work and pick up the second colour. Allow the yarn to sit loosely behind the work you have just knitted.

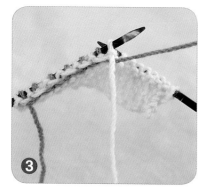

④ Knit the stitches of the second colour and then pick up the first colour again. Try to keep the lighter colour on top of the darker colour, so that the carried threads don't twist together.

Ideally, yarn should not be carried across more than 5 or 6 stitches at a time. If there are more stitches than this, twist the carried yarn with the working yarn at the back of the work, every few stitches.

COLOUR YOUR WORLD

Whether you're starting with simple stripes, moving on to blocks of colour or tackling complex Fair Isle designs, multicolour knitting not only adds pizzazz to your fabric but gains you kudos for your knitting skills.

Stripes

NARROW HORIZONTAL STRIPES

Narrow horizontal stripes, here in two colours, in stocking stitch fabric.

Pattern repeat: 4 rows

Working in stocking stitch, knit 2 rows of the first colour and then join the second colour of yarn at the side edge.

Work 2 rows of the second colour.

When there are only 2 or 4 rows between stripes of the same colour, you can simply carry the yarn loosely at the side edge to the next stripe. The carried yarn will be hidden in the seam allowance.

Repeat these four rows as many times as you like: work two or three stripes and then continue in the main colour, or cover the whole fabric in narrow horizontal stripes.

Narrow horizontal stripes

WIDE HORIZONTAL STRIPES

Wide horizontal stripes in stocking stitch fabric, here in three colours.

Pattern repeat: 18 rows (6 rows of each colour)

Working in stocking stitch, knit 6 rows of the first colour and then join the second yarn colour at the side edge. Break off the first colour yarn, leaving a tail of about 10 to 15 cm (4 to 6 in).

Work 6 rows of the second colour, then join the third colour and break off the second colour as before.

Work 6 rows of the third colour.

Repeat these 18 rows until you have the required length of fabric.

Wide horizontal stripes

GARTER STITCH STRIPES

Stripes in two colours in garter stitch fabric. Even though garter stitch is usually reversible, the back looks very different from the front.

Pattern repeat: 4 rows

Working in garter stitch (all rows knit), knit 2 rows of the first colour and then join the second colour of yarn at the side edge.

Work 2 rows of the second colour.

When there are only 2 or 4 rows between stripes of the same colour, you can simply carry the yarn loosely at the side edge to the next stripe. The carried yarn will be hidden in the seam allowance.

Repeat these four rows as many times as you like: work two or three stripes and then continue in the main colour, or cover the whole fabric in narrow horizontal stripes.

Garter stitch stripes

Single-row stripes

SINGLE-ROW STRIPES

Using double-pointed needles (DPNs) allows you to knit just one stripe of colour at a time without joining a new colour of yarn at every row.

There are so many options for these single stripes. To work alternate stripes of two colours, knit a stripe of one colour, then join the second colour at the right-hand edge and knit a stripe. Now turn the work and purl a stripe of each colour. (See page 74 for step-by-step pictures.) You can work in repeats of three colours by knitting a row in the first colour, joining the second colour yarn at the right-hand edge and knitting a row; then join the third yarn at the right-hand edge and knit a row. Now turn the work and purl three rows in the same order as before.

In the example, a more complex pattern of single stripes is shown. Colours can be carried along the side edges when not in use.

Narrow vertical stripes

NARROW VERTICAL STRIPES

The difficulty with knitting stripes vertically is to ensure the tension of the yarn carried at the back of the work is just right, so that the wales of colour remain close together.

Pattern repeat: 6 stitches
Work in stocking stitch (knit right-side rows and purl wrong-side rows).
Row 1: K2 in main colour (MC), * K2 in contrast colour (CC), K4MC *, repeat * to * to last 4 stitches, K2CC, K2MC. Carry yarn behind stitches.
Row 2: P2MC, * P2CC, P4MC *, repeat * to * to last 4 stitches, P2CC, P2MC.
Repeat these two rows until you have the required length of fabric.

Two-colour brioche (front)

TWO-COLOUR BRIOCHE

Using double-pointed needles (DPNs), you can work brioche stitch as a double-sided striped fabric. Although we've knitted it with contrasting colours here, this stitch looks particularly effective using a dark and light shade of the same colour.

Pattern repeat: any even number + 2 extras
Cast on in colour 1 (C1).
Foundation row: Don't turn work. Join colour 2 (C2) at right-hand edge. P1, * with yarn in front of work, slip 1 purlwise, yon, P1 *, repeat * to * to last stitch, P1. Note that the yarn must go right around the needle and back to the front before you work the purl stitch.

Row 1: Turn work and use C1. P1, * slip 1 wyif, yon, P2tog *, repeat * to * to last stitch, P1. Slip all the slipped stitches purlwise in this and following rows.

Row 2: Don't turn work and use C2. K1, * K2tog, yfwd, slip 1, yon *, repeat * to * to last stitch, K1.

Row 3: Turn work and use C1. K1, * K2tog, yfwd, slip 1, yon *, repeat * to * to last stitch, K1.

Row 4: Don't turn work and use C2. P1, * slip1 wyif, yon, P2tog *, repeat * to * to last stitch, P1.

Repeat these four rows until you have the required length of fabric. Cast off in either colour, in pattern: purl the two stitches together but knit the stitches between rather than slipping them and putting the yarn over the needle. If you feel adventurous, you could try casting off in alternate colours to carry on the striped effect.

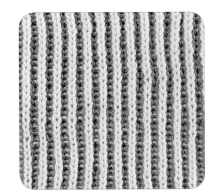

Two-colour brioche (back)

DIAGONAL STRIPES

These diagonal bands are worked in stocking stitch in stripes 4 stitches wide, and can be slanted in either direction by offsetting the pattern by 1 stitch in each row. Make the bands as wide or narrow as you like: if they're wider than 6 stitches, use separate strands of yarn rather than carrying the unused yarn across the back of the work.

Diagonal stripes

Pattern repeat: 8 stitches

Row 1: * K4 in main colour (MC), K4 in contrast colour (CC) *, repeat * to * to end.

Row 2: P3CC, * P4MC, P4CC *, repeat * to * to last 5 stitches, P4MC, P1CC.

Row 3: K2CC, * K4MC, K4CC *, repeat * to * to last 6 stitches, K4MC, K2CC.

Row 4: P1CC, * P4MC, P4CC *, repeat * to * to last 7 stitches, P4MC, P3CC.

Row 5: * K4CC, K4MC *, repeat * to * to end.

Row 6: P3MC, * P4CC, P4MC *, repeat * to * to last 5 stitches, P4CC, P1MC.

Row 7: K2MC, * K4CC, K4MC *, repeat * to * to last 6 stitches, K4CC, K2MC.

Row 8: P1MC, * P4CC, P4MC *, repeat * to * to last 7 stitches, P4CC, P3MC.

Repeat these 8 rows until you have the required length of fabric.

Changing colours

Patchwork

Blocks of colour

PATCHWORK

Large blocks of colour must be worked with separate strands of yarn, twisting the yarn together behind the work where the colours intersect.

Pattern repeat: any number of stitches
Work in stocking stitch.

Row A1: Knit in colour 1 (C1) to the changeover point. Join colour 2 (C2) and knit. Knot the C2 yarn loosely behind the work if you find it easier. After you've knitted a few rows, undo the knot and darn in the tail of the C2 yarn.

Row A2: Purl in C2, then pass the C2 yarn once around the C1 yarn and purl in C1 to end.

Repeat these two rows, twisting the two yarns together on the wrong side at the changeover point, until you have the required length of fabric. Break off both yarns, leaving tails to be darned into the fabric later.

Row B1: Join C2 at side edge of work and knit across C1 stitches in C2 yarn. Join C1 yarn and knit across C2 stitches in C1 yarn.

Row B2: Purl in C1 until you reach the crossover point, then twist the yarns together and continue purling in C2 to the end of the row.

Repeat these two rows, twisting the two yarns together on the wrong side at the changeover point, until you have the required length of fabric.

COLOURED CHEQUERBOARD

These four-stitch squares are small enough for you to carry the yarn across the back of the work. For larger squares, use a separate strand of yarn for each colour in each pair of squares.

Pattern repeat: 8 stitches

Row 1: * K4 in main colour (MC), P4 in contrast colour (CC) *, repeat * to * to end. Carry unused yarns behind work.

Row 2: * K4CC, P4MC *, repeat * to * to end.

Rows 3 and 4: Repeat rows 1 and 2.

Row 5: * P4CC, K4MC *, repeat * to * to end.

Row 6: * P4MC, K4CC *, repeat * to * to end.

Rows 7 and 8: Repeat rows 5 and 6.

Repeat these 8 rows until you have the required length of fabric.

Coloured chequerboard

HOUNDSTOOTH CHECK

Patterns that have a regular repeat of two or more colours that are not in blocks of colour are called mosaics. This mosaic is based on the traditional woven houndstooth check design. Look at the picture below right to see how the yarn should be carried across the back of the work.

Pattern repeat: 4 stitches

Row 1: K1 in main colour (MC), * K1 in contrast colour (CC), K3MC *, repeat * to * to last 3 stitches, K1CC, K2MC.

Row 2: * P3CC, P1MC *, repeat * to * to end.

Row 3: * K3CC, K1MC *, repeat * to * to end.

Row 4: P1MC, * P1CC, P3MC *, repeat * to * to last 3 stitches, P1CC, P2MC.

Repeat these 4 rows until you have the required length of fabric.

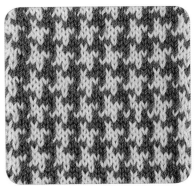

Houndstooth check (right side)

Geometrics

COLOURED DIAMONDS

An all-over pattern of coloured diamonds is worked in a stocking stitch fabric.

Pattern repeat: 6 stitches

Row 1: K3 in main colour (MC), * K1 in contrast colour (CC), K5MC *, repeat * to* to last 3 stitches, K1CC, K2MC. Carry unused yarn behind work.

Row 2 and all even rows: Purl all stitches, using the same colours as the previous row.

Row 3: K2MC, * K3CC, K3MC *, repeat * to * to last 4 stitches, K3CC, K1MC.

Row 5: * K1MC, K5CC *, repeat * to * to end.

Row 7: K30CC. Carry MC at side edge to Row 9.

Row 9: Repeat Row 5.

Row 11: Repeat Row 3.

Row 13: Repeat Row 1.

Row 15: K30MC.

Repeat these 16 rows until you have the required length of fabric.

Houndstooth check (wrong side)

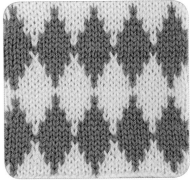

Coloured diamonds

Knitting basics

Two-tone cushion

Brioche stitch gives this cushion both its lovely tonal appearance and its soft, stretchy texture.

YOU WILL NEED:

* Two 50 g balls of 8-ply yarn in a dark shade (C1)
* Two 50 g balls of 8-ply yarn in a lighter shade of the same colour (C2)
* Pair of 4 mm (UK 8, US 6) DPNs
* Wool needle or 3.5 mm crochet hook
* Scissors

CONSTRUCTION:

Cast on 52 stitches in the dark shade.

FOUNDATION ROW: Don't turn work. Join the lighter shade (C2) at right-hand edge. P1, * with yarn in front of work, slip 1 purlwise, yon, P1 *, repeat * to * to last stitch, P1. Note that the yarn must go right around the needle and back to the front before you work the purl stitch. You should now have both working yarns at the left-hand side of the work.

Row 1: Turn work and use C1. P1, * slip 1 wyif, yon, P2tog *, repeat * to * to last stitch, P1. Slip all slipped stitches purlwise in this and following rows.
Row 2: Don't turn work and use C2. K1, * K2tog, yfwd, slip 1, yon *, repeat * to * to last stitch, K1.
Row 3: Turn work and use C1. K1, * K2tog, yfwd, slip 1, yon *, repeat * to * to last stitch, K1.
Row 4: Don't turn work and use C2. P1, * slip 1 wyif, yon, P2tog *, repeat * to * to last stitch, P1.
Repeat these 4 rows twenty-eight times, for 112 rows in total (approximately 30 cm in length).

CAST OFF USING THE DARKER SHADE: purl 2 stitches together as before, but knit the stitches between rather than slipping them and putting the yarn over the needle.

Work a second square of fabric the same as the first one.

MAKING UP:

Lay the two squares with wrong sides together and pin them around all edges. Using the darker shade of yarn in the wool needle, work whip stitch (see page 104) or blanket stitch to create a decorative seam on the outside of the cushion, or work ladder stitch (see page 105) to make an invisible seam.

Begin at one corner and work around three sides of the cushion. When you have stitched three of the sides together, unpin the fourth side and place the cushion insert in the cushion. Pin the fourth side closed and stitch the edges together as before, enclosing the insert. Darn the tail of the yarn into the seam.

If you know how to crochet, you can work double crochet to join the two pieces of fabric, as in the sample in the photograph. When you get to a corner, work two chain stitches, then turn the corner and work the first double crochet into the same stitch.

Coloured 3D blocks

COLOURED 3D BLOCKS

Based on the 3D boxes on page 130, this version uses different colours instead of different textures to define the spaces.

Pattern repeat: 10 stitches

Cast on in colour 1 (C1). Join a strand of colour 2 (C2) at side edge.

Row 1: K1C2, K8C1, join a strand of colour 3 (C3) and K1C3. Join a new strand of C2 and K1C2, K8C1, join a new strand of C3 and K1C3. Continue in pattern (K1C2, K8C1, K1C3), joining a new strand of C2 and C3 for each pattern repeat and carrying C1 yarn across the back of the work when not in use.

Row 2: * P2C3, pass C3 around C1, P6C1, pass C2 around C1, P2C2, pass C2 around C3 *, repeat * to * to end, working with the relevant strands of yarn in each block of colour and carrying C1 yarn across the back of the work when not in use.

Row 3: * K3C2, pass C2 around C1 at back of work, K4C1, pass C3 around C1 at back of work, K3C3, pass C3 around C2 and C1 at back of work *, repeat * to * to end, working with the relevant strands of yarn in each block of colour and carrying C1 yarn across the back of the work when not in use.

Row 4: * P4C3, pass C3 around C1, P2C1, pass C2 around C1, P4C2, pass C2 around C3 and C1 *, repeat * to * to end, working with the relevant strands of yarn in each block of colour and carrying C1 yarn across the back of the work when not in use.

Rows 5 and 7: Drop C1 yarn at edge of work (you will not use it for the next four rows). * K5C2, pass C2 around C3 at back of work, K5C3, pass C3 around C2 at back of work *, repeat * to * to end, working with the relevant strands of yarn in each block of colour.

Rows 6 and 8: * P5C3, pass C3 around C2, P5C2, pass C2 around C3 *, repeat * to * to end, working with the relevant strands of yarn in each block of colour.

Row 9: Twisting yarns together at the back of the work as before, pick up C1 yarn, * K1C1, K4C2, K4C3, K1C1 *, repeat * to * to end, working with the relevant strands of yarn in each block of colour and carrying C1 yarn across the back of the work when not in use.

Row 10: * P2C1, P3C3, P3C2, P2C1 *, repeat * to * to end, working with the relevant strands of yarn in each block of colour and carrying C1 yarn across the back of the work when not in use.

Row 11: * K3C1, K2C2, K2C3, K3C1 *, repeat * to * to end, working with the relevant strands of yarn in each block of colour and carrying C1 yarn across the back of the work when not in use.

Row 12: * P4C1, P1C3, P1C2, P4C1 *, repeat * to * to end, working with the relevant strands of yarn in each block of colour and carrying C1 yarn across the back of the work when not in use.

Row 13: * K4C1, pick up C3 from next colour block, K1C3, pick up C2 from previous colour block, K1C2, K4C1 *, repeat * to * to end, working with the relevant strands of yarn in each block of colour and carrying C1 yarn across the back of the work when not in use.

Row 14: * P3C1, P2C2, P2C3, P3C1 *, repeat * to * to end, working with the relevant strands of yarn in each block of colour and carrying C1 yarn across the back of the work when not in use.

Row 15: * K2C1, K3C3, K3C2, K2C1 *, repeat * to * to end, working with the relevant strands of yarn in each block of colour and carrying C1 yarn across the back of the work when not in use.

Row 16: * P1C1, P4C2, P4C3, P1C1 *, repeat * to * to end, working with the relevant strands of yarn in each block of colour and carrying C1 yarn across the back of the work when not in use.

Rows 17 and 19: Drop C1 yarn at side of work until Row 21: * K5C3, K5C2 *, repeat * to * to end, working with the relevant strands of yarn in each block of colour.

Rows 18 and 20: * P5C2, P5C3 *, repeat * to * to end, working with the relevant strands of yarn in each block of colour and carrying C1 yarn across the back of the work when not in use.

Row 21: Pick up C1 yarn, * K4C3, K2C1, K4C2 *, repeat * to * to end, working with the relevant strands of yarn in each block of colour and carrying C1 yarn across the back of the work when not in use.

Row 22: * P3C2, P4C1, P3C3 *, repeat * to * to end, working with the relevant strands of yarn in each block of colour and carrying C1 yarn across the back of the work when not in use.

Row 23: * K2C3, K6C1, K2C2 *, repeat * to * to end, working with the relevant strands of yarn in each block of colour and carrying C1 yarn across the back of the work when not in use.

Row 24: P1C2, break off C2 yarn from this block, P8C1, P1C3 (don't break off yarn), * P1C2 (don't break off yarn), P8C1, P1C3 *, repeat * to * to end, working with the relevant strands of yarn in each block of colour and carrying C1 yarn across the back of the work when not in use. At the end of the row, break off C3 yarn from last block.

Repeat these 24 rows—join the C2 yarn you broke off in the first repeat of Row 24 to begin the first block of colour, then join the C3 yarn you broke off at the end of Row 24 to work the final block of colour—until you have the required length of fabric.

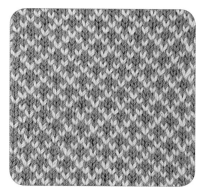
Two-colour Fair Isle

M	C	M	C
M	M	C	M
M	C	M	C
C	M	M	M

When reading the tables, begin in the bottom right-hand corner. Blank squares should be knitted in the main colour.

Argyles

Fair Isle knitting

Fair Isle is a real place: it's a tiny island off the northernmost tip of the United Kingdom's mainland. Fair Isle is well known for the colourful patterns that have traditionally been knitted with the local wool.

TWO-COLOUR FAIR ISLE

This all-over diamond pattern in two colours is a simple way to get started in Fair Isle knitting.

Pattern repeat: 4 stitches

Cast on in the main colour (M)—in our example, leaf green.

Row 1: * K3M, K1C (cream) *, repeat * to * to end.

Row 2: * P1M, P1C, P1M, P1C *, repeat * to * to end.

Row 3: * K1M, K1C, K2M *, repeat * to * to end.

Row 4: Repeat Row 2.

Repeat these 4 rows until you have the required length of fabric.

ARGYLES

Argyles are a traditional pattern of diamonds crossed with fine lines. Although they aren't from Fair Isle, the techniques are the same.

Pattern repeat: 24 stitches for three colours (You could work a 12 stitch repeat in two colours.)

You can carry yarn across the back of the work between the diagonal lines and the diamonds, but use a separate strand of yarn for each colour repeat. In our example, the main colour (MC – blank squares) is cream, contrast colour 1 (C1) is plum and contrast colour 2 (C2) is green.

Row 1: * K1C1, K5MC, K1C1, K5MC, K1C2, K5MC, K1C2, K5MC *, repeat * to * to end.

Row 2: * P1C2, P3MC, P3C2, P3MC, P1C2, P1MC, P1C1, P3MC, P3C1, P3MC, P1C1, P1MC *, repeat * to * to end.

Row 3: * K2MC, K1C1, K1MC, K5C1, K1MC, K1C1, K3MC, K1C2, K1MC, K5C2, K1MC, K1C2, K1MC *, repeat * to * to end.

2			2	2	2				2		1			1	1	1				1			
	2		2	2	2	2		2				1		1	1	1	1	1		1			
		2		2	2	2		2					1		1	1	1		1				
	2	2	2		2		2	2	2			1	1	1		1		1	1	1			
2	2	2	2	2		2	2	2	2	2	1	1	1	1	1		1	1	1	1	1		
	2	2	2		2		2	2	2			1	1	1		1		1	1	1			
		2		2	2	2		2					1		1	1	1		1				
	2		2	2	2	2		2				1		1	1	1	1	1		1			
2			2	2	2				2		1			1	1	1				1			
			2					2						1					1				1

Row 4: * P2MC, P1C1, P1MC, P3C2, P1MC, P1C2, P5MC, P1C1, P1MC, P3C1, P1MC, P1C1, P3MC *, repeat * to * to end.

Row 5: * K2MC, K3C1, K1MC, K1C1, K1MC, K3C1, K3MC, K3C2, K1MC, K1C2, K1MC, K3C2, K1MC *, repeat * to * to end.

Row 6: * P5C2, P1MC, P5C2, P1MC, P5C1, P1MC, P5C1, P1MC *, repeat * to * to end.

Row 7: Repeat Row 5.

Row 8: Repeat Row 4.

Row 9: Repeat Row 3.

Row 10: Repeat Row 2.

Repeat these 10 rows, swapping C1 and C2 so that colours alternate in each repeat, until you have the required length of fabric.

Three-colour Fair Isle

THREE-COLOUR FAIR ISLE

A basic diamond design alternates lines and blocks of colour.

Pattern repeat: 8 stitches

Work the design as a strip in a stocking stitch background in the main colour (MC)—cream.

Start Fair Isle pattern:

Row 1: Knit all stitches in contrast colour 1 (C1).

Row 2: Purl all stitches in C1.

Row 3: Knit all stitches in MC.

Row 4: Purl all stitches in MC.

Row 5: Join contrast colour 2 (C2) at edge of row. * K3C1, K1MC, K1C2, K1MC, K2C1 *, repeat * to * to end.

Row 6: * P1C1, P1MC, P3C2, P1MC, P2C1 *, repeat * to * to end.

Row 7: * K1C1, K1MC, K2C2, K1MC, K2C2, K1MC *, repeat * to * to end.

Row 8: P2C2, P1MC, P1C1, P1MC, P2C2, P1MC *, repeat * to * to end.

Row 9: * K2C2, K1MC, K3C1, K1MC, K1C2 *, repeat * to * to end.

Row 10: * P1MC, P5C1, P1MC, P1C2 *, repeat * to * to end.

Row 11: Repeat Row 9.

Row 12: Repeat Row 8.

Row 13: Repeat Row 7.

Row 14: Repeat Row 6.

Row 15: Repeat Row 5. Break off C2 at end of row.

Row 16: Purl all stitches in MC.

Row 17: Knit all stitches in MC.

Row 18: Purl all stitches in C1.

Row 19: Knit all stitches in C1.

Continue knitting the stocking stitch fabric in MC until you have the required length of fabric.

1	1	1	1	1	1	1	1
1	1	1	1	1	1	1	1
1	1			2		1	1
1		2	2	2		1	1
	2	2		2	2		1
2	2		1		2	2	
2		1	1	1		2	2
	1	1	1	1	1		2
2		1	1	1		2	2
2	2		1		2	2	
	2	2		2	2		1
1		2	2	2		1	1
1	1			2		1	1
1	1	1	1	1	1	1	1
1	1	1	1	1	1	1	1

Knitting basics

Fair Isle necktie

This man's necktie is knitted in fine cotton or wool yarn with a traditional Scandinavian snowflake design.

YOU WILL NEED:

* 50 g ball of 4-ply cotton yarn in each of the three colours (maroon, ice blue and lemon gelato)
* Pair of 2.25 mm (UK 13, US 1) knitting needles
* Small wool needle and scissors

CONSTRUCTION:

Cast on 3 stitches in the main colour.

Row 1: Knit all stitches.
Row 2: Purl all stitches.
Row 3: K1, inc in next stitch using your preferred method (see page 80), knit to last 2 stitches, inc in next stitch, K1.
Row 4: Purl all stitches.
Repeat rows 3 and 4 eleven more times, until you have 27 stitches on the needle. Begin knitting the Fair Isle pattern according to the chart on the following page, while still increasing one stitch at each end of every knit row until you have 51 stitches. Knit 11 rows of stocking stitch in pattern according to the chart and then begin to decrease as follows:
Next row: K1, K2tog, knit in pattern to last 3 stitches, K2tog, K1.
Work 9 rows stocking stitch in pattern according to the chart. When you have completed the chart, continue in the main colour.
Next row: K1, K2tog, knit to last 3 stitches, K2tog, K1.
Work 7 rows stocking stitch.
Next row: K1, K2tog, knit to last 3 stitches, K2tog, K1.

Work 5 rows of stocking stitch and continue decreasing in every 6th row until you have 25 stitches.
Work 11 rows of stocking stitch and continue decreasing in every 12th row until you have 21 stitches.
Continue on these 21 stitches until the work measures 120 cm (47¼ in).

Decrease one stitch at each end of every knit row until you have 3 stitches left. Cast off.

Darn the ends of the yarn into the edges of the fabric. Press the tie flat from the back, being careful not to catch the loose threads at the back of the work. Fold the two side edges to the middle and press.

Use ladder stitch (see page 105) to sew the two edges together at the centre back.

If you have DPNs in the correct size, you can knit the tie on the DPNs and it won't be necessary to break off colours and rejoin them as many times as with a pair of needles. If you do this, make sure you keep track of your row numbers for increasing and decreasing.

You could also knit this tie in any 4-ply yarn, such as wool, acrylic or silk.

NOTE: Do not knit blank squares. Start at bottom right and, when you reach the centre stitch, repeat the pattern in reverse to the other edge.

```
M  M  M  M  M  M  M  M  M  M  M  M  M  M  M  M  M  M  M  M  M  M  M  M  M  M  M  M  .  .
M  M  M  M  M  M  M  M  M  M  M  M  M  M  M  M  M  M  M  M  M  M  M  M  M  M  M  .  .  .
B  M  M  M  B  M  M  M  M  B  M  M  M  M  B  M  M  M  M  B  M  M  M  M  B  M  M  M  M  B
M  B  M  B  M  B  M  B  M  B  M  B  M  B  M  B  M  B  M  B  M  B  M  B  M  B  M  B  M  .
B  M  B  M  B  M  B  M  B  M  B  M  B  M  B  M  B  M  B  M  B  M  B  M  B  M  B  M  B  .
M  M  M  M  M  M  M  M  M  M  M  M  M  M  M  M  M  M  M  M  M  M  M  M  M  M  M  M  .  .
Y  Y  Y  Y  Y  Y  Y  Y  Y  Y  Y  Y  Y  Y  Y  Y  Y  Y  Y  Y  Y  Y  Y  Y  Y  Y  Y  Y  .  .
M  M  M  M  M  M  M  M  M  M  M  M  M  M  M  M  M  M  M  M  M  M  M  M  M  M  M  M  M  M
M  M  M  B  M  M  M  M  M  B  M  M  M  M  M  B  M  M  M  M  M  B  M  M  M  M  M  M  M  M
M  M  B  B  B  M  M  M  M  B  B  B  M  M  M  M  B  B  B  M  M  M  M  B  B  B  M  M  M  M
M  B  B  M  B  B  M  B  B  M  B  B  M  B  B  M  B  B  M  B  B  M  B  B  M  B  B  M  B  .
B  B  M  M  M  B  B  B  M  M  M  B  B  B  M  M  M  B  B  B  M  M  M  B  B  B  M  M  B  B
B  M  M  M  M  M  B  M  M  M  M  M  B  M  M  M  M  M  B  M  M  M  M  M  B  M  M  M  B  M
M  M  M  M  M  M  M  M  M  M  M  M  M  M  M  M  M  M  M  M  M  M  M  M  M  M  M  M  M  .
Y  Y  Y  Y  Y  Y  Y  Y  Y  Y  Y  Y  Y  Y  Y  Y  Y  Y  Y  Y  Y  Y  Y  Y  Y  Y  Y  Y  Y  .
M  M  M  M  M  M  M  M  M  M  M  M  M  M  M  M  M  M  M  M  M  M  M  M  M  M  M  M  M  .
B  M  B  M  B  M  B  M  B  M  B  M  B  M  B  M  B  M  B  M  B  M  B  M  B  M  B  M  .  .
M  B  M  B  M  B  M  B  M  B  M  B  M  B  M  B  M  B  M  B  M  B  M  B  M  B  M  B  M  B
M  M  M  M  M  M  M  M  M  M  M  M  M  M  M  M  M  M  M  M  M  M  M  M  M  M  M  M  M  M
M  M  M  Y  M  M  M  M  M  M  M  Y  M  M  M  M  M  M  M  Y  M  M  M  M  M  M  M  M  M  .
M  M  M  Y  M  M  M  M  M  M  Y  Y  M  M  M  M  M  Y  Y  M  M  M  M  M  M  M  M  Y  M  .
M  Y  Y  Y  M  M  M  M  M  Y  Y  Y  M  M  M  M  Y  Y  Y  M  M  M  M  M  Y  M  M  M  .  .
M  Y  Y  M  Y  Y  Y  Y  M  Y  Y  Y  M  Y  Y  M  Y  Y  Y  M  Y  Y  Y  M  Y  M  M  Y  Y  .
M  Y  M  Y  Y  Y  M  M  M  M  Y  Y  Y  M  Y  M  Y  Y  M  Y  Y  Y  M  M  M  .  .  .  .  .
M  M  Y  Y  Y  M  M  M  M  M  Y  Y  Y  Y  M  M  Y  Y  M  M  M  Y  Y  Y  M  M  M  .  .  .
B  M  M  M  M  M  M  M  B  M  M  M  M  M  M  M  B  M  M  M  M  M  M  M  M  B  .  .  .  .
M  M  Y  Y  Y  M  M  M  M  M  Y  Y  Y  M  M  M  M  M  Y  Y  M  M  M  M  .  .  .  .  .  .
M  Y  M  Y  Y  Y  M  M  M  M  M  Y  Y  Y  M  Y  M  Y  Y  Y  M  M  M  .  .  .  .  .  .  .
M  Y  Y  Y  M  Y  Y  Y  M  M  M  M  Y  Y  Y  M  Y  Y  Y  M  Y  Y  Y  .  .  .  .  .  .  .
M  Y  Y  Y  M  M  M  M  Y  M  M  M  M  Y  Y  Y  M  Y  Y  Y  M  M  .  .  .  .  .  .  .  .
M  M  Y  Y  M  M  M  M  M  Y  M  M  M  M  Y  Y  Y  M  Y  Y  M  M  .  .  .  .  .  .  .  .
M  M  Y  Y  M  M  M  M  M  M  Y  M  M  M  M  Y  Y  M  M  Y  M  .  .  .  .  .  .  .  .  .
M  M  M  M  M  M  M  M  M  M  M  M  M  M  M  M  M  M  M  M  .  .  .  .  .  .  .  .  .  .
M  B  M  B  M  B  M  B  M  B  M  B  M  B  M  B  M  B  .  .  .  .  .  .  .  .  .  .  .  .
B  M  B  M  B  M  B  M  B  M  B  M  B  M  B  M  B  M  .  .  .  .  .  .  .  .  .  .  .  .
Y  Y  Y  Y  Y  Y  Y  Y  Y  Y  Y  Y  Y  Y  Y  Y  Y  Y  .  .  .  .  .  .  .  .  .  .  .  .
M  M  M  M  M  M  M  M  M  M  M  M  M  M  M  M  M  .  .  .  .  .  .  .  .  .  .  .  .  .
B  M  M  B  M  B  M  M  B  M  M  M  B  M  M  M  .  .  .  .  .  .  .  .  .  .  .  .  .  .
M  B  M  M  B  M  M  B  M  M  B  M  M  M  .  .  .  .  .  .  .  .  .  .  .  .  .  .  .  .
B  M  M  B  M  B  M  M  B  M  M  B  M  M  .  .  .  .  .  .  .  .  .  .  .  .  .  .  .  .
```

Four-colour Fair Isle: band 1 (bottom) and band 2 (top).

FOUR-COLOUR FAIR ISLE

Adding a fourth colour to a Fair Isle pattern opens up a whole realm of possibilities. This example shows two different bands of pattern.

Pattern repeat: 6 stitches

Work stocking stitch in main colour (MC)—in this example, cream.

Begin Fair Isle band 1:

Row 1: Knit all stitches in contrast colour 1 (C1)—plum.

Row 2: Join contrast colour 2 (C2)—leaf green. * P1C1, P1C2 *, repeat * to * to end. Break off C2.

Row 3: Knit all stitches in MC.

Row 4: Join contrast colour 3 (C3)—deep plum. * P3MC, P1C3, P2MC *, repeat * to * to end.

Row 5: * K1MC, K1C3, K1C1, K1C3, K2MC *, repeat * to * to end.

Row 6: Join C2 at edge of work. * P1MC, P1C3, P1C1, P1C2, P1C1, P1C3 *, repeat * to * to end. Break off C2.

Row 7: Repeat Row 5.

Row 8: Repeat Row 4. Break off C3.

Row 9: Repeat Row 3.

Row 10: Repeat Row 2.

Row 11: Repeat Row 1.

These 11 rows form the diamond band.

Work fabric in stocking stitch in MC for desired number of rows.

Begin Fair Isle band 2:

Row 1: Join C2. * K5MC, K1C2 *, repeat * to * to end.

Row 2: * P2C2, P3MC, P1C2 *, repeat * to * to end.

Row 3: Join C1. * K2C2, K1MC, K2C2, K1C1 *, repeat * to * to end. Break off MC.

Row 4: * P2C1, P3C2, P1C1 *, repeat * to * to end.

Row 5: Join C3. * K2C1, K1C2, K2C1, K2C3 *, repeat * to * to end. Break off C2.

Row 6: * P2C3, P3C1, P1C3 *, repeat * to * to end.

Row 7: Join MC. * K2C3, K1C1, K2C3, K1MC *, repeat * to * to end. Break off C1.

Row 8: * P2MC, P3C3, P1MC *, repeat * to * to end.

Row 9: * K2MC, K1C3, K3MC *, repeat * to * to end. Break off C3.

These 9 rows form the zigzag band.

Resume stocking stitch in main colour until you have the required length of fabric.

1	1	1	1	1	1
1	2	1	2	1	2
			3		
		3	1	3	
	3	1	2	1	3
		3	1	3	
			3		
1	2	1	2	1	2
1	1	1	1	1	1

Four-colour Fair Isle band 1.

		3			
	3	3	3		
	3	3	1	3	3
3	3	1	1	1	3
3	1	1	2	1	1
1	1	2	2	2	1
1	2	2		2	2
2	2				2
2					

Four-colour Fair Isle band 2.

Intarsia

Intarsia is another name for knitting in large areas of colour, particularly if there are pictorial designs involved.

HEART MOTIF

Pattern repeat: 19 stitches (heart only)

Work stocking stitch fabric in main colour (MC) to the motif starting point.

Row 1: K9MC, join contrast colour (CC), K1CC, K9MC. (Work more stocking stitch in MC either side of the motif to complete the row.)

Row 2: P8MC, P3CC, join new strand of MC, P8MC. You are now working with two separate strands of MC, one on each side of the motif. Don't forget to twist the yarns around each other each time you change colour in the following rows.

Row 3: K8MC, K3CC, K8MC.

Row 4: P7MC, P5CC, P7MC.

Row 5: K6MC, K7CC, K6MC.

Row 6: P6MC, P7CC, P6MC.

Row 7: K5MC, K9CC, K5MC.

Row 8: P4MC, K11CC, P4MC.

Row 9: K4MC, K11CC, K4MC.

Row 10: P3MC, P13CC, P3MC.

Row 11: K2MC, K15CC, K2MC.

Row 12: P2MC, P15CC, P2MC.

Row 13: K1MC, K17CC, K1MC.

Row 14: P1MC, P17CC, P1MC.

Row 15: K1MC, K17CC, K1MC.

Row 16: P19CC.

Row 17: K19CC.

Row 18: Repeat Row 16.

Row 19: Repeat Row 17.

Row 20: Repeat Row 16 again.

Row 21: K1MC, K8CC, join new strand of MC (you will now have three separate strands of MC), K1MC, K8CC, K1MC. Carry CC yarn across central MC stitches behind work in this and following rows.

Row 22: P1MC, P7CC, P3MC, P7CC, P1MC.

Row 23: K2MC, K6CC, K3MC, K6CC, K2MC.

Row 24: P3MC, P4CC, P5MC, P4CC, P3MC.

Row 25: K3MC (break off MC), K3CC, K7MC (break off MC), K3CC (break off CC), K3MC.

These 25 rows form the motif. Continue with the remaining strand of MC to knit the stocking stitch fabric beyond the motif.

Heart motif

				c	c	c								c	c	c				
				c	c	c	c						c	c	c	c				
			c	c	c	c	c	c				c	c	c	c	c	c			
		c	c	c	c	c	c	c				c	c	c	c	c	c	c		
		c	c	c	c	c	c	c	c		c	c	c	c	c	c	c	c		
	c	c	c	c	c	c	c	c	c	c	c	c	c	c	c	c	c	c	c	
	c	c	c	c	c	c	c	c	c	c	c	c	c	c	c	c	c	c	c	
	c	c	c	c	c	c	c	c	c	c	c	c	c	c	c	c	c	c	c	
	c	c	c	c	c	c	c	c	c	c	c	c	c	c	c	c	c	c	c	
	c	c	c	c	c	c	c	c	c	c	c	c	c	c	c	c	c	c	c	
		c	c	c	c	c	c	c	c	c	c	c	c	c	c	c	c	c		
		c	c	c	c	c	c	c	c	c	c	c	c	c	c	c	c	c		
		c	c	c	c	c	c	c	c	c	c	c	c	c	c	c	c	c		
			c	c	c	c	c	c	c	c	c	c	c	c	c	c	c			
			c	c	c	c	c	c	c	c	c	c	c	c	c	c	c			
				c	c	c	c	c	c	c	c	c	c	c	c	c				
					c	c	c	c	c	c	c	c	c	c	c					
					c	c	c	c	c	c	c	c	c	c	c					
						c	c	c	c	c	c	c	c	c						
							c	c	c	c	c	c	c							
							c	c	c	c	c	c	c							
								c	c	c	c	c								
									c	c	c									
									c	c	c									
										c										

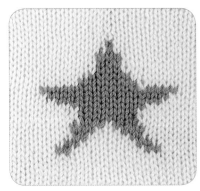

Star motif

STAR MOTIF

Start the legs of this star motif with two bobbins of coloured yarn.
Work the design on a background of stocking stitch in the main colour.

Pattern repeat: 15 stitches (star only)

Work stocking stitch in MC until you are ready to start the star motif.

Row 1: K1MC, join a strand of contrast colour (CC), K2CC, K9MC, join a second strand of CC, K2CC, K1MC. Carry the MC yarn across the back of the work in this and following rows until Row 6.

Row 2: P2MC, P2CC, P7MC, P2CC, P2MC.

Row 3: K3MC, K2CC, K5MC, K2CC, K3MC.

Row 4: P3MC, P3CC, P3MC, P3CC, P3MC.

Row 5: K4MC, K3CC (break off yarn), K1MC, K3CC (don't break off yarn), K4MC.

Row 6: P4MC, P7CC, join new strand of MC, P4MC.

Row 7: K5MC, K5CC, K5MC.

Row 8: P5MC, P5CC, P5MC.

Row 9: K4MC, K7CC, K4MC.

Row 10: P2MC, P11CC, P2MC.

Row 11: K1MC, K13CC, K1MC (break off MC).

Row 12: P15CC.

Row 13: Pick up MC from **Row 11**, K5MC, K5CC, K5MC (carry MC yarn across at back).

Row 14: P6MC, P3CC, P6MC.

Row 15: K6MC, K3CC, K6MC.

Row 16: Repeat Row 14.

Row 17: K7MC, K1CC, K7MC.

Row 18: P7MC, P1CC, P7MC.

These 18 rows make up one star motif. Continue to knit stocking stitch fabric in MC until you have the required length of fabric.

							C							
							C							
						C	C	C						
						C	C	C						
						C	C	C						
					C	C	C	C	C					
C	C	C	C	C	C	C	C	C	C	C	C	C	C	C
	C	C	C	C	C	C	C	C	C	C	C	C	C	
		C	C	C	C	C	C	C	C	C	C	C		
			C	C	C	C	C	C	C					
				C	C	C	C	C						
				C	C	C	C	C						
			C	C	C		C	C	C					
			C	C	C			C	C	C				
			C	C	C			C	C	C				
		C	C	C					C	C	C			
		C	C							C	C			
	C	C									C	C		

Flower motif

FLOWER MOTIF

Using three colours, this simple flower is an easy entry into the world of pictorial intarsia.

Pattern repeat: 28 stitches (flower only)

Work the flower motif on stocking stitch fabric in the main colour (MC). Each petal should have its own bobbin of contrast colour 1 (C1).

Begin motif (chart on following page):

Row 1: K11MC, join C1, K3C1, join new strand of MC, K14MC.

Row 2: P14MC, P5C1, P9MC.

Row 3: K8MC, K7C1, K13MC.

Row 4: P13MC, P9C1, P6MC.

Row 5: K6MC, K10C1, K12MC.

Row 6: P4MC, join new strand of C1, P4C1, carry MC across behind stitches, P4MC, P10C1, P6MC.

Row 7: K7MC, K9C1, K4MC, K5C1, join new strand of MC, K3MC.

Row 8: P2MC, P7C1, P3MC, P9C1, P7MC.

Row 9: K9MC, K7C1, K3MC, K8CC, K1MC.

Row 10: P10C1, P3MC, P5C1, P4MC, join new strand of C1, P4C1, P2MC.

Row 11: Continue working stocking stitch to the right of the motif with the MC yarn. K8C1 (carry MC across behind work, twisting it with the C1 yarn after four stitches), K3MC, K4C1 (don't break off yarn, you will use this yarn for the flower centre), K3MC, K10C1.

Row 12: P1MC, P10C1, P1MC (don't break off yarn), join contrast colour 2 (C2), P5C2, P1MC, P10C1 (carry MC across behind work, twisting it with the C1 yarn after five stitches).

Row 13: K10C1, K7C2, K9C1, K2MC.

Row 14: P4MC, P7C1, P2C2, pick up C1 yarn from first flower petal, P3C1, P2C2, P10C1.

Row 15: K10C1, K2C2, K2C1, K2C2, pick up MC yarn from two rows below, K1MC, K4C1 (don't break off yarn), K6MC.

Row 16: P11MC, P2C2, P3C1 (don't break off yarn), P2C2, join new MC, P1MC, P8C1, P1MC with yarn from right-hand side.

Row 17: K1MC, K6C1, K3MC, K7C2, K1MC, pick up C1 from petal below, K3C1, carry MC yarn across behind work, K7MC.

Row 18: P3MC, P9C1, P5C2 (break off yarn), pick up C1 yarn from flower centre, P2C1, P3MC (break off yarn), P4C1, P2MC.

Row 19: K8MC, K5C1, join new MC, K2MC, K11C1, K2MC.

Row 20: P2MC, P11C1, P2MC, P5C1, P8MC.

Row 21: K7MC, K7C1, K2MC, K10C1, K2MC.

Row 22: P3MC, P9C1, P2MC, P7C1, P7C1.

Row 23: K6MC, K8C1, K4MC, K7C1, K3MC.

Row 24: P4MC, P5C1, P5MC, P8C1, P6MC.

Row 25: K7MC, K7C1, K6MC (break off yarn), K3C1 (break off yarn), K5MC.

Row 26: P15MC (break off yarn), P4C1 (break off yarn), P9MC.

These 26 rows make up one flower motif. Continue to knit stocking stitch fabric in MC until you have the required length of fabric.

														1	1	1	1								
			1	1	1								1	1	1	1	1	1	1						
		1	1	1	1	1							1	1	1	1	1	1	1	1					
			1	1	1	1	1	1					1	1	1	1	1	1	1	1					
			1	1	1	1	1	1	1	1			1	1	1	1	1	1	1						
		1	1	1	1	1	1	1	1	1	1		1	1	1	1	1	1	1						
		1	1	1	1	1	1	1	1	1	1	1		1	1	1	1	1							
		1	1	1	1	1	1	1	1	1	1			1	1	1	1	1							
			1	1	1	1	1	1	1	1	2	2	2	2	2	1	1			1	1	1	1		
				1	1	1			2	2	2	2	2	2	2				1	1	1	1	1	1	
									2	2	1	1	1	2	2		1	1	1	1	1	1	1	1	
				1	1	1	1		2	2	1	1	1	2	2	1	1	1	1	1	1	1	1	1	1
			1	1	1	1	1	1	1	2	2	1	1	1	2	2	1	1	1	1	1	1	1	1	1
		1	1	1	1	1	1	1	1	2	2	2	2	2	2	2	1	1	1	1	1	1	1	1	1
	1	1	1	1	1	1	1	1	1		2	2	2	2	2		1	1	1	1	1	1	1	1	1
1	1	1	1	1	1	1	1	1	1			1	1	1	1			1	1	1	1	1	1	1	1
1	1	1	1	1	1	1	1	1	1			1	1	1	1	1			1	1	1	1			
	1	1	1	1	1	1	1	1				1	1	1	1	1	1	1							
		1	1	1	1	1	1	1				1	1	1	1	1	1	1	1	1					
			1	1	1	1	1					1	1	1	1	1	1	1	1						
				1	1	1	1					1	1	1	1	1	1	1	1	1					
												1	1	1	1	1	1	1	1	1					
												1	1	1	1	1	1	1							
												1	1	1	1	1									
												1	1	1											

JOLLY ROGER

Any pirate would be happy to fly this gruesome flag, or wear it.

Jolly Roger

Pattern repeat: 25 stitches (motif only)

Work the skull and crossbones in cream yarn (CC) on a charcoal background (MC) in stocking stitch. The instructions are for the motif only, so knit in stocking stitch until you are ready to start the design.

Row 1: K2MC, join CC yarn, K2CC, K17MC, join a new strand of CC yarn, K2CC, K2MC. Carry the MC yarn across at the back of the work until you get to the main part of the skull.

Row 2: P1MC, P3CC, P17MC, P3CC, P1MC.

Row 3: K6CC, K13MC, K6CC.

Row 4: P3MC, P5CC, P9MC, P5CC, P3MC.

Row 5: K5MC, K5CC, K5MC, K5CC, K5MC.

Row 6: P7MC, P5CC, P1MC, P5CC, P7MC.

Row 7: K9MC, K5CC, twist CC with MC and other CC strand, continue with second CC strand, K4CC, K9MC.

Row 8: P9MC, P5CC, twist CC with MC and other CC strand, continue with first CC strand, P4CC, P9MC.

Row 9: K8MC, K4CC, K1MC, K4CC, K8MC.

Row 10: P6MC, P4CC, P5MC, P4CC, P6MC.

Row 11: K4MC, K4CC, K9MC, K4CC, K4MC.

Row 12: P1MC, P5CC, P5MC, join new strand of CC, P3CC, P5MC, P5CC, P1MC.

Row 13: K4CC, K5MC, K7CC, K5MC, K4CC.

Row 14: P3CC, P5MC, P2CC, P5MC, P2CC, P5MC, P3CC.

Row 15: K1MC, K1CC (break off yarn), K6MC, K1CC, K2MC, K3CC, K2MC, K1CC, K6MC, K1CC (break off yarn), K1MC.

Row 16: P9MC, P7CC, P9MC.

Row 17: K8MC, K3CC, K3MC, K3CC, K8MC.

Row 18: P7MC, P5CC, P1MC, P5CC, P7MC.

Row 19: K7MC, K11CC (twist MC with CC at the back of the work every four stitches), K7MC.

Row 20: P6MC, P3CC, P2MC, P3CC, P2MC, P3CC, P6MC.

Row 21: K6MC, K2CC, K4MC, K1CC, K4MC, K2CC, K6MC.

Row 22: P6MC, P2CC, P4MC, P1CC, P4MC, P2CC, P6MC.

Row 23: K5MC, K3CC, K4MC, K1CC, K4MC, K3CC, K5MC.

Row 24: P5MC, P4CC, P2MC, P3CC, P2MC, P4CC, P5MC.

Row 25: K5MC, K15CC, join new MC, K5MC.

Row 26: P5MC, P15CC, P5MC.

Row 27: Repeat Row 25.

Row 28: P6MC, P13CC, P6MC.

Row 29: K6MC, K13CC, K6MC.

Row 30: P7MC, P11CC, P7MC.

Row 31: K9MC, K7CC, K9MC.

Row 32: P10MC (break off yarn), P5CC, P10MC.

These 32 rows make up one motif. Continue to knit stocking stitch fabric in MC until you have the required length of fabric.

1	2	3	4	5	6	7	8	9	10	11	12	13	14	15	16	17	18
							C	C	C	C	C						
						C	C	C	C	C	C	C					
					C	C	C	C	C	C	C	C	C	C			
				C	C	C	C	C	C	C	C	C	C	C	C		
				C	C	C	C	C	C	C	C	C	C	C			
			C	C	C	C	C	C	C	C	C	C	C	C	C		
			C	C	C	C	C	C	C	C	C	C	C	C	C		
			C	C	C	C	C	C	C	C	C	C	C	C	C		
			C	C	C	C			C	C	C		C	C	C	C	
			C	C	C				C				C	C	C		
			C	C					C				C	C			
			C	C					C				C	C			
			C	C	C				C	C	C		C	C	C		
				C	C	C	C	C	C	C	C	C	C	C			
				C	C	C	C	C			C	C	C	C	C		
					C	C	C				C	C	C				
					C	C	C	C	C	C	C						
	C					C			C	C	C			C			C
C	C	C				C	C					C	C			C	C	C
C	C	C	C			C	C	C	C	C	C	C		C	C	C	C
	C	C	C	C	C		C	C	C			C	C	C	C	C	C
		C	C	C	C							C	C	C	C		
			C	C	C	C						C	C	C	C		
				C	C	C	C			C	C	C	C				
				C	C	C	C	C	C	C							
				C	C	C	C	C	C	C							
			C	C	C	C	C			C	C	C	C	C			
		C	C	C	C	C					C	C	C	C	C		
	C	C	C	C	C						C	C	C	C	C		
C	C	C	C	C	C								C	C	C	C	C
	C	C	C												C	C	C
		C	C													C	C

11

Garment care

* Troubleshooting * Wet washing

* Treating stains * Dry-cleaning

* Drying knitwear * Storing knitwear

Washing and drying

Yes, small our household is, I own, Yet must I see to it. No maid we keep, And I must cook, sew, knit, and sweep, Still early on my feet and late.

Margaret, in Johann Wolfgang von Goethe's FAUST. PART I

The proper care of hand knits is very important. When you've put so much effort into creating a one-off masterpiece, it would be a shame to have it shrink, stretch or be otherwise unwearable after the first time you wear it. Washing and drying hand-knitted garments and accessories needn't be a pain: sure, you can't just throw them in the washing machine with your T-shirts and jeans, but they don't all need to be handled with kid gloves by professionals, either.

If you've been careful to use only fibres of the same or similar types in a garment, care is much easier. The label of the yarn you used should have recommended care instructions printed on it, and you should follow these instructions. If you've lost the label, or you never had one, the information in this chapter will help you decide the best method of cleaning and caring for your garment.

Troubleshooting

LOST LABEL

What if you've lost the label of the yarn, and you can't even remember what type of fibre it is? There's a simple test you can do to identify the basic fibre content of a yarn. You need to burn a small piece of the yarn (carefully!) to see how it burns, what it smells like and what kind of residue is left behind. Perform the test in a safe place, preferably outdoors or well away from any flammable items, and make sure there is a container of water on hand to extinguish any flames or embers.

Cut a short length of yarn, about 5 cm (2 in) long, if you have some unused yarn left over. If you only have a finished garment, try to find a tail of yarn from inside a seam and snip off a small piece: even a centimetre of yarn is better than nothing. Over a flameproof surface—

such as an old dinner plate—hold the fibre firmly using a pair of tweezers or small kitchen tongs to keep it away from your fingers. Use a stove lighter or a match to light the end of the fibre; allow ash to fall onto the plate as it burns and then drop any remaining pieces of fibre into the bucket of water.

From top: wool, cotton, bamboo viscose, acrylic, mixture (50% wool, 30% acrylic, 20% alpaca).

* **Cotton** burns with a steady flame, smells like burning leaves and leaves a crumbly ash.
* **Linen** burns in a similar way to cotton but will take longer to ignite. It doesn't matter if you can't tell them apart as the basic washing and drying instructions are the same.
* **Wool** is difficult to ignite, but once it is lit it burns with a steady flame and smells like burning hair.
* **Silk** burns more readily than wool and also smells like burning hair, but the flame will flicker and the ash is more easily crumbled than wool ash.
* **Acrylic** fibres burn rapidly with an acrid smell and form a hard ash.
* **Nylon** will melt and then continue to burn rapidly, with a smell like burning plastic.
* **Polyester** melts and burns at the same time and leaves a sticky ash, which will bond quickly to any surface it falls on, so be careful. The black smoke will have a sweet smell.
* **Rayon**, because of its cellulose content, burns quickly and leaves a light, crumbly ash. It smells like burning leaves, similar to cotton and linen.

Blends of two fibres can be difficult to identify by this method, because they should have the characteristics of all the fibres they comprise. If you can identify at least one type of fibre in a blend, you'll have some idea how it should be treated.

TENSION SQUARES

If you're concerned about the method of washing a finished project, use the tension square as a test swatch. Wash it according to the manufacturer's instructions or the advice in this chapter for the fibre type. If you're not completely happy with the result, modify the process or have the item dry-cleaned.

The table below covers the best ways of cleaning, washing, rinsing and drying the main fibre types.

FIBRE OR YARN COMPOSITION	TREATMENT
Cotton and linen (These fibres are stronger when wet and so they can be scrubbed and twisted during the washing process.)	Soak in cold water with a little detergent. Wash in hot water in a washing machine. Spin until almost dry. Dry flat in shade or on low heat in a tumble dryer until just damp. Iron while still damp, using a hot iron on the wrong side. Don't allow the fabric to stretch.
Silk	Soak 15 minutes only in lukewarm water with a little detergent. Wash in lukewarm water by hand or in a muslin bag in a washing machine. Do not spin. Dry by rolling in a towel to absorb excess water. Iron while still damp, using a warm iron on the wrong side. Don't allow the fabric to stretch.
Wool (Wool fibres are felted by a combination of soap, friction and heat—see Chapter 13—so be careful when washing.)	Soak 15 minutes only in lukewarm water with a little detergent. Wash in warm water with mild detergent. In a machine, use a muslin bag. If washing by hand, don't lift the garment out of the water as the weight will stretch and damage the fibres. Spin gently in a washing machine but stop while still wet. Never twist or wring. Dry flat in shade, shaking the item occasionally to fluff up the fibres. When it's touch dry, air for a further 24 hours. Iron while still slightly damp, using a warm iron on the wrong side. Don't allow the fabric to stretch.
Rayon (Rayon fibres are very short and so the yarn is weaker when wet. Treat it gently.)	Soak 15 minutes only in lukewarm water with a little detergent. Wash in lukewarm water by hand or in a muslin bag in a washing machine. Do not spin. Dry by rolling in a towel to absorb excess water. Iron while still damp, using a medium–hot iron on the wrong side. Don't allow the fabric to stretch.
Nylon (Nylon is just as strong when wet as dry and so it can be washed normally. As it is usually blended with another fibre, wash it according to the instructions for the other fibre.)	Wash in hot water in a washing machine. Spin dry. Dry flat in shade. Ironing should not be necessary, but use a cool iron.
Polyester and acrylics	Soak in warm water with a little detergent. Wash in hand-hot water by hand or in a washing machine. Rinse in cold water. Spin dry for a short time after rinsing. Dry flat in shade. Ironing should not be necessary, but use a cool iron.

 Knitting basics

Wet washing

Advances in manufacturing technology mean that many yarns are safe to machine wash, and the label will usually tell you whether this is the case. However, that doesn't mean that you can simply throw it into the washing machine on a standard wash cycle. In general, knitted items need to be treated gently so that they don't shrink or stretch during the washing process. A protective muslin bag or a pillowcase is recommended for any piece of knitwear to help keep it in shape in a washing machine. Drying is also an issue, as spin-drying can twist and break fibres or pull garments out of shape, and line-drying garments that are heavy with water can lead to stretching and loss of elasticity in the knitted fabric.

There are two basic kinds of cleaning agent used in the laundry: acids and alkalis (bases). The basic rule of thumb to remember is that animal fibres like wool and silk can be damaged by alkalis, while acids can neutralise the effects; cotton and linen—plant fibres—are damaged by acids but the effects can be neutralised by alkalis.

Laundry soap is alkaline and so is preferable for cleaning cotton and linen but not recommended for wool. Washing detergents are generally pH neutral but they can contain bleaching agents such as sodium perborate or sodium hypochlorate that can damage wool and silk. Specialised wool washing detergents are widely available and recommended for washing wool and silk.

Treating stains

Stains and discoloration can spoil the look of your knitted clothing and accessories. If possible, it's best to treat stains as soon as they occur, before they have time to soak into the fibre and spread or dry into the fibre. Wash or dry-clean the item as soon as possible after the initial treatment, so that the substance you used to remove the stain doesn't do further damage to the fibres.

Lemon juice and salt are your allies in stain removal.

There are a few main types of stain: vegetable stains, animal or protein stains, greasy stains, pigment stains, and other stains. Initial treatment differs according to the type of stain, but all treatments should be followed up with thorough washing of the whole garment or item, unless dry-cleaning is recommended. The following table will help you work out how to treat different stains on different fibres.

Garment care

STAIN TYPE	FIBRE TYPE	TREATMENT
Vegetable stains: fruit juice, wine, tea, coffee, grass	All fabrics	Cover with salt to stop the stain spreading; then wash.
	Cotton and linen only	Stretch the fabric gently over a basin and cover with salt; then pour boiling water through the stained area into the basin; then wash.
Grass stains only	All fabrics	Dab with methylated spirits; then wash.
Protein stains: blood, egg, milk	All fabrics	Cover with salt and soak in cold water; then wash.
Greasy stains: oil, fat, lipstick	Cotton and linen	Soak in hot water with sodium percarbonate (NapiSan—see Bleach, below); then wash.
	Wool, silk, synthetics	Wash immediately in warm water with sodium percarbonate (see Bleach, below) and mild detergent.
	All non-washable fabrics	Dry-clean.
Pigment stains: paint (oil-based or acrylic), nail varnish	All fabrics	Oil-based paint: dab gently with turpentine; then wash.
		Acrylic paint: soak in cold water; then wash.
	All fabrics except acetate	Nail varnish: dab gently with acetone (nail polish remover).
Other: ink	Cotton and linen	Cover with a paste of salt and lemon juice; then wash.
	Wool, silk, synthetics	Soak in milk or methylated spirits for 15 minutes; then wash.
Other: organic stains such as perspiration and mildew	All fabrics	Soak in potassium permanganate; this will leave a brown stain that can be removed by soaking in diluted hydrogen peroxide (see Bleach, below).

BLEACH

Bleach is a common way to remove stains from white or light-coloured items. You must be careful, though, not to remove the colour along with the unwanted stain. Test a hidden area of the item before using any bleaching agent on a whole garment.

Bleaching is a process of oxidation: it allows oxygen to combine with the molecules of the stain to remove them from the fibres. Sunlight is a bleaching agent— a very mild one that is suitable for many fibres—although prolonged exposure to direct sunlight will fade most colours and weaken natural fibres.

Other oxidising bleaches include hydrogen peroxide, which can be used on silk and wool fibres, and potassium permanganate (blue bags), which can also be used on silk and wool as well as cotton and linen. Sodium hyperchlorite is the basis of most chlorine bleaches, which are suitable for cotton, linen and rayon but must not be used on wool and silk or nylon. The mild bleaching or brightening agent that is in most laundry detergents—including soaking additives such as NapiSan—is sodium perborate or sodium percarbonate and this is suitable for most fibre types.

FABRIC	BLEACHING AGENT
Cotton, linen and rayon	Chlorine bleach may be used, but rinse well.
Silk and wool	Diluted hydrogen peroxide may be used. Never use chlorine bleach.
Nylon	Do not bleach.
Polyester and acrylics	Sodium perborate or sodium percarbonate (NapiSan) may be used.

Dry-cleaning

Most knitted items can be dry-cleaned if you prefer not to risk the stretching and agitation of washing in water. Dry-cleaners use a solvent called tetrachloroethylene (perchloroethylene), which is safe for most fibre types. You can purchase dry-cleaning fluid to use as a spot remover at home. Other solvents you can try for spots are hydrocarbon-based solvents such as kerosene, alcohol and turpentine, although these are all very flammable and must be used and stored carefully. They can also leave behind a slight odour.

Drying knitwear

It is rarely a good idea to tumble dry knitted items after washing them. Some fibres will withstand the heat, agitation and friction, but it's better to be safe than sorry and dry all of your knitwear flat and away from direct sunlight. Hanging wet knitwear on a clothesline is not recommended, because the weight of the water in the damp garment will tend to pull the stitches out of shape.

You can purchase jumper drying racks, which are usually metal frames with a light nylon mesh fabric stretched between them to hold the knitted item away from the flat surface so that air can circulate all around it. If you don't have one of these, lay a towel over a folding laundry rack or on a suitable surface in a protected place where there's plenty of air circulating but no direct sunlight. Turn the item over and fluff it up gently a few times during the drying process to encourage the stitches to return to their normal shape and elasticity.

Most knits will not need ironing, although you can press them lightly from the back of the fabric with a steam iron (see the table on page 214 for temperature suggestions) to help restore their shape after washing and drying, if you like.

VODKA SPRITZER
To freshen up knitwear between washes or trips to the dry-cleaner, hang the garment on a padded hanger out of direct sunlight and mist it all over with vodka from a spray bottle. The alcohol dissolves any particles of odour or dirt and doesn't leave a nasty smell behind.

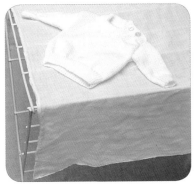

Dry knitwear flat in a shaded area.

Storing knitwear

The great thing about knitted garments is that you can fold them up and store them in a drawer, and when you take them out they are ready to wear without creases or fold marks. Here's a quick tutorial on how to fold jumpers nice and flat for storage.

1. Lay the jumper face down on a flat surface.
2. Fold the sides of the jumper in to the middle.
3. Fold the sleeves down at the shoulder so they are parallel with the sides.
4. Fold the jumper in half with the neck opening on top and place it in a drawer or on a shelf.

Knitted garments can be hung in a wardrobe, too, providing you choose a padded hanger to prevent bumps in the shoulders. Avoid hanging heavy knits, even when they are dry, because they will tend to stretch and drop. These should be folded and placed in a drawer.

Scarves and shawls can be folded flat and placed in drawers or on shelves, along with hats and mittens, or hung loosely on hooks or over a rail.

LONG-TERM STORAGE

If you're putting your woollies away for the summer, or storing a favourite hand knit as a keepsake after a child has grown out of it, make sure the item is clean and dry before you store it. Cotton, linen and synthetic fabrics can be stored in a dry place with no further preparation.

Wool and silk, however, can attract moths and other creatures that like to nibble away at them when you're not looking. Place clean, dry garments in a polythene bag (such as a dry-cleaner's bag) and

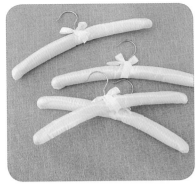

Padded coathangers help knits keep their shape.

Hang scarves on a hook or over a rail.

squash as much of the air out as you can before sealing the bag with tape or an elastic band.

Putting it in mothballs

Mothballs are a chemical insecticide designed to rid your stored clothing of pests, but they do leave a pungent smell behind. If you have cleaned and sealed your woollens in an airtight bag, you shouldn't have too much trouble with moths. Some alternatives to chemical mothballs include cedar balls (you could try storing your knitwear in a cedar chest), or sprigs of lavender and rosemary. These act as a repellent rather than as a pesticide, and the effect will fade over time as they lose their strong scent, so make sure you refresh them regularly.

Polythene storage bags for knitwear help keep moths at bay.

Chemical deterrents can also be used.

Garment care

12

Mending wool

✳ Filling holes

✳ Swiss darning ✳ Patchwork

✳ Unravelling and reknitting ✳ Alterations

Making amends

Darn it! That's not only the expletive you utter when you find a hole in your favourite jumper, it's also what you can do to fix it.

Filling holes

When you find a small hole in a piece of knitted fabric, mending it is a simple process. If you still have some of the yarn you used to knit the piece, you can mend it invisibly. If you don't still have the yarn and can't find a close match, you might need to make a feature of the repair work.

The item should be clean and dry when you start mending it, but the laundering process can make small holes larger and so you might need to do some preparatory or temporary mending before you wash it. At the very least, pass a length of yarn through all the loose loops around the hole and knot the yarn: you can cut it off later, but in the meantime it will prevent any more stitches from unravelling.

BASIC MENDING EQUIPMENT

For mending knitted items, the basic requirements include:
* a small pair of sharp scissors or snips (for cutting seams and yarn)
* darning or wool needles in various sizes
* leftover yarn from projects you have made
* sewing needles and sewing thread in various colours
* a small crochet hook
* stitch holders
* yarn bobbins (for winding unravelled yarn).

Swiss darning

In Swiss darning the stitches you make with a wool needle and yarn follow the loops of the stitches in the fabric, so that they look like knitted stitches. If you use the same yarn as the fabric, the darning is almost invisible. This type of darning is also used to embroider designs on knitted fabric.

1. Thread a wool needle with a piece of yarn the same as or matching the yarn in the fabric. Darn one end into the back of the fabric and lay strands of yarn across the hole (one strand of yarn across each row of knitting), passing the yarn through any loose loops around the hole to prevent any further unravelling. (The example shows a contrasting yarn so that you can see the stitching, although you would usually use a matching yarn.)

2. Bring the needle and yarn to the front of the fabric near the bottom right of the area to be mended. Following the loops of the knitted fabric, pass the needle behind the stitch above so the new stitch will sit over the strand of yarn.

3. Still following the loops of the knitted fabric, pass the needle behind the stitch next to the first darned stitch.

4. Continue across the row. When you have passed to the left of the area to be mended, bring the needle up behind the fabric to the row above and work back across the hole, still following the loops of the knitted fabric.

(Continued over page)

Mending wool

(5) When you're stitching over the actual hole in the fabric, continue passing the darning yarn through the loops as though you were following the missing knitted stitches.

(6) If a hole is large, you might have to make a new loop in one row as you stitch, without any loops of knitted fabric to stitch it to.

(7) In the next row of darning, catch the new loop as you stitch past it.

(8) Continue until you have completely covered the hole and several surrounding stitches, and then darn the tail of the yarn into the back of the fabric to finish.

EMBROIDERY

Swiss darning, as shown in the previous example, is also a way of working surface embroidery on knitted fabric. If you can't match the yarn to mend a hole invisibly, use contrasting colours to make a feature of the darning. Some simple motifs you could use are shown below, and you could also use these to embroider undamaged fabric if you like.

Monogram

Strawberry patch

		V	V	V			
	V	V	V	V	V		
V	V	V	A	V	V	V	
V	V	A	V	A	V	V	
V	V	A	V	A	V	V	
V	V	A	A	A	V	V	
V	V	A	V	A	V	V	
	V	V	V	V	V		
		V	V	V			

		G		G		
			G			
		V	V	V		
	V	W	V	W	V	
	V	V	W	V	V	
	V	W	V	W	V	
		V	W	V		
		V	V	V		
			V			

W	W	W	W	B	B	B	B	B
W	W	W	W	B	B	B	B	B
W	W	W	W	B	B	B	B	B
W	W	W	W	B	B	B	B	B
B	B	B	B	B	B	B	B	B
B	B	B	B	B	B	B	B	B
B	B	B	B	B	B	B	B	B

Be patriotic and wave your country's flag on your knitwear. I've stitched an Australian flag, but you can make the flag of your choice.

Patchwork

There are certain areas of a knitted garment that are subject to more wear and tear than others, such as at the elbows. In these places, darning will work for a while but then it will wear through. If a large hole has developed, darning will be difficult and tedious. In these cases, stitching a larger patch over the damage may be the answer.

You can patch knitted fabric with more knitted fabric, or with a woven or bonded fabric, such as wool felt. Wool felt is a good choice for patching wool. Alternatively, leather patches can add character to a garment. If you choose a woven fabric, you'll need to hem the edges of the patch properly before you use it. Try to keep to the same type of fabric for the patch as for the garment—use wool with wool, cotton with cotton, synthetic with synthetic—if you will be laundering the item at any time after mending it.

PREPARATION

Before you sew on a patch, you will need to secure all the loose ends of the knitted fabric. Use a piece of yarn as closely matching the fabric as possible to stitch in back stitch (see page 104) through every stitch around the hole. You may now trim away any loose pieces of yarn from the hole.

PATCHING

Use the stitching around the hole as a guide for the size and shape of the patch. The patch should be larger than the hole and have an even outline, such as a rectangle or oval.

① Stitch around the edges of the hole using back stitch. (The example shows a contrasting yarn so that you can see the stitching, although you would usually use a matching yarn.)

② Cut a patch of a bonded fabric such as felt or leather, just larger than the stitched border around the hole. Place the patch over the hole—make sure that all of the back stitch is hidden under the edges of the patch—and pin it in place.

③ Stitch around the edges of the patch and through the knitted fabric using strong sewing thread and a sharp needle. You can use any stitch you like; in the example, blanket stitch helps define the edges of the patch. If you can place the item on a sewing machine, you can sew the patch that way (although this is difficult with the sleeves of jumpers!).

Unravelling and reknitting

Some of the areas of a knitted garment that get the most wear and tear are around the cuffs, collars and hemlines. If the edges of the fabric start to fray in these areas, you can unravel the ribbing and reknit it. See page 89 for unravelling and unknitting instructions. You may be able to reuse the yarn from the existing ribbing, if it's not too damaged: the ribbing might end up a row or two shorter than the original, so remember if you choose this method to mend one cuff, you'll need to shorten the other cuff to match.

Alternatively, if you still have some of the project yarn left over, you can reknit the ribbing at the full length; however, if the garment is well worn, the new yarn might stand out from the old yarn, so use this option judiciously. If the yarn is too damaged to be reused and you don't have any of the same yarn left over, another option is to reknit the ribbing in a contrasting yarn.

① To unravel a section of knitting on a collar, cuff or hem, you will first need to undo any seams near the area. Stretch the two sides of the seam apart near the edge of the fabric and snip the yarn with sharp, pointed scissors, being careful not to accidentally cut any of the knitted yarn. Undo the seam a few centimetres past the end of the ribbing.

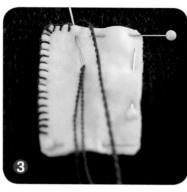

② Snip the yarn at one edge of the fabric at the top of the cuff (if a new colour is used, as in our pictures, simply find the darned-in tail) and use a small crochet hook to pull it free of the fabric and work it loose. Continue using the crochet hook to undo the last row of the cuff. To unravel a collar, start at the top and unpick the cast-off edge.

③ If you want to reuse the same yarn, unravel the cuff after you have detached it from the sleeve and wind it loosely onto a bobbin or into a small ball.

④ Using a knitting needle of the correct size for the ribbing, pick up the stitches on the edge of the sleeve.

⑤ With the right side of the sleeve fabric facing you, join the yarn for the cuff and knit all the stitches in the new yarn.

⑥ Knit in the ribbing pattern until you have the required number of rows.

⑦ Finish the reknitting by casting off and then restitching any seams.

Mending wool

Before: ribbed turtleneck

After: soft cotton collar

Alterations

There are occasions when reknitting is required for other reasons than damage. A collar may be too tight: you can unravel it and reknit it with more stitches or on larger needles, with a looser cast-off row. (Note that you'll need more yarn for this than you unravel, or you'll need to knit fewer rows.) Perhaps you've changed your mind about a garment: you thought you liked the long-sleeved version but now you think that shorter sleeves (or no sleeves) would be more practical.

A top or skirt may turn out to be too long or too short: my father had a favourite fisherman's rib jumper that was perfect for working around our farm in icy winter weather, but he complained that it left his kidneys exposed when he was sitting on the tractor or bending and lifting bales of hay. He had another jumper just like it, so one day he simply cut off the ribbing of the first jumper and cut off the body of the second jumper below the sleeves; he then sewed the two together. This rough two-tone look was fine for farm work, but I was always tempted to take it apart, unravel both jumpers up to the sleeves and reknit the bottom parts in a stripey pattern.

Here's another example: the mohair turtleneck jumper shown is soft and snuggly, but the hairy collar can be irritating on the skin of the neck. A collar conversion is required: by unravelling the ribbed neckline (carefully, because mohair is easily tangled) the collar could be refinished without any ribbing, by simply casting off loosely around the neck, or reknitted as a shorter and looser version of the original. In the example, I've used a contrasting slubby cotton yarn to knit a collar that softens the jumper's neckline and is more comfortable around the wearer's neck.

13
Felting and fulling

✳ Making felt ✳ Knitting for felting

✳ Adding decoration ✳ Needlefelting

A fibre blast!

Making felt

Woollen fibres are covered in microscopic scales, which are the reason that wool is so cosy, as they help trap a layer of warm air in the fabric. They are also the reason that wool must be treated so carefully when you are washing and drying it (see Chapter 11, page 211). High temperatures, moisture and agitation cause the scales to catch on each other and on the scales of other fibres, so that the wool fibres interlock and become matted. This is the main action in felt-making; most of the time, you don't want it to happen to your knitted woollen fabrics.

There are times when felting is a desirable result: if you want a firm fabric with a smoother surface than a knitted fabric, you can deliberately cause the fibres to mesh together. An interesting result of felting is that, although the fabric is firmer and denser than unfelted wool, it is actually less capable of retaining warm air, because the spaces between the

Roved and dyed wool and silk fibres for felting.

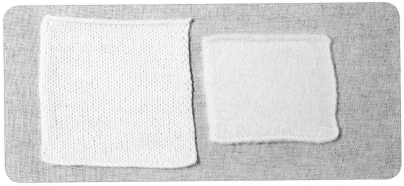

The felted swatch of the right was originally the same size as the knitted swatch on the left.

fibres and between the stitches have been closed up. So felt is a slightly cooler fabric to wear than knitted or woven wool.

The term 'felt' is really only correctly used when talking about a fabric that is bonded from roved wool fibres. The process begins with roved fibres being laid out parallel to each other, and then more fibres are added at right angles to the first layer. Several layers can be laid in alternating directions, depending on the desired final thickness of the fabric. These fibres are wetted with soapy water and agitated lightly until they begin to cling together in a fabric.

After the mesh is stable, the agitation becomes more violent, and hot water and soap are continually applied to the fabric to encourage the fibres to interlock and felt up. This part of the process can be done by hand (by vigorously rolling the fabric on a hard surface) but it's hard work—believe me, I've tried it! It can also be done in a washing machine, although the benefit of reducing labour must be balanced against the loss of control over the final shape and density of the fabric.

The final stage of felting is fulling, where the fabric is beaten into its final, firm shape. When you are felting knitted woollen fabric, you are really only doing the fulling part of the process. This, too, can be done by hand—by throwing, rolling and beating

the fabric until it stops shrinking down—or in a washing machine.

Any woollen fabric can be felted by fulling. Once it is fulled, the fabric is stable and can be cut into different shapes without fraying at the cut edges.

Knitting for felting

To create new knitted fabric for the purpose of felting, you need to start with the right sort of yarn. Check the label: many yarns are treated with special coatings that protect against felting, and so avoid yarns that say 'machine washable'. Only wool yarn will felt, although—as in nuno felting—that doesn't mean you have to avoid blends completely, as long as the main fibre in the yarn is wool.

Some yarn shops sell yarn that is specifically designed to be knitted for felting, labelled 'felting yarn' or something similar. I've had good results from 100 per cent wool 'hand wash only' yarns as well as wool and other animal fibre blends.

It is important to remember that fabric shrinks during the felting and fulling process, and so if you are creating fabric for the purpose of felting it, make sure that you know approximately how much it will shrink. The best way to find this out is to knit a test swatch and felt it.

Before: this wool jumper was washed in too-hot water; the fulling process has begun but is not complete.

A deliberate hot-water wash completes the felting process.

After: The jumper was cut apart and the fabric used to make a soft toy.

The two sample swatches in the photograph on the previous page are knitted in 8-ply felting wool yarn using 4 mm (UK 8, US 6) needles, 30 stitches across and 40 rows high. The unfulled swatch measures 15 cm wide x 15 cm high; the felted piece is 13 cm wide x 11 cm high. Note that the fabric has shrunk more in height than in width—keep this in mind when planning your felted projects. The fulled piece is 65 per cent of the size of the original; although it's nearly 90 per cent of the original width, it's just 75 per cent of the height.

When you're knitting fabric for felting, you can either knit a piece of flat fabric, full it and then cut it into shape and sew it together, or you can knit shaped fabric and sew it or join it before you full it. The second method makes a sturdier item, as seams and decorations are felted into the fabric.

SECOND-HAND ROSE

Jumpers and other woollen clothing that has passed its use-by date can be felted so that the fabric can be recycled for other projects. Dig old favourites out of the back of your wardrobe or scour the local op shop for woollen garments. Make sure they are not labelled 'machine washable', as this means that the yarn has been treated to prevent felting

and, although they will felt up a little bit, you won't achieve the dense, flat surface of a well-felted fabric.

Cut off any buttons or zippers and other non-wool components of the garment. Put the garments in a washing machine with some washing detergent and set the machine on the hottest cycle. Don't forget to add some vinegar to the rinse cycle to neutralise the soap (see Chapter 11, page 211). Remove the shrunken garments from the machine and dry them in a tumble dryer or flat in the shade. You can now cut the garment apart, removing seams and any damaged areas or unwanted parts.

Here are some ideas for things to make with felted fabric pieces:

* tablewear: placemats, table runners, napkin rings
* stuffed toys
* blankets—cut equal-sized squares from coordinating coloured felts and sew them together
* egg cosies, teapot cosies, mug holders
* cushion covers
* fashion items such as bags, belts, bangles, scarves and hats.

See also the pattern for the felted pin and needle holder on pages 30–31.

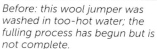

Close up of nuno decoration.

Greek key embroidery stitched in back stitch before felting.

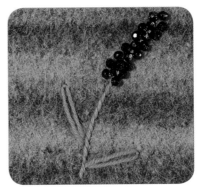

Beaded decoration.

Adding decoration

Decorative elements can be added to felted fabric either before or after fulling. The main thing to remember is that, if you are going to add them before fulling, they must be able to withstand the temperature and agitation of the washing machine. For this reason, beads and other baubles should probably be added at the end of the process.

EMBROIDERY

Embroidery with wool yarns can be worked before fulling. The yarns will shrink down with the fabric and become bonded into it. You can also work embroidery in other fibres that will not shrink with the fabric, which might result in some interesting effects. On the nuno felt scarf above, for example, I laid a piece of silk and mohair yarn in a curve across the wool. By the time the fulling was done, the smooth curve of yarn had crinkled up into a wriggly line.

Surface stitching may also be completed after the fabric is felted, or even after the project is assembled, to add the finishing touch.

BEADING

Beads, buttons and baubles of all shapes and sizes may be stitched onto the felted surface as decorations. As mentioned above, this type of decoration should be applied after fulling, so that the beads will not be damaged by the hot water, soap and agitation. Ribbons, lace and metal findings such as belt buckles, brooch backs and hair clips can also be attached.

Knitting basics

Felted handbag

Knitted in a multi-coloured blend of mohair and wool, this bag can be sewn together before you felt it in the washing machine—then just add the handles.

YOU WILL NEED:

* Three 50 g balls of 12-ply feltable wool
* 5.5 mm (UK 5, US 9) knitting needles
* Wool needle and scissors
* Handles to fit (see below)

CONSTRUCTION:

FRONT, BASE AND BACK: Cast on 45 stitches, knit in stocking stitch for 112 rows and then cast off. This rectangle will measure approximately 27 x 50 cm (10½ x 19½ in) and use most of the first two balls of yarn.

SIDE GUSSETS: Cast on 16 stitches and begin knitting in stocking stitch.
Decrease one stitch at each end of every 8th row, five times in all, until 6 stitches remain.
Work 6 more rows of stocking stitch and then cast off. Make another side gusset to match.

SEWING UP:

Fold the main piece of knitted fabric in half, with the cast-on and cast-off rows meeting. Place a pin on the fold at each side edge and open the fabric out flat. With the fabric lying right side up on a flat surface, place each side gusset, right side down, on top of the fabric so that the cast-on edge of the gusset is aligned with the side edge of the fabric and the gusset is centred over the pin. Pin the gussets in place and join them to the main piece along the cast-on edge of the gusset using back stitch.

With the main piece still right side up, fold each gusset piece forward so that the front side edge matches the front side edge of the main piece. Ease the pieces if necessary (see page 102) so that the top edges are level. Pin and stitch the seams on each side of the front and then repeat with the back side seams. Turn the bag right side out now.

NOTE that you can darn in the tails of the yarn if you wish, or simply cut them off after felting.

FELTING:

Place the bag in a washing machine set on a hot wash cycle with a little detergent. Add some vinegar to the rinse water. The felting process will shrink the bag down to approximately 10 cm high x 20 cm wide (4 x 8 in) and will lock the seams together for extra strength. While the bag is still wet, pull it into shape and stuff it with bubble wrap to hold the desired shape while it dries.

HANDLES:

Handles like the bamboo ones used here can be purchased from craft stores, but I recommend you felt the bag first before purchasing the handles, to make sure you get the right size. Other options for handles could be to knit a strip of matching yarn and attach it to the bag before felting, or to attach handles such as twisted cords, leather straps or chains after felting.

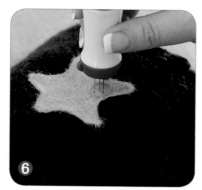

Needlefelting

Needlefelting is another way of making felt objects from wool roving; primarily, it's used to create three-dimensional felt items. Instead of agitating wool in hot water and soap, a very sharp burred felting needle is used to poke into a mass of roving and encourage the wool fibres to matt together.

① Needlefelting can be used to decorate felted fabric such as the fabric produced by knitting. Lay the fabric flat on a foam brick or felting brush (this protects your table top from damage).

② Use a template if you like.

③ Arrange the wool roving roughly in the desired shape on the surface.

④ Begin poking the felting needle through the roving and fabric around the outline of the shape.

⑤ Poke the roving all over within the borders of the template, until the roving is bonded with the fabric.

⑥ Remove the template and smooth any loose roving fibres into the centre, poking them into the fabric with the needle. Continue poking the decoration with the felting needle until you are happy that the fibres are well bonded.

3D FELTED DECORATIONS

Once you've felted the fabric, you can cut it into all sorts of shapes and stitch or glue them to other items as decorations. You can use felted fabric as patches on damaged knitwear (see pages 225–226) or make brooches and hair accessories by cutting shapes and attaching them to metal findings (available from craft shops and beading suppliers).

To make the headband pictured, cut out a multitude of small flower shapes and a few leaf shapes from felted fabric and arrange them on a headband, sewing through the centre of each flower with a cross stitch in a contrasting embroidery thread. These small flowers are made of thin felted fibre fabric; if you're using thicker knitted and fulled fabric you might need to make the flowers a little larger.

Knitting basics

Felted belt

Make this belt to match your felted handbag, or to add zing to your favourite little black dress.

YOU WILL NEED:
* Two 50 g balls of 12-ply feltable wool
* 6 mm (UK 4, US 10) knitting needles
* Buckle to fit (see right)
* Scissors, sewing needle and thread to match the belt

CONSTRUCTION:
To calculate the required length for your belt, take your waist measurement and multiply it by 1.25 to work out the required length of the belt after felting; for example, if your waist measures 85 cm (33 in), multiply by 1.25 to get a finished belt length of 106.25 cm (41¼ in). This amount is sixty per cent of the length you need to knit, to allow for shrinkage during felting, so to find the full length divide (do not multiply) that figure by 0.6; for example, 106.25 cm divided by 0.6 means you will need to knit 177.08 cm of fabric (or 41¼ divided by 0.6 gives 68¾ in).

Cast on 16 stitches and knit in stocking stitch without increasing or decreasing until you have the required length of fabric for your belt. Knit the first and last stitch of every purl row, so that the fabric strip will not curl in on itself at the edges. When you have the required length of fabric, cast off.

Put the belt in a washing machine set on a hot wash cycle with a little detergent, and add vinegar to the rinse water. When the cycle is complete, pull the belt into a straight line and lay it flat on a towel or other flat surface to dry completely.

BUCKLE IT UP:
It's best to leave the purchase of the buckle until after you have felted the belt, so that you can choose one that fits. The fabric will be quite thick, so make sure there's room in the buckle for the thickness of the fabric as well as the width. Trim the ends of the belt if necessary, and fold one end around the buckle bar. Use a sewing needle and strong sewing thread to stitch it securely in place. If your buckle has a tongue, simply punch holes as required in the other end of the belt using a sharp pair of scissors or an awl.

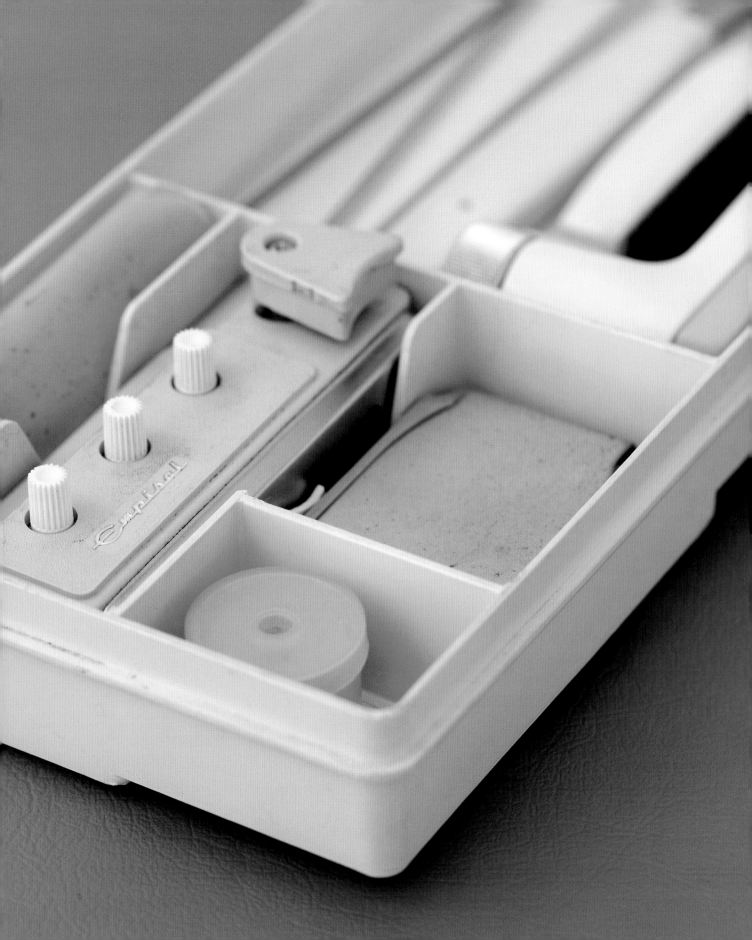

14

Knitting machines

* How a knitting machine works

* Caring for your machine

* Yarn for machine knitting * Join the club

Fast and furious

L ike the Spinning Jenny and the flying shuttle, the knitting machine helped to revolutionise the textile industry and spark the Industrial Revolution. It wasn't until the early twentieth century, though, that knitting machines suitable for domestic use went into production.

I love my washing machine and my sewing machine, because they make tedious chores faster and easier, but I've never had much time for machines that take the fun out of doing craft. A colleague once tried to interest me in a computerised sewing machine that cost almost as much as my car: the supposed attraction was that you could load the fabric into a hoop, place a spool of thread on the rack, press a pre-programmed button and then walk away and do the dishes while the machine did your embroidery. Where's the fun in that?

I'm equally wary of knitting machines. Even when I was first learning to knit, I could appreciate the fun of throwing yarn over the needles and watching the fabric gradually grow. The feel of the yarn, the intricacy of the stitch pattern, the satisfaction of a job well done—even the quiet rhythm of the repetitive motions—are all part of the attraction of the hand-knitting process.

The satisfaction in using knitting machines, my machine-knitting friends tell me, is not just in the speed of the machine. Knitting by machine takes skill, just as hand knitting does, and as you learn more about the process you can begin to create your own patterns and designs with as much creativity as any hand knitter. Machine knitting also has the advantage of producing more uniform stitches than hand knitting, if that's the look you're after, particularly over large areas of stocking stitch and along hems and edges.

Needle-bed of a knitting machine.

Close up of the latch-hook needles. *Yarn carriage.* *Yarn tensioner.*

How a knitting machine works

The first knitting machine was called an Instant Knitter, which is said to have been invented in Japan in 1924. This machine required the yarn to be laid across the bed of hooks for every row; modern knitting machines have a tension unit that automatically feeds the yarn into the machine as you knit. Get to know your knitting machine and how it works by reading the manufacturer's instruction book carefully. If you've bought or received a machine second-hand, without a book, many of the instructions are available on the Internet or in books that you can borrow from the library or buy.

The functional parts of a knitting machine are a needle-bed, which holds hundreds of individual latch-hooks (one for each stitch), and a carriage or cam-box that moves across the needle bed and provides the action that forms the knitted stitches. The yarn tensioner has dials to adjust the tension and spring loops for feeding the yarn through.

You will still need to knit a tension square on a knitting machine, so it doesn't save you from that part of the process!

Most home machines are single-bed machines that can only knit single-sided fabric in knit and purl stitches. Many have a ribbing attachment that can be purchased separately; other machines have a double-bed built in that allows you to make ribbing and other decorative fabrics. Knitting machines come in several gauges: fine gauge (for 1- to 3-ply yarn), standard gauge (2- to 6-ply), mid-gauge (4- to 10-ply) and bulky (8- to 14-ply).

The process of making a stitch is much the same as in French knitting.

① The yarn is wrapped over the shaft of the needle. When the hook is pushed through the loop, the latch falls open and the yarn slips behind it.

② The yarn for the next row of stitches is laid in the hook, manually or by the machine.

③ As the needle moves back, the old stitch moves forward under the latch, closing it over the yarn in the hook.

④ The hook, with the latch closed, pulls the new stitch through the loop, which drops off the needle.

PATTERNS FOR MACHINES

Instead of written instructions, patterns for knitting machines often look like graphs filled with mathematical symbols such as x, o, \, /, dashes and lines. These patterns, when followed manually by the machine knitter, indicate where stitches are to be knitted as right-side or wrong-side stitches, where a different colour is to be added, and how to make lacy fabric as well as cables and Fair Isle designs. Some machines have a punch-card style system that locates the needles and stitches that need to be manipulated, while modern machines are often controlled by a computer rather than by punch cards.

Patterns designed for hand knitting can also be knitted on a knitting machine by an experienced operator.

A sample of machine-knitted fabric using feather-and-fan stitch.

CASTING ON

Casting on in a knitting machine is a simple process. Starting with all of the needles in neutral position, you select the required number of needles (one for each stitch) in the centre of the needle-bed, bringing them forward to the working position. Using a manual latch-hook tool (there should be one with the machine), you hook the yarn over itself and onto the next needle, making an edge that looks very much like one that's knitted by hand. You can also knit doubled hems and decorative hems on a knitting machine, as well as ribbing (the manufacturer's instruction book will give details on how to do this).

Knitting machines enable you to knit neat edges and fancy patterns.

INCREASING AND DECREASING

Increasing and decreasing is also done manually. When increasing, you use a transfer hook (which comes with the machine) to pick up the first loop on the edge of the fabric and move it across to the first empty needle beside the work. You can then pick up the next stitch and move it across by one hook. This leaves a hook free three stitches into the fabric. Now you can pick up the back of the stitch in the previous row of the next wale and slip it onto the spare hook. When you pass the carriage over the needle-bed, this will be knitted as an extra stitch.

If you need to increase by a number of stitches at the edge in one row, as in hand knitting you simply manually cast on new stitches before you pass the carriage across the needles.

To decrease a stitch, you take the last stitch of the row and use the transfer hook to lift it off the needle and onto the needle on top of the next stitch in line. When you pass the carriage over the needle-bed, there will be one fewer stitch knitted. To decrease several stitches at a time, see Casting off (below).

CASTING OFF

One way of casting off from a knitting machine is to use a large wool needle to pass the yarn through the final row of loops using a back stitch motion. While the last row is still on the hooks, pass the needle through the second stitch and then the first and draw the yarn through (not too tightly); now pass the needle through the third stitch, then the second and draw the yarn through. Continue across the row until all stitches have been caught and then lift the stitches off the hooks carefully. A crochet hook can also be used to catch all the stitches and cast them off after the fabric has been removed from the machine.

Note the neatness of the yarns on the reverse side of the fabric.

FINISHING A PROJECT

Knitting machines can be used to knit trim, such as ribbed necklines, as well as to sew up seams. Most machine knitters finish their projects by hand, using the same methods as for hand knits. See Chapter 6 (page 93) for methods of sewing seams and finishing knitted projects.

Caring for your machine

It's important to cover your knitting machine when it's not in use to prevent dust getting into the mechanism. You can use a vacuum cleaner with a brush extension to gently clean the needle-bed if necessary.

The machine also needs to be oiled carefully, so that oil doesn't transfer to the knitted fabric. Follow the manufacturer's instructions about where to apply oil. Basically, any moving part may be oiled, particularly the rails that the carriage runs on and the needle butts (but not the latches).

Some manufacturers recommend that you 'run in' a new machine by working only in 4-ply yarn for the first few garments, before moving on to 8-ply yarns.

Don't leave unfinished knitting hanging from the needles for more than a few minutes, as the weight of the fabric will drag on the yarn, spoiling the tension, and can also cause the hooks to flex. If you must leave a piece unfinished, lift it so that the loops remain on the hooks but the weight of the fabric is supported.

Yarn for machine knitting

Knitting machines are really only suitable for wool yarns with a standard twist. The mechanism of the latch-hook system and the automatic tensioner will not work as effectively with less elastic yarns, such as cotton and even acrylic, especially if they are also quite thick. The gauge of the machine (fine, standard, mid or bulky) will determine the thickness of the yarn you can use. Novelty yarn is not suitable for knitting in machines.

CONES AND BALLS

Yarn for machine knitting is usually bought on cones or in balls with the working yarn coming from the centre. You can wind yarn bought in hanks or balls onto a cone yourself, using a manual winding machine, or use the yarn straight from a commercially wound ball (make sure you take the yarn from the centre, not the outside). You should never use yarn directly from a hank, or from a hand-wound ball.

If you're using a commercially wound ball of yarn, place it in a jar or other heavy container near the machine, to keep the ball in place as the tension mechanism pulls the yarn from it. Cones will stand under their own weight.

Yarn on cones for machine knitting.

WAXING

The hairy fibres of woollen yarns can cause friction with the carriage mechanism, and so many yarns designed for machine knitting are waxed lightly by simply running the yarn over a candle or a block of wax before it feeds through the tensioning unit. You can buy yarns designed for machine knitting that are already waxed and wound onto cones, or you can wind yarn onto cones or balls yourself, using a winding machine, and waxing it as you go.

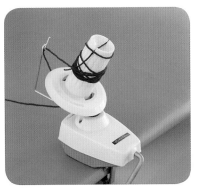

A manual yarn winder prepares yarn for feeding into the machine.

Join the club

The best way to find out more about machine knitting—whether you already own and use a machine or are thinking about trying one—is to join a local machine-knitting club or association. You can find the nearest club by searching the Internet, or asking in your local knitting supplies store.

Membership is usually quite inexpensive and offers benefits such as access to books and patterns, advice from more experienced machine knitters and contacts for machine servicing and parts.

You can also join chat groups on the Internet. Knitting machines may not be as portable as hand knitting, but they can make you friends all around the world!

15

Basic patterns

✴ Baby's jumper pattern ✴ Child's jumper pattern

✴ Woman's jumper pattern ✴ Man's jumper pattern

The patterns in this chapter are for basic jumpers with ribbing bands and stocking stitch fabric. There is no shaping for sleeves or armholes, although there is a little bit of shaping around the neckline and shoulders. You can use these patterns as a starting point for making jumpers featuring the stitch patterns in Chapters 7 to 10 of this book.

Remember to knit a tension square using the stitch pattern of your choice to check the size. You will probably find that some lacy stitches knit up at a looser tension than is recommended. This may be acceptable if you don't mind a softer drape for the body of the garment, as this can show off lacy fabric.

Cable stitches, on the other hand, knit up into a fabric that is about 20 per cent smaller than plain stocking stitch. One or two cables on an otherwise plain jumper shouldn't make too much difference, but if you are knitting a number of cables or several wide braids, it would be wise to add some extra stitches. You can do this by knitting the ribbing bands of the jumper in the correct size and then increasing evenly across the last row of ribbing until you have the desired number of stitches. As a rough guide, add 1 extra stitch for every 4-stitch cable, 2 extra stitches for 6- or 8-stitch cables, and 3 or 4 stitches for a braid. Remember to take the extra stitches into account when you cast off stitches for the neck and shoulders, casting them off evenly across the width of the garment.

With these four basic patterns, you can make jumpers for everyone in your family!

Baby's jumper pattern

This pattern is for a plain stocking stitch jumper in 3-ply yarn. You can use it with any of the decorative stitches and patterns in Chapters 7, 8, 9 and 10 of this book. The sizes given will fit most babies from newborn to about one year.

Tension
31 stitches to 10 cm (4 in) for stocking stitch.

Size
(Measure around the chest under the arms.)

Fits chest	35	40	45	50 cm
	14	16	18	20 in
Actual size	38.5	44	49.5	55 cm
	15	17¼	19½	21¾ in
Length	21	25	28	31 cm
	8¼	9¾	11	12¼ in
Sleeve	26	29	34	39 cm
	10¼	11½	13¼	15¼ in

Materials
* 2 [2, 3, 3] balls of 3-ply yarn (50 g balls). Quantities are approximate as they vary between knitters.
* One pair each of 3 mm (UK 11, US 3) and 2.25 mm (UK 13, US 1) needles or the sizes required to give the correct tension
* Row markers
* Wool needle and scissors
* Two small stitch holders
* 2 [2, 3, 3] small flat buttons for shoulder

Back

Using 2.25 mm needles, cast on 61 [71, 79, 87] stitches.

Row 1: K2, * P1, K1 *, repeat * to * to last stitch, K1.

Row 2: K1, * P1, K1 *, repeat * to * to end.

Repeat these 2 rows six more times until you have 14 rows of ribbing.

Change to 3 mm needles and stocking stitch. Work in stocking stitch (odd rows knit, even rows purl) until the work measures 13 [16, 18, 20] cm (5 [6¼, 7¼, 8] in) from beginning, ending with a purl row.

Use row markers or pieces of coloured yarn tied through the stitches at each end of the row to make beginning of the armholes. There is no armhole shaping.

Work a further 30 [34, 40, 44] rows stocking stitch.

Shape shoulders

Cast off 6 [7, 8, 9] at beginning of each of the next four rows and then 5 [7, 8, 9] stitches at beginning of the following 2 rows. Leave the remaining 27 [29, 31, 33] stitches on a stitch holder.

Front

Work as for the back until you reach beginning of the armholes and place the row markers.

Work a further 12 [16, 22, 24] rows of stocking stitch.

Shape neck

Knit 24 [28, 31, 35] stitches, turn work. Continue on these stitches for the left front shoulder.

Decrease by 1 stitch at the neck edge in every row until 20 [24, 27, 31] stitches remain, then in alternate rows until 18 [22, 25, 28] stitches remain. Work 1 row.

Shape left shoulder

Cast off 6 [7, 8, 9] stitches at beginning of next row and following alternate row, at the same time decrease at the neck edge in the first row.

Work 1 row. Cast off.

Slip next 13 [15, 17, 17] stitches onto a stitch holder and leave. Join yarn to remaining stitches and knit to end. Continue on these 24 [28, 31, 35] stitches for the right front shoulder.

Decrease by 1 stitch at the neck edge in every row until 20 [24, 27, 31] stitches remain, then in alternate rows until 17 [21, 24, 27] stitches remain. Work 8 rows stocking stitch.

Shape right shoulder

Cast off 6 [7, 8, 9] stitches at beginning of next row and following alternate row. Work 1 row. Cast off.

NOTE: The left front shoulder is shorter than the right to allow for the button placket that will help make dressing baby easier.

Sleeves

Both sleeves are the same.

Using 2.25 mm needles, cast on 37 [39, 41, 43] stitches.

Work 14 rows ribbing as for Back.

Change to 3 mm needles and stocking stitch.

Rows 1 to 4: Work stocking stitch.

Row 5: K2, increase in next stitch, knit to last 2 stitches, increase in next stitch, K2.

Continue in stocking stitch, increasing as for row 5 at each end of the following 8th [6th, 6th, 6th] rows until there are 43 [49, 55, 61] stitches.

Continue in stocking stitch without shaping until work measures 11 [13, 16, 19] cm (4½ [5, 6¼, 7½] in) from beginning, ending with a purl row.

Cast off 4 stitches at beginning of each of the next 8 [10, 12, 12] rows. Cast off remaining stitches.

Neck

Use a wool needle, a length of the same yarn and back stitch to join the front and back along the right shoulder seam (longer side of the front).

With right side facing you, use 2.25 mm needles to knit up 73 [77, 81, 87] stitches evenly around the neck, including stitches from stitch holders: that is, knit up 11 stitches on the left side of the neck, 13 [15, 17, 17] stitches from stitch holder at front of neck, 22 stitches on the right side of the neck and 27 [29, 31, 33] stitches from the stitch holder at the back of the neck.

Work 25 rows ribbing as for Back, beginning with

Row 2: Cast off loosely in rib.

Fold the neckband in half onto the wrong side and slip stitch the cast off edge to the backs of the stitches that you knitted up around the neck. Darn the tail of the yarn into the seam allowance.

Front shoulder band

With right side facing you, use 2.25 mm needles to knit up 27 [31, 35, 37] stitches evenly along the left front shoulder, working through both thicknesses of the neckband.

Row 1: K1, * P1, K1 *, repeat * to * to end.

Row 2: K2, * P1, K1 *, repeat * to * to last stitch, K1.

Row 3: Repeat **Row 1**.

Row 4: Rib 10 [14, 6, 8] as for **Row 2**, * yon, K2tog, rib 10 *, repeat * to * 0 [0, 1, 1] times, yon, K2tog, rib 3. This makes 2 [2, 3, 3] buttonholes.

Work 5 rows rib. Cast off loosely in rib.

Back shoulder band

With right side facing you, use 2.25 mm needles to knit up 27 [31, 35, 37] stitches evenly along the left back shoulder, working through both thicknesses of the neckband.

Row 1: K1, * P1, K1 *, repeat * to * to end.

Row 2: K2, * P1, K1 *, repeat * to * to last stitch, K1.

Repeat these 2 rows three more times, and then repeat Row 1 again (9 rows in total).

Cast off loosely in rib.

Make up

Lay front shoulder band over back shoulder band on the right side and whip stitch together (see page 104) at the armhole edge.

Lay the jumper flat with right side up, place a sleeve between the row markers for the armholes and use back stitch to sew the sleeve to the jumper, easing if necessary. Repeat for the other sleeve.

With the jumper right sides facing, use back stitch to sew up the side seams and underarm seams. Darn in the tails of yarn. Turn right side out. Sew buttons to the back shoulder band under the buttonholes.

Child's jumper pattern

This pattern is for a plain stocking stitch jumper in 8-ply yarn. You can use it with any of the decorative stitches and patterns in Chapters 7, 8, 9 and 10 of this book. The sizes given will fit children from about four to eight years old.

Tension

22 stitches to 10 cm (4 in) using 4 mm (No 8) needles and stocking stitch.

Size

(Measure around the chest under the arms.)

Fits chest	60	65	70 cm
	24	*26*	*28 in*
Actual size	72	77	82 cm
	28¼	*30¼*	*32¼ in*
Length	40	44	48 cm
	15¾	*17¼*	*19 in*
Sleeve	28	33	38 cm
	11	*13*	*15 in*

Materials

✱ 9 [9, 10] balls of 8-ply yarn (50 g balls). Quantities are approximate as they vary between knitters.

✱ One pair each of 4 mm (UK 8, US 6) and 3.25 mm (UK 10, US 3) needles or the sizes required to give the correct tension.

✱ One set of 3.25 mm (UK 10, US 3) DPNs (optional)

✱ Row markers

✱ Wool needle and scissors

✱ Two stitch holders

Back

Using 3.25 mm needles, cast on 81 [87, 93] stitches.
Row 1: K2, * P1, K1 *, repeat * to * to last stitch, K1.
Row 2: K1, * P1, K1 *, repeat * to * to end.
Repeat these 2 rows five more times until you have 12 rows of ribbing.
Change to 4 mm needles and stocking stitch.
Knit in stocking stitch until work measures 21 [24, 26] cm [8¼ [9½, 10¼] in) from beginning of stocking stitch, ending with a purl row.
Tie a small piece of contrast coloured yarn at each end of this row to mark beginning of the armholes. There is no other shaping for the sleeves.
Continue in stocking stitch until work measures 36 [40, 44] cm (14 [16, 18] in) from beginning of the stocking stitch.

Shape shoulders

Cast off 8 [8, 9] stitches at beginning of next 4 rows, then 7 [9, 9] stitches at beginning of following 2 rows. 21 [23, 23] stitches remain; leave these on a stitch holder for the neckband.

Front

Work as for the back until you reach beginning of the armholes and place the row markers. Continue in stocking stitch until you have 12 [14, 14] rows fewer than for the Back at beginning of the shoulder shaping.

Shape neck

Next row: K27 [30, 32], turn work and continue on these stitches for left side.
Dec 1 stitch at neck edge in following alternate rows 3 [4, 4] times, then in following 4th row once—23 [25, 27] stitches.

Shape shoulder

Cast off 8 [8, 9] stitches at beginning of next and following alternate row. Work 1 row. Cast off rem 7 [9, 9] stitches.
Slip next 13 stitches onto a stitch holder for the neckband (same for all sizes).
Join the yarn to the remaining 27 [30, 32] stitches for the right side. Work 1 row.

Shape neck and shoulder to match the left side.

Sleeves

Both sleeves are the same.
Using 3.25 mm needles, cast on 39 [39, 41] stitches.
Row 1: K2, * P1, K1 *, repeat * to * to last stitch, K1.
Row 2: K1, * P1, K1 *, repeat * to * to end.
Repeat these 2 rows five more times until you have 12 rows of ribbing.
Change to 4 mm needles and stocking stitch. Knit in stocking stitch, increasing 1 stitch at each end of following 7th rows until there are 59 [63, 73] stitches. Continue without further increase until work measures approx. 24 [29, 34] cm (9½ [11½, 133/8] in) from beginning of stocking stitch, ending on a purl row.

Shape top

Cast off 7 [7, 8] stitches at beginning of next 6 rows, then cast off 5 [6, 8] stitches at beginning of next 2 rows. Cast off remaining 7 [9, 9] stitches.

Neck

Use a wool needle, a length of the same yarn, and back stitch to join the front and back along the shoulder seams.
NOTE: if you are not using DPNs, leave the left shoulder seam unstitched, knit the neckband and then sew the seam.
Using 3.25 mm DPNs, begin at the left shoulder seam. Knit up 16 [18, 18] stitches evenly along the left front of the neckline, knit across the 13 stitches from the front stitch holder, knit up 16 [18, 18] stitches evenly along the right front neckline and then knit across the 21 [23, 23] stitches from the back stitch holder: 66 [72, 72] stitches.
Row 1: * K1, P1 *, repeat * to * to end of row.
Row 2: Repeat Row 1 (this works for both knitting in the round or flat knitting).
Repeat these two rows twice more. Cast off loosely in rib.

Make up

Lay the jumper flat with right side up, place a sleeve between the row markers for the armholes and use back stitch to sew the sleeve to the jumper, easing if necessary. Repeat for the other sleeve.

With the jumper right sides facing, use back stitch to sew up the side seams and underarm seams. Darn in the tails of yarn. Turn right side out.

Woman's jumper pattern

This pattern is for a plain V-neck stocking stitch jumper in 8-ply yarn. You can use it with any of the decorative stitches in Chapters 7, 8, 9 and 10.

Tension

22 stitches to 10 cm (4 in) using 4 mm (No 8) needles and stocking stitch.

Size

(Measure around the chest under the arms.)

Fits chest	80	85	90 cm
	32	*34*	*36 in*
Actual size	90	95	100 cm
	35½	*37½*	*39¼ in*
Length	60	60	61 cm
	23½	*23½*	*24 in*
Sleeve	43	43	43 cm
	17	*17*	*17 in*

Materials

* 11 [12, 12] balls of 8-ply yarn (50 g balls). Quantities are approximate as they vary between knitters.
* One pair each of 4 mm (UK 8, US 6) and 3.25 mm (UK 10, US 3) needles or the sizes required to give the correct tension
* One set of 3.25 mm (UK 10, US 3) DPNs
* Row markers
* Wool needle and scissors
* One stitch holder

Back

Using 3.25 mm needles, cast on 104 [108, 114] stitches.

Row 1: K2, * P1, K1 *, repeat * to * to last stitch, K1.
Row 2: K1, * P1, K1 *, repeat * to * to end.
Repeat these 2 rows six more times until you have 14 rows of ribbing.
Change to 4 mm needles and stocking stitch.
Knit in stocking stitch until work measures 30 cm (12 in) from beginning of stocking stitch, ending with a purl row.
Tie a small piece of contrast coloured yarn (or use a row marker) at each end of this row to mark beginning of the armholes. There is no other shaping for the sleeves.
Work a further 66 [66, 70] rows.

Shape shoulders

Cast off 7 [7, 8] stitches at beginning of next 8 rows, then 6 [7, 6] stitches at beginning of following 2 rows. Place the remaining 36 [38, 38] stitches on a stitch holder.

Front

Work as for the back until you reach beginning of the armholes and place the row markers.
Work a further 12 rows of stocking stitch.

Divide for neck

Next row: K52 [54, 57], turn work and continue on these stitches for left side.
Dec at neck edge in alternate rows until 42 [42, 47]

stitches remain, then in following 4th rows until 34 [35, 38] stitches remain.

Work 1 row.

Shape shoulder

Cast off 7 [7, 8] stitches at beginning of next and alternate rows four times in all. Work 1 row.

Cast off rem 6 [7, 6] stitches.

Join the yarn to the remaining 52 [54, 57] stitches for the right side.

Shape neck and shoulder to match left side, working 2 rows instead of 1 before shaping the shoulder.

Sleeves

Both sleeves are the same.

Using 3.25 mm needles, cast on 50 [50, 52] stitches.

Row 1: K2, * P1, K1 *, repeat * to * to last stitch, K1.

Row 2: K1, * P1, K1 *, repeat * to * to end.

Repeat these 2 rows five more times until you have 12 rows of ribbing.

Change to 4 mm needles and stocking stitch.

Knit in stocking stitch, increasing 1 stitch at each end of following 4th rows until there are 60 [60, 68] stitches, then in following 6th rows until there are 90 [90, 94] stitches.

Continue without further increase until work measures approx. 37 cm (14½ in) from beginning of stocking stitch, ending on a purl row.

Shape top

Cast off 9 stitches at beginning of next 8 rows, then cast off remaining 18 [18, 22] stitches.

Neck

Use a wool needle, a length of the same yarn and back stitch to join the front and back along the shoulder seams.

Using 3.25 mm DPNs, begin at the left shoulder seam. Knit up 55 [55, 57] stitches evenly along the left front of the neckline, knit up one stitch at the point of the V, knit up 55 [55, 57] stitches evenly along the right front neckline, then knit the 36 [38, 38] from the stitch holder for the back neck:

147 [149, 153] stitches.

Row 1: * K1, P1 *, repeat * to * to end of round.

Row 2: Repeat **Row 1** to within 1 stitch of centre of V—54 [54, 56] stitches in this round. With yarn at back of work, slip 1, K2tog, psso, continue in ribbing to end of round.

Row 3: Rib to within 1 stitch of centre of V, ybk, slip 1, P2tog, psso, continue in ribbing to end of round. Repeat rows 2 and 3 four more times. Cast off loosely in rib.

Make up

Lay the jumper flat with right side up, place a sleeve between the row markers for the armholes and use back stitch to sew the sleeve to the jumper, easing if necessary. Repeat for the other sleeve.

With the jumper right sides facing, use back stitch to sew up the side seams and underarm seams. Darn in the tails of yarn. Turn right side out.

Man's jumper pattern

This pattern is for a plain stocking stitch jumper in 8-ply yarn with an option for a crew (round) neck or a turtleneck. You can use it with any of the decorative stitches and patterns in Chapters 7, 8, 9 and 10.

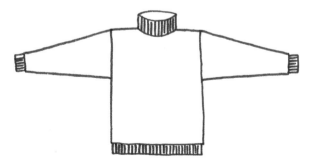

Tension

22 stitches to 10 cm (4 in) using 4 mm (No 8) needles and stocking stitch.

Size

(Measure around the chest under the arms.)

Fits chest	97–102	107–112	117–122 cm
	38–40	*42–44*	*46–48 in*
Actual size	108	119	129 cm
	42½	*46¾*	*50¾ in*
Length	68	69	70 cm
	26¾	*27*	*27½ in*
Underarm seam	48	48	48 cm
	18¾	*18¾*	*18¾ in*

Materials

* 16 [17, 18] balls of 8-ply yarn (50 g balls). Quantities are approximate as they vary between knitters.
* One pair each of 4 mm (UK 8, US 6) and 3.25 mm (UK 10, US 3) needles or the sizes required to give the correct tension
* One set of 3.25 mm (UK 10, US 3) DPNs
* Row markers
* Wool needle and scissors
* Two stitch holders
* Scissors

Back

Using 3.25 mm needles, cast on 121 [133, 143] stitches.

Row 1: K2, * P1, K1 *, repeat * to * to last stitch, K1.

Row 2: K1, * P1, K1 *, repeat * to * to end.

Repeat these 2 rows until the band measures 7 cm (2¾ in) from beginning.

Change to 4 mm needles and stocking stitch.

Knit in stocking stitch until work measures 35 cm (13¾ in) from beginning of stocking stitch, ending with a purl row.

Tie a small piece of contrast coloured yarn (or use a row marker) at each end of this row to mark beginning of the armholes. There is no other shaping for the armholes.

Continue in stocking stitch until work measures 60 [61, 62] cm (23½ [24, 24½] in) from beginning of stocking stitch, ending with a purl row.

Shape shoulders

Cast off 11 [13, 14] stitches at beginning of next 6 rows, then 12 [11, 12] stitches at beginning of following 2 rows. Place the remaining 31 [33, 35] stitches on a stitch holder.

Front

Work as for the back until you reach beginning of the armholes and place the row markers.

Continue in stocking stitch until there are 22 [22, 24] rows fewer than for the Back to shoulder shaping—approximately 50.5 [51.5, 51] cm (19¾ [20¼, 20] in) from beginning of stocking stitch.

Shape neck

Next row: K52 [58, 63], turn work and continue on these stitches for left side.

Dec 1 stitch at neck edge in alternate rows until 45 [50, 54] stitches remain.

Work 5 rows.

Shape shoulder

Cast off 11 [13, 14] stitches at beginning of next and following alternate rows three times in all.

Work 1 row. Cast off rem 12 [11, 12] stitches.

Slip next 17 stitches onto a stitch holder.

Join the yarn to the remaining 52 [58, 63] stitches for the right side.

Shape neck and shoulder to match the left side.

Sleeves

Both sleeves are the same.

Using 3.25 mm needles, cast on 77 stitches.

Row 1: K2, * P1, K1 *, repeat * to * to last stitch, K1.

Row 2: K1, * P1, K1 *, repeat * to * to end.

Repeat these two rows until the band measures 7 cm (2¾ in) from beginning.

Change to 4 mm needles and stocking stitch.

Knit in stocking stitch, increasing 1 stitch at each end of 7th row and following 6th [4th, 4th] rows until there are 113 [91, 97] stitches, then (for second and third sizes only) in following 6th rows until there are [117, 119] stitches.

Continue without further increase until the sleeve

edge measures approx. 48 cm (18¾ in) from beginning of stocking stitch, ending on a purl row.

Shape top

Cast off 11 [11, 12] stitches at beginning of next 8 rows, then cast off remaining 25 [29, 23] stitches.

Neck

Use a wool needle, a length of the same yarn, and back stitch to join the front and back along the shoulder seams.

Using 3.25 mm DPNs, begin at the left shoulder seam with right side facing. Knit up 25 [25, 26] stitches evenly along the left front of the neckline, knit up 17 stitches from the front stitch holder, knit up 25 [25, 26] stitches evenly along the right front neckline, then knit the 31 [33, 35] stitches from the stitch holder for the back neck: 98 [100, 104] stitches.

Row 1: * K1, P1 *, repeat * to * to end of round.

For turtleneck

Repeat Row 1 until neckband measures 15 cm (6 in) or the length desired. Use one of the 4 mm needles to cast off loosely in rib.

For crew neck

Repeat Row 1 until neckband measures 6 cm (2½ in). Cast off loosely in rib.

Make up

Lay the jumper flat with right side up, place a sleeve between the row markers for the armholes and use back stitch to sew the sleeve to the jumper, easing if necessary. Repeat for the other sleeve.

For the crew neck version only: double the ribbed collar over on the wrong side and stitch the cast-off edge to the back of the knitted-up stitches using slip stitch.

With the jumper right sides facing, use back stitch to sew up the side seams and underarm seams. Darn in the tails of yarn. Turn right side out.

CHANGING SIZES

If you want to make minor adjustments to a pattern—for example, by changing the neckline from a crew neck to a V-neck style—it can be very helpful to find some graph paper and a pencil. Draw up the jumper on the graph paper using a square to represent a stitch (or, if there are too many stitches to fit, you can use a square to represent 2 stitches and 2 rows). This way, when you make your changes, you can work out in advance where you'll need to knit differently from the pattern.

Glossary

alt abbreviation used in patterns for alternate

ball a ball of yarn is an amount of yarn, usually measured by weight and length, that is a convenient size for hand knitting

basque a band of ribbing stitch, usually at the hem of a jumper or sleeve

beanie a knitted cap that stretches to fit the head. Also known as a toque

beg abbreviation used in patterns for beginning

bind off See cast off

bonded fabric fabrics such as felt in which the fibres are held together with a physical or chemical bond rather than being knitted or woven

break off yarn cut the yarn, leaving a tail about 10 to 15 cm (4 to 6 in) long for darning in later

brocade fabric with a raised decorative design on the surface. See page 128 for examples of brocade

carriage the moving part of a knitting machine that lays the yarn across the needle-bed

cast off to finish a piece of fabric by taking the active stitches off the needles in a way that prevents them from unravelling (see page 94). Also known as bind off

cast on make stitches and place them on the left-hand needle for knitting (see page 67)

circular needle a pair of knitting needle points joined by a length of metal or plastic wire so that stitches can be knitted in either direction or in a circle (see page 90)

CN abbreviation used in patterns for cable needle

cont abbreviation used in patterns for continue

darning needle See wool needle

dec abbreviation used in patterns for decrease

DK abbreviation used in patterns for double knitting (yarn type)

DPN double-pointed needle

dye lot a single batch of dyed yarn or fabric. Even if the fibre is the same, the dye recipe is the same and the process is the same, yarn dyed in different dye lots can vary in colour

fabric the material that is produced by knitting is a type of fabric

Fair Isle traditional style of knitting in coloured patterns from Fair Isle, United Kingdom

foll abbreviation used in patterns for following

fwd abbreviation used in patterns for forward

garter stitch a stitch pattern produced by knitting every stitch, in rows going in both directions

gusset a piece of fabric, usually triangular in shape, inserted into another piece of fabric to give shape or movement

hank a large amount of yarn wound loosely into a twisted loop. In manufacturing, a hank is a specific length, which varies depending on the composition of the fibre

inc abbreviation used in patterns for increase

incl abbreviation used in patterns for including

intarsia knitting with large areas of different coloured yarn, usually to create a picture or motif

K abbreviation used in patterns for knit (right-side stitch)

K1 abbreviation used in patterns for knit 1 stitch (knit 1 right-side stitch)

K2tog abbreviation used in patterns for knit 2 stitches together

knitwise as though you were making a knit (right-side) stitch; that is, with the tip of the right-hand needle inserted in the front of the stitch

latch-hook needle a metal hook with a small latch that flips up or down to hold and release the yarn. These can be used manually for hooking rugs, but the latch-hook is the main mechanism in a knitting machine

M1 abbreviation used in patterns for make 1 extra stitch

MB abbreviation used in patterns for make bobble

needle-bed the mechanism of a knitting machine with rows of metal latch-hook needles

no. abbreviation used in patterns for number

nuno felt roved wool fibres are laid on a woven mesh and felted

P abbreviation used in patterns for purl (wrong-side stitch)

P1 abbreviation used in patterns for purl 1 stitch (knit 1 wrong-side stitch)

p2sso abbreviation used in patterns for pass 2 slipped stitches over

P2tog abbreviation used in patterns for purl 2 stitches together

patt abbreviation used in patterns for pattern

pattern repeat the number of stitches (or rows) before the instructions repeat themselves

pb abbreviation used in patterns for place bead

pfb abbreviation used in patterns for purl into the front, then the back of the stitch

pompom a three-dimensional ball made of (usually) wool yarn

psso abbreviation used in patterns for pass slipped stitch over

purlwise as though you were making a purl (wrong-side) stitch; that is, with the tip of the right-hand needle inserted through the back of the stitch

rem abbreviation used in patterns for remaining

rep abbreviation used in patterns for repeat

row a horizontal line of stitches on knitted fabric

RS abbreviation used in patterns for right side

rev st st abbreviation used in patterns for reverse stocking stitch; also known as reverse stockinette stitch and wrong-side stitch

selvedge on woven fabric, the selvedge is the double-woven edge of the fabric; on knitted fabric it is the side edges of a piece of work (rather than the cast-on or cast-off edge)

sk abbreviation used in patterns for skip

skein an amount of wound yarn that is not supported by a reel or bobbin. A ball of yarn is a skein

skpo abbreviation used in patterns for slip 1, knit 1, pass slipped stitch over

sl abbreviation used in patterns for slip

sl1 abbreviation used in patterns for slip 1 stitch

SSK abbreviation used in patterns for slip 1 knitwise, slip another stitch knitwise, place the left-hand needle through the front of the slipped stitches and knit the two together

SSP abbreviation used in patterns for slip 1 stitch purlwise, slip another stitch purlwise, return the stitches to the left-hand needle and purl the two together

st abbreviation used in patterns for stitch

stocking stitch

sts abbreviation used in patterns for stitches

st st abbreviation used in patterns for stocking stitch; also known as stockinette stitch and right-side stitch

tail a short length of yarn left hanging at the beginning or end of a section of yarn. The tail is darned into the fabric after the knitting is complete

tbl abbreviation used in patterns for through back of loop

tension the looseness or tightness of knitted fabric; tension is measured by counting the number of stitches

in a row or rows in a wale over the space of 10 cm (4 in). More stitches than recommended mean a tighter tension, fewer stitches mean the tension is looser

tog abbreviation used in patterns for together

turtleneck a long band of ribbing on a round neckline that is folded in half and covers most of the neck when worn

V-neck a V-shaped neckline

wale a vertical row of stitches on knitted fabric

wool needle a large needle with a blunt point, used for sewing in ends of yarn and stitching projects together

working yarn the yarn coming from the ball or skein that is used to knit the next stitch

WS abbreviation used in patterns for wrong side

wyib abbreviation used in patterns for with yarn at the back of the work; also wyb

wyif abbreviation used in patterns for with yarn at the front of the work; also wyf

yarn a general term for spun fibre that is used for knitting; however, it can also describe non-spun fibres and materials such as plastic and paper (see Chapter 3)

yb abbreviation used in patterns for yarn back

yfwd abbreviation used in patterns for yarn forward

yon abbreviation used in patterns for yarn over needle

yrn abbreviation used in patterns for yarn round needle

Index

Acknowledgements

I'm indebted to my grandmothers, mother and aunts for their patience in teaching me to knit.

I'd like to thank Silvana Holler for teaching me how to knit Continental style.

I could not have made this book without the enthusiastic assistance, advice and mistake-spotting of Anne Lewis.

Thank you to Macknit Inc—the NSW Machine Knitters Association, particularly Fay Butcher and June Fortunat, who allowed me to photograph their machine-knitted garments for Chapter 14. http://mkansw.org.au/

Quotations used in this book:

Page 6: Grimm, Jacob and Wilhelm. *Household Tales*. Vol. XVII, Part 2. The Harvard Classics. New York: P.F. Collier & Son, 1909–14; Bartleby.com, 2001. www.bartleby.com/17/2/. 5th April 2011.

Page 10: Cather, Willa. *One of Ours*. New York: D. Appleton, 1920; Bartleby.com, 2000. www.bartleby.com/1006/. 5th April 2011.

Page 17 and 66: Austen, Jane. *Pride and Prejudice* 1813; Penguin Red Classic, 2006

Page 20: Fontane, Theodor. *Trials and Tribulations*. Vol. XV, Part 4. Harvard Classics Shelf of Fiction. New York: P.F. Collier & Son, 1917; Bartleby.com, 2000. www.bartleby.com/315/4/. 5th April 2011.

Page 38: Craig, W.J., ed. "All's Well that Ends Well." *The Complete Works of William Shakespeare*. London: Oxford University Press: 1914; Bartleby.com, 2000. www.bartleby.com/70/. 12th October 2011.

Page 54: Storm, Theodor. *The Rider on the White Horse*. Vol. XV, Part 3. Harvard Classics Shelf of Fiction. New York: P.F. Collier & Son, 1917; Bartleby.com, 2000. www.bartleby.com/315/3/. 5th April 2011.

Page 94: Thackeray, William Makepeace. *Vanity Fair, A Novel without a Hero*. Vols. V & VI. Harvard Classics Shelf of Fiction. New York: P.F. Collier & Son, 1917; Bartleby.com, 2000. www.bartleby.com/305/. 5th April 2011.

Page 212: Goethe, J.W. von. *Faust. Part I*, translated by Anna Swanwick. Vol. XIX, Part 1. The Harvard Classics. New York: P.F. Collier & Son, 1909–14; Bartleby.com, 2001. www.bartleby.com/19/1/. 5th April 2011.

Page 232: Grimm, Jacob and Wilhelm. *Household Tales*. Vol. XVII, Part 2. The Harvard Classics. New York: P.F. Collier & Son, 1909–14; Bartleby.com, 2001. www.bartleby.com/17/2/. 5th April 2011.

Published in 2012 by Murdoch Books Pty Limited

Murdoch Books Australia
Pier 8/9
23 Hickson Road
Millers Point NSW 2000
Phone: +61 (0) 2 8220 2000
Fax: +61 (0) 2 8220 2558
www.murdochbooks.com.au
info@murdochbooks.com.au

Murdoch Books UK Limited
Erico House, 6th Floor
93–99 Upper Richmond Road
Putney, London SW15 2TG
Phone: +44 (0) 20 8785 5995
Fax: +44 (0) 20 8785 5985
www.murdochbooks.co.uk
info@murdochbooks.co.uk

For Corporate Orders & Custom Publishing contact Noel Hammond, National Business
Development Manager Murdoch Books Australia

Publisher: Tracy Lines
Designer: Debra Billson
Layout Designer: Katy Wall
Photographer: Natasha Milne
Project Editor: Kit Carstairs
Editor: Christine Eslick
Production: Joan Beal
Printer: 1010 Printing International Limited, China.

National Library of Australia Cataloguing-in-Publication Data
    Lord, Melody.
    Knitting basics / Melody Lord.
    ISBN 9781742664347 (pbk.)
    Includes index.
    Knitting
    Knitting—Technique
746.432

A catalogue record for this book is available from the British Library.